TEACHING LIBERATION

TEACHING LIBERATION

Essays on Social Justice, Animals, Veganism, and Education

AGNES TRZAK, EDITOR

LANTERN PUBLISHING & MEDIA • BROOKLYN, NY

2020
Lantern Publishing & Media
128 Second Place
Brooklyn, NY 11231
www.lanternpm.org

Copyright © 2020/2019 Agnes Trzak

All rights reserved. No part of this book may be reproduced, stored in a retrieval system, or transmitted in any form or by any means, electronic, mechanical, photocopying, recording, or otherwise, without the written permission of Lantern Publishing & Media.

This title was previously published by Booklight Inc. (DBA Lantern Books). In December 2019, Booklight Inc. transferred all its assets, including this book, to Lantern Publishing & Media, a new company dedicated to the same publishing mission as Lantern Books. Lantern Publishing & Media's printing of this book remains the same as the Lantern Books' version, unless otherwise indicated.

Printed in the United States of America

Library of Congress Cataloging-in-Publication Data

Names: Trzak, Agnes, editor.
Title: Teaching liberation : essays on social justice, animals, veganism, and education / Agnes Trzak, editor.
Description: New York : Lantern Books, [2019] | Includes bibliographical references.
Identifiers: LCCN 2019019011 (print) | LCCN 2019981389 (ebook) | ISBN 9781590565926 (paperback) | ISBN 9781590565933 (ebook)
Subjects: LCSH: Humane education. | Animal rights—Study and teaching. | Veganism—Study and teaching. | Social justice—Study and teaching.
Classification: LCC HV4712 .T34 2019 (print) | LCC HV4712 (ebook) | DDC 179/.3071—dc23
LC record available at https://lccn.loc.gov/2019019011
LC ebook record available at https://lccn.loc.gov/2019981389

To those who teach us—human and animal
And to those willing to learn

Contents

Acknowledgments ix

Agnes Trzak
Introduction: Making Animals Relevant in Education xi

Sarah Rose Olson
1: Dismantling the Human/Animal Divide in Education:
  The Case for Critical Humane Education 1

Beti Scott Brown
2: Our Bodies, Complex and Connected: Analyzing Interconnected
  Oppressions as a Methodological Basis for a Liberating Pedagogy 19

Jacqueline Adamescu
3: Modeling Dissent:
  Teachers as Protectors, Activists, and Public Intellectuals 37

Riley J. Taylor
4: Including an Anti-speciesist Practice in My Work
  with Neurodiverse Youth 51

Susan M. Roberts
5: Learning about Animals:
  How We Are Taught to Ignore Animal Oppression 61

Liz Tyson and Nicola O'Brien
6: What Zoos Teach Us: Speciesism, Colonialism, Racism,
  and Capitalism in the Captive Animal Industry 73

Tanja Badalič
7: Ecocriticism in the Classroom and at Home: Generating a New Ethical
  and Ecological Consciousness through Fairy Tales 89

**Tânia Regina Vizachri, Adriana Regina Braga,
and Luís Paulo de Carvalho Piassi**
8: Including Non-Vegans in Developing and Delivering
  an Anti-Speciesist Pedagogy to Children 105

Heather Fraser and Nik Taylor
9: "The Things We Choose to Teach Are Political Decisions.
So, Embrace That.": Neoliberalism, the Academy,
and Critical Animal Studies Educators 121

Will Boisseau
10: What We Can Learn about Vegan Education from
Anarchist Philosophy and Animal Liberation Activists 137

Agnes Trzak
11: Teaching Men: What Men (and All of Us) Need to Consider
when Communicating for Veganism 157

Blane Abercrombie
12: Muscles, Meat, and Masculinity:
Obstacles to a Vegan Teaching Practice in the Sports Sciences................ 173

Terry Hurtado
13: Working with the Imagination and a Corporeal Pedagogy
to Foster Interspecies Empathy 187

Notes 203
Glossary 223

About the Authors
About the Publisher

Acknowledgments

This book would obviously not exist without the wonderful contributors. I thank you for the trust you showed me by sharing such intimate and revolutionary work. I thank you for bearing witness to the injustices of the world and for doing the best you can to fight them. You all give me hope and I am honored to be able to present your groundbreaking work to the world.

A special thank you to Lex Kartanė, for your friendship, everlasting support, and generous feedback during the editing of this book. Thank you, Casey Tufnell, for the motivation and support you have given me throughout this process. I am also grateful to my partner, Alex Annetts, for being my forever first reader and the most valuable editor. Thank you for being a driving force in my work and my life, for over a decade. Your involvement and dedication shine through every word I write.

Lastly, words cannot begin to express the appreciation and gratitude I have for my parents, Aldona Trzak and Reinhart Przygoda-Trzak, who never cease to shower me with their unconditional love and generosity and who, with their loving words, patience, knowledge, hard work, and warm meals empower and inspire me to reach my potential, every day: Niemożliwym jest wyrazić słowami wdzięczność i miłość, jaką darzę moich rodziców Aldonę Trzak i Reinhart a Przygodę-Trzak, którzy nieprzerwanie obdarzają mnie bezwarunkową miłością i wsparciem oraz których ciepłe słowa, cierpliwość, wiedza, ciężka praca i ciepłe posiłki, każdego dnia dodają mi sił w osiąganiu powziętych celów oraz inspirują mnie w wyznaczaniu nowych.

Introduction

Making Animals Relevant in Education

Agnes Trzak

As educators in any capacity, we take the responsibility of providing our audiences with tools to help them coexist with others. We offer suggestions on how to understand the world around us and how to communicate with those in it. This is why animals, their lives, and their moral standing in human society must be made relevant in a pedagogical context. Simply put, animals are part of this co-dependent existence we as social beings lead, which is why they deserve a place in our pedagogies. As activist educators, it is also our intent to share critical-thinking skills with our audiences and help them contribute to a collective and personal process of emancipation from the concept of *power over*, that is, power over individual bodies, groups, and societies. In line with this, we could say that we teach for social justice, illustrating to our audiences the ways that power works to undermine. Animals are but one constructed identity group that falls victim to that undermining power generated in *human* society.

As will become clear throughout this book, Eurocentric society operates on a very narrow definition of "humanity" and so grants different degrees of privilege to all of us who share this planet, simply due to the nature of our being and the architecture of the system we are placed in. As is the case with all those oppressed, animals are also represented through distorted symbols generated by those deemed "human-enough" in our world. The image of "the animal" that we derive from our understanding of farmed animals, animals in zoos and circuses, or of those used in the medical and other industries, and even wild animals, is tainted by the caricature that those deemed "human-enough" turned "the animal" into.

It is our responsibility as educators to critically engage our audiences in order for them to recognize that artificial categories of animalization, just like those of racialization, sexualization, and other forms of objectification, serve to undermine most of us and enable only a few of us. If all our community has ever been exposed to is a distorted image of what "the animal" is supposed to be, it is up to us educators to remedy that. Thus, when discussing the moral consideration of animals in our everyday lives, we do not only have to explore the *why* but also the *how*. This book shines a light on both of these questions from different perspectives, uniting all contributions under the idea of "the animal" (and with it "the human") as being a speciesist construct. Thus, together with the authors of this book, I invite you, the reader, to become part of a critical education that is concerned with social justice, not only for animals and the planet, but for all of us.

Teaching Liberation is a collection of deeply personal and intimate reflections by people who at times make themselves vulnerable to us—a gift I am truly grateful for. The authors tell us how they incorporate a vegan ethics and an anti-speciesist ideology into their teaching practice and their everyday lives. As readers, we are invited to learn about their innermost thoughts, their past experiences, and their outlooks on the world and its darker sides. Occasionally, we will read not only about cruelty towards animals but also violence towards humans. More importantly, we will read about remedies to issues of violence and oppression and we will hopefully close the book encouraged and inspired to do what we can in our classrooms, with our children, and with all other audiences we encounter, in order to dismantle the speciesist problems we perceive in our communities and society at large. It should be noted that this book is not graphic and the descriptions of (mostly structural) violence serve to remind us all why our work as educators is urgent. Foremost, *Teaching Liberation* gives us tools to dismantle the cruelty towards animals, humans, and the environment that we observe—and with these tools comes hope.

The strategies proposed by the authors enhance the tool belt of any educator, vegan or not. We are coming together through the pages of this book to propose and exchange methods that make our co-existence with one another, including animals and the environment, gentler and kinder. This is something that in the times of the Anthropocene—when all social fronts, such as culture, politics, the economy, the environment, and our health and education systems, are overshadowed by a dense gray cloud—is more urgent than ever.

All contributors to *Teaching Liberation* are vegan and are interested in remedying the ills of the world, not only by practicing anti-speciesism, but also by including an otherwise emancipatory stance in their writing, politics, and actions. This makes the volume very relevant for any and all teachers, activists, parents, and guardians, as well as social workers or anybody who interacts with other humans in any context. It was specifically important to me to facilitate a space for *vegan* educators, as being vegan can often be a lonely and difficult condition for us as social beings, especially if we are also involved in human liberation work. Not only are we aware of the ubiquity of speciesist violence without being able to share the trauma induced from this awareness with our carnist colleagues, friends, and families, but we find ourselves vulnerable to continuous questioning, teasing, or even bullying by them. Especially in an educational context, these realities can make it hard to truthfully represent our anti-oppression values, as addressed by some of the contributors in this volume.

All of us who are part of *Teaching Liberation* recognize that, not only as vegans but as advocates for social justice, we can encounter several obstacles in our teaching practices. When it comes to navigating our responsibility to teach critical thinking and the pressures from the institutions we are part of, and which too often sabotage our efforts to do so, we find ourselves in often existential dilemmas. Nonetheless, now more than ever, it is necessary to express emancipatory politics in any context possible, and the authors in *Teaching Liberation* encourage all of us to do so. Therefore, I hope, besides providing educators with tools to make a significant and positive impact in this world, the chapters of this book will tell any and all of you that you are indeed making a difference and that your work *does* bear fruit, even if you only rarely get a chance to experience the results of your influence.

A *Vegan* Education?

Before we delve into the collection of essays, let us begin by responding to the following questions: "What is education?" and "What exactly makes education *vegan*?" Although most of the authors in this volume work within the education sector in a professional capacity as teachers, lecturers, and key and support workers, the education they participate in doesn't only take place in the classroom setting. Nor do you have to be a professional pedagogue to have an educative role. Other potential scenarios in which we see ourselves as instructors, mentors, or knowledge facilitators could be when we are parenting, child minding, producing art and media, campaigning, or in fact communicating with others in *any* capacity. Any moment of interaction is educational, not only in children's lives but also in those of adults. You don't need to have children of your own to exchange knowledge, contribute to forming your own opinions and those of others, and help to guide them in their lives. Instead of asking, "What *is* education?" it would perhaps be more plausible then to ask ourselves, somewhat rhetorically, "What *isn't* education?"

Education isn't only the transfer of knowledge from one person to another. It is the opening up of a space in which both the educator and their audience can learn (about) skills, values, and whole belief systems from one another. And this is the key here: We learn *from one another*. As educators we should always remain open and willing to learn from our students, especially in times when the line between teacher and student is increasingly being eroded and the binary is being made obsolete. A stark insistence on the teacher being the knowledgeable authority figure in their field, whereas the students are their inferiors, learning only at the teacher's mercy so to speak, inhibits the learning process. This attitude makes the teacher unapproachable as a person, and so makes the learning experience unnecessarily impersonal. It takes away the interpersonal aspects of education, which are, arguably, the most important pedagogical elements today.

These days, most of us can become students anytime we like, for example by enrolling in an online course or simply though consulting our search engines on a topic we desire to learn about. We don't need an interpersonal relationship to simply extract the knowledge we crave. So, the traditional Eurocentric understanding we have of a teacher imparting knowledge that their students might only access through them becomes obsolete, and the student/teacher distinction is rendered useless. Such a situation also indicates that as educators we are always already students or learners ourselves. Thus, we could even say that any and all interactions we have, inside or outside a schooling context, are pedagogical in and of themselves.

This becomes particularly clear when we navigate the world as social justice advocates, where our ethics are so ingrained in our everyday lives that all our interactions become guided by our ulterior motive of making the world a better place through passing on the knowledge we have gathered about its state so far and possible alternatives to it. Any interaction then becomes one of unlearning our own oppressive habits that contribute to the ills of the world, while simultaneously modeling the emancipatory practices we have picked up along the way.

This is not only the role that teachers of ethics or political science should play in our lives. Take a minute to reflect upon the teachers you've had, who truly made an impact on you. Chances are, you're thinking of a person who didn't simply teach you everything you needed to know about trigonometry or the anatomy of the human body. In fact, you're probably remembering this person for not only being very knowledgeable in their field, but for being personable, approachable, encouraging, and supportive. They probably allowed you to make mistakes and guided you on your path to finding your own answers to the problems of the world. They showed you an array of options and let you invent your own ones, too.

As our morals are an integral part of our selves, albeit a flexible and ever-changing part, we cannot simply take them off like our coats, for instance, when we enter the classroom. When we interact with people, we act as a whole person, opinions and flaws included. There's no point attempting and no need to try to establish a teaching persona that is detached from our innermost beliefs. On the contrary, our characteristics are useful and needed when educating. Even if our convictions are antagonistic to those of our audiences, or if they perhaps seem out of context, we can find ways of revealing our beliefs and perhaps even engaging others in a conversation about them. I'm not suggesting here that as a physical education teacher, for instance, you should forcibly integrate lessons on environmental degradation into your syllabus (although I can think of many creative ways to include the topic). However, as educators we have a responsibility towards those we interact with: to guide them and aid their development and, especially, their own emancipation.

When we approach people not as students but simply as another person, we will find ways of integrating our moral imperatives into situations and subjects that might not seem to offer any space for ethical guidance. In *Teaching Liberation*, you will find examples of organic conversations surrounding veganism and animals that at first glance might seem out of place. Any educator and parent with strong opinions, be they based in anti-racism and decolonization, feminist or queer liberation, or in anti-speciesism, knows how naturally these issues come up in any social context. Moral considerations and social justice issues are so ubiquitous that those of us, dedicating our lives to them, don't just find ways of integrating them into our curricula, but feel more responsible to address them in any context imaginable. This book focuses on ways of integrating anti-speciesist thought into educational contexts. It illustrates from a complex variety of viewpoints how deeply anti-speciesism is embedded in the overall effort for social justice.

In the chapters of this book we find out what a specifically *vegan* education can look like. The authors will show you its many different facets—all as unique and individual as the authors themselves. The common denominator, however, is that vegan education is far more than the imparting of knowledge about what veganism is. By "vegan education" we don't only mean the active unlearning of carnist ideals and habits. As vegan educators we go beyond teaching our audiences where to buy their soymilk and vegetables and how to make a healthy meal out of them. That, perhaps, is in fact the smallest part of vegan pedagogy.

Introduction

When we write about veganism in this book, we do, of course, mean the boycotting of animal products for ethical reasons. The ethical reasons encompass, but are not limited to, a respect for animals, which makes our veganism an expression of our anti-speciesist ideologies. Further, the authors agree that an anti-speciesist veganism also includes a concern for our fellow humans and the environment. The book makes clear why vegan pedagogy must include an overall discussion against oppression and *power over*. Every page of this book makes the case for anti-speciesism to explicitly include an active stance against the violence of objectification in any form, be it that of animalization, racialization, infantilization, or feminization.

Thus, a vegan educator does not fulfill their task when all knowledge about the cruelty we inflict upon animals is made accessible to their students. In fact, we might not know all the gory details of how a slaughterhouse operates or the ways penguins are treated at our local zoo. Similarly, a vegan education goes beyond instructions on the logistics of a vegan lifestyle. Many of us might not even know anything about cooking or where to get our protein from! Hearing that a number of our students are going vegetarian and would like to know how to stop consuming dairy and eggs (which indeed, in Eurocentric capitalism is initially a hard task to figure out), does fill our vegan hearts with pride. However, this can only be considered a small side effect of our excellent teaching skills.

Remember, It's a Process

In all seriousness, of course we want our audiences to reject carnism. Nonetheless, let it be explicitly said that we are not guiding their thoughts towards veganism to achieve a sense of power over them. The image of the preachy vegan, imposing their beliefs upon everyone, is still very much a stereotype held by many. Our aim is not to achieve power over carnists by converting them into vegan disciples. Instead, we are interested in mending the broken elements of society: the ontological constructions and their physical manifestation that harm humans, animals, and the environment. It must not be our goal to change the identities of our audiences; we are rather focused on guiding them towards discovering new ideas and beliefs. The separation between inherent identity and learned idea, between the person and their habitual actions, is something we must keep in mind as we communicate and organize for social justice.

It is easy to get frustrated when we notice that, although our audience may apparently understand our thoughts on the state of society, they won't adjust their behavior accordingly. To avoid frustration and its next-door neighbor hopelessness, we vegan educators must remember how hard it actually is to become vegan. We need always to bear in mind that when trying to convey anti-speciesist values, especially in a world saturated by Eurocentric, neoliberal ideas, we are working with people who have most likely been exposed to carnism their whole lives. All institutions we pass through are based on carnist traditions, which are greatly reinforced by a generalized speciesist attitude through the elevation of some individuals over others. Additionally, our differing cultural backgrounds, economic possibilities, and bodily and mental abilities create an uneven playing field when it comes to (psychosocial and physical) accessibility to veganism, making veganism a more obvious and easier option for some than for others. In capitalism, however, none of us can leave the house, gaze at our digital devices, or prepare a meal without being confronted with some sort of advertising for, or normalization of, speciesism.

It is one thing to start realizing the injustice in speciesism and another to adjust our behaviors accordingly. Both of these processes are evoked through education. For me, going vegan was a conscious process that stretched out over months—subconsciously probably even over years—induced through the education I soaked up from my vegan friends as well as at university. With every little thing I consumed as a new vegan, I realized how everything was made for carnists. If vegan options existed, they were very well hidden. I remember going into a big supermarket and not being able to find soymilk because I didn't really know what I was searching for, how the packaging looked, what aisle it would be in, and on which shelf it would be placed. (I wasn't surprised to find only a few cartons on a bottom shelf, whereas the dairy shelves were full with all sorts of familiar brands of cow's milk.) I'm sure many readers have similar memories.

As experienced vegans, we forget this very quickly. We navigate the aisles in the grocery or drug store as if we were at home. We're familiar with what symbols and ingredients to look for on product labels; we already know where we can buy an edible take-away option or treat ourselves to coffee and dessert. All of this information is potentially overwhelming and exhausting for new vegans. We need to keep this in mind when we get frustrated at those who understand the ethical ramifications of consuming somebody's flesh but have trouble adjusting their behaviors to reflect their beliefs.

Another factor making veganism initially hard to practice is the social aspect of sharing meals together, or perhaps even going shopping for clothes and make-up, something many of our adolescent students will spend their time on. Carnist social traditions are something that even experienced vegans struggle with, so imagine how hard it must be for our audiences. Many of us know the feeling of struggling with social situations in which we inevitably become the "attention-seeking vegan" in a restaurant or at a dinner party demanding special treatment, "unnecessarily complicating things," and perhaps even compromising the carefree atmosphere by inadvertently confronting our company with their own carnist guilt that seems to arise simply through our presence. As a result, some of us might be teased or even harassed for our veganism.[1] These are significant aspects to bear in mind when we find ourselves getting frustrated in our vegan teaching practice, in the classroom, doing outreach, or at a family gathering.

Whenever I get disheartened, I remind myself that although I might be the only vegan teacher or even vegan person at my institution, I'm not alone in my ethical and pedagogical practice. There are so many others working hard to protect animals, Earth, and our fellow humans. I am certain that we must be doing something right, as veganism is on the rise across the globe, sanctuaries are appearing everywhere, and dairy farms are shutting down. Zoos and aquaria are experiencing one controversy after another with respect to animal cruelty, and the pharmaceutical industry is investing in alternatives to animal experimentation. There is even more than a single brand of plant-based milk on our supermarket shelves.

Seeing that our education methods are guided by a concern for the individual and, indeed, the world as a whole, we must bear in mind the complexity of our audience: that is, their unique way of experiencing the world, of processing information, and of adapting to the newly found knowledge. No interaction is the same as a previous one, even with the same class of students. Each person we communicate with has their own idiosyncrasies that are also flexible and depend on the context the person is placed in. This is not only true for our students but also for us. Thus, as educators, we must never assume anything about the position our students find themselves in.

This is of particular significance when we teach anti-speciesism, as it is a highly sensitive subject, where much of what we learn concerns violence towards animals. Not only do our students have to cope with the trauma of learning about the plight of the animals, be it structural or corporeal, but they also have to grapple with their own complicity in that trauma and the guilt that arises with it. This makes anti-speciesism, even when taught within a scientific context, a very emotionally challenging subject that demands a lot from our students and ourselves. Therefore, despite the urgency of an anti-speciesist practice, the biggest virtue we as educators have to bring with us is patience. Some chapters in this book touch upon this and other kinds of sensitivities in a vegan-teaching context.

Solidarity Instead of Shame

Anti-speciesism is a complex ideology, not only useful for dismantling animal oppression but also addressing human struggles; it is embedded in the wider social justice context. If we don't realize this as educators, we can potentially do more harm than good by hurting and traumatizing members of our audiences who might themselves be facing hardships in a capitalist, ableist, white supremacy, dominated by cis-gendered men. Our anti-speciesist pedagogies specifically focus on allowing everyone to understand concepts such as autonomy, difference, uniqueness, and plurality as desirable, for humans and animals. It is useful, or even *necessary*, to keep this in mind when we relate to our students, as well as when we relate to other people who are also in educating roles.

The vegan community can often be very self-critical. We might expect every spokesperson for the cause to be perfectly versed in veganism and political correctness. Communicating perfectly in this context means expressing the right thing in the right moment to generate a prefigurative moment of political utopia. In other words, as social justice advocates, we're always striving to behave in the way we'd like the whole world to behave, by continuously unlearning the oppressive actions we have internalized. When we cross the line from unlearning to denying that we, too, are perpetuating harmful practices and that we, too, are placed within the context of a kyriarchy, we run the risk of expecting too much of ourselves and others. We often become very strict with ourselves, questioning and overthinking every moment in which we failed to generate the perfect prefigurative moment, a utopian bubble in a world of cruelty.

Especially as educators, we might feel a responsibility to lead by example and become dissatisfied with our own teaching practice if it doesn't perfectly reflect the ideals we set out to teach our students about. Often, this comes at the expense of excluding, sometimes even shaming, valuable voices, including our own. So, I want to remind us all to remain gentle, kind, and patient in our teaching practice with our students, fellow social justice educators, and ourselves. I am not asking us to excuse or justify oppressive behavior. In fact, a vital part of a gentle pedagogy is to suggest corrections and point out mistakes—be they in the form of a wrong solution to a math problem or harmful behavior in an interpersonal and sociopolitical context. It's part of our responsibility as teachers to point out and challenge the inexcusable. Nonetheless, when approaching one another, we mustn't forget that we're all part of an oppressive structure, and that unlearning the behaviors we have learned within it is a process. However, before shutting down our students or fellow teachers by shaming them (even inadvertently), let us focus on a solidarity practice in which we encourage the things we like about the way they construct their worlds, while approaching that which is harmful with passion but with care.

Contributions

By giving us a glimpse of their teaching ethics and practices, the authors in this volume invite us to reflect on our own methods and attitudes. You'll read about the methods contributors employ to make anti-speciesism and veganism a topic with their audiences. You'll read about the obstacles their institutions create for them and the ways they overcome them. All of the chapters are products of personal experiences, which is why I believe *Teaching Liberation* is such a valuable volume.

Sarah Rose Olson's contribution, "Dismantling the Human/Animal Divide in Education: The Case for Critical Humane Education," serves as a good introduction to the pedagogical theories that pave the way for an anti-speciesist education to arise. Olson fuses the fields of Humane Education and Critical Pedagogy to show us a space where interspecies justice can be taught in an interdisciplinary format. The chapter takes us on a brief tour of decolonial, queer, vegan, feminist thought to remind us how to undo our own oppressive features to be better teachers and activists. After introducing the concept of Critical Humane Education, Olson then combines the principles of individual self-awareness and criticality with the axiom of holistic nonviolence.

Similar to Olson, Beti Scott Brown also provides an excellent thematic introduction to those of us who are beginning to recognize the overlaps in structural and corporeal systematic violence across ability and species, as well as race, gender, and class. In the chapter "Our Bodies, Complex and Connected: Analyzing Interconnected Oppressions as a Methodological Basis for a Liberating Pedagogy," these themes are seamlessly interwoven with an account of Scott Brown's own experience with disability as well as her scholarship in the field, making clear that identity and oppression cannot be compartmentalized. Scott Brown believes that pedagogy should be intimate, accessible, radical, and empowering, which she reflects in the tone of her chapter. She begins her narrative with a personal introduction of herself and illustrates how her socially engaged fiber art acts as a tool for an anti-oppressive pedagogy. Her chapter serves as an identity politics and language toolkit for vegan educators, artists, and activists.

Introduction

Jacqueline Adamescu likewise gives us a very personal insight into her world of education in her chapter "Modeling Dissent: Teachers as Protectors, Activists, and Public Intellectuals." The anarcha-feminist tone of this chapter reflects Adamescu's radical stance towards education as a tool for liberation. The essay itself is an appeal for more educators, who aren't white men, to transgress, radicalize, and pass on an ethic of care in their classrooms—for humans and animals. To counter the corporate attack on public education, Adamescu provides an eleven-point plan to make knowledge more accessible and available.

Riley J. Taylor also gives us a very intimate look at her work accompanying autistic youth in their school lives. In her chapter, "Including an Anti-speciesist Practice in my Work with Neurodiverse Youth," Taylor relates to us the effects of poverty and disability upon her students' freedom of choice and autonomy. She reminds us that the popular vegan slogan YOU HAVE A CHOICE does not always apply. This chapter echoes the work of Olson and Adamescu in that Taylor emphasizes that as mentors we are not free from our identities and beliefs. Concretely, this chapter is a reminder that the language we use and the dialogue strategies we apply must be student-led, critically engaged, and guide rather than prescribe.

Susan M. Roberts teaches the principles of veganism to audiences of primary school children, youth as well as adults. In her chapter, "Learning about Animals: How We are Taught to Ignore Animal Oppression," she combines personal anecdotes from her teaching experience with her scholarly affinity for philosophy. Roberts invites us to reflect on the way we learn at different stages of our lives. This chapter provides a direct comparison between the ways children and adults reflect upon moral questions regarding animals and our relationship to them. In doing so, Roberts stresses the importance of working with young children to effectively undo carnism for an anti-speciesist long-term future. In essence, Roberts paints a vivid picture of the general rapport children have with animals, the empathy they feel for them, and the ways the adult world directs their morals towards speciesism.

The two subsequent chapters offer very specific examples of how education determines the ways children ethically interact with the world.

First, Liz Tyson and Nicola O'Brien critically engage with the pedagogical value of zoos. In their chapter, "What Zoos Teach Us: Speciesism, Colonialism, Racism, and Capitalism in the Captive Animal Industry," Tyson and O'Brien show us how zoos are often considered valuable and even essential in the context of Eurocentric childhood education. The authors share their urgent work on debunking commonly accepted "truths" about zoos by analyzing industry rhetoric that upholds pedagogical myths. Something I am particularly grateful for is the authors' reference to their own experience of visiting zoos and bearing witness to the cruelty endured by the animals held captive there. This chapter gives any teacher, parent, or guardian the means to uncover and address how zoos perpetuate a speciesist ideology to our children, one based on racist and capitalist exploitation.

Similar to the zoo as a foundation of Eurocentric education, fairy tales also play a role in teaching children about animals. Tanja Badalič's chapter, "Ecocriticism in the Classroom and at Home: Generating a New Ethical and Ecological Consciousness through Fairy Tales," provides us with the valuable tool that is *ecocriticism*, which allows us to critically engage children (as well as adults) when it comes to human–animal relations. Badalič reminds us that literature and the physical world are not separate, and she shines a light upon the importance of critically engaging with anthropocentric stories. Specifically, Badalič introduces us to the fairy-tale worlds created by the Slovenian author Svetlana Macarovič. This chapter beautifully illustrates the kindness and compassion in Makarovič's stories and presents examples of ecocriticism that can serve as inspiration for language and literature teachers as well as parents, guardians, and childminders.

In their chapter, "Including Non-Vegans in Developing and Delivering an Anti-Speciesist Pedagogy to Children," the team of educational researchers made up of Tânia Regina Vizachri, Adriana Regina Braga, and Luís Paulo de Carvalho Piassi focus on the importance of educating children to foster a future free of animal cruelty. They relate their work on a wonderful science outreach project for children, within which their team trained university students in animal ethics in preparation for providing schoolchildren with an education in animal advocacy. This chapter offers an interesting insight into the difficult task that is preparing and providing workshops and discussions to be held with children at primary school and sufficiently equipping adult carnists with methods to teach anti-speciesism to these youngsters. The authors show the scientific approach they took in developing their teaching materials and give us concrete examples for anti-speciesist classroom activities, while including charming anecdotes from their own teaching experiences. Although frustration and obstacles are addressed, the overall message the team has for any vegan teacher is to approach our audiences with patience, love, and curiosity.

Exchanging personal experiences and reminding ourselves that we aren't alone in our vegan teaching practice is a valuable habit that ensures our pedagogies are ever evolving and sustainable. Heather Fraser and Nik Taylor remind us of this urgency with their contribution, "'The Things We Choose to Teach are Political Decisions. So, Embrace That.': Neoliberalism, the Academy, and Critical Animal Studies Educators." The authors present us with the results of a survey they conducted among Critical Animal Studies scholars working in higher education, and they offer insight into our fellow educators' opinions on neoliberalism, the academy, and classroom scholar-activism. We find out about the possibilities and challenges our colleagues face as well as about the strategies they use to ensure the effectiveness of their pedagogies. Fraser and Taylor provide us with ideas and methods we can apply in our own teaching and the message they pass on encourages us to build alliances with colleagues, to be patient with our students, and to invite our audiences to join an anti-speciesist journey, rather than expecting to "convert" them.

In "What We Can Learn about Vegan Education from Anarchist Philosophy and Animal Liberation Activists," Will Boisseau also presents interviews with animal activists. Instead of asking them questions about how they *teach* veganism, as seen in the previous chapter, he investigates how they *learned* it. We find out about the common denominators that encouraged these activists to go vegan, which tells us what we should bear in mind when conveying the importance of animal liberation in a teaching context. Boisseau's reflections are embedded in his interest in anarchist punk, a subculture strongly grounded in the principles of anti-hierarchy, autonomy, and liberation. Boisseau preludes the reflections on vegan anarchism with a short history and critique of the anarchist canon of thinkers, and reminds us of the feminists who even today are paving the way for anarchism to become an inclusive movement truly informed by principles of liberation.

Too often those of us who aren't white, cis, non-disabled men share experiences of being made to feel unwelcome or inadequate in a movement that in academia, education, and activism is dominated by men. So, my chapter, "Teaching Men: What Men (and All of Us) Need to Consider when Communicating for Veganism," provides guidelines to make everyone's (and not only men's) teaching practices as well as their veganism more inviting. In this chapter, I make clear why it is so urgent that we reform our language, our attitudes, and our behaviors, to shift away from masculinized forms of expression when it comes to communicating for veganism, and how we can begin to do so.

Blane Abercrombie gives us an insight into the academic world of sport sciences as well as bodybuilding culture and the toxic masculinity and carnism it's connected to. As Abercrombie writes in his chapter, "Muscles, Meat, and Masculinity: Obstacles to a Vegan Teaching Practice in the Sports Sciences," bodybuilding acts as an extension of puberty, which intends to shape *boys'* bodies into those of *men's*. So, the sport acts as a reinforcement of masculinity, which is closely linked to the consumption of animal protein. Abercrombie analyzes bodybuilding culture by applying a feminist critique of gendered food habits. Presenting anecdotes from his own experience with the resistance to animal liberation and women's accessibility to the sport of bodybuilding as well as academic sciences, the author uses this chapter to appeal to sport scientists to do away with the oppressive and carnist nature of sports and academia alike.

Terry Hurtado offers a valuable closing chapter to this book with "Working with the Imagination and a Corporeal Pedagogy to Foster Interspecies Empathy." Hurtado utilizes knowledge about the neurology and the psychosocial process of learning empathy to show us that a common practice used to encourage anti-speciesism can indeed be counterproductive. Exposing audiences to gory images of animal cruelty to create empathy towards animals and so encourage veganism might not be the best method in our vegan pedagogy toolbox. Noticing a lack of positive, life-affirming depictions of animals in vegan education, the author has successfully tried to expand the vegan education toolbox by developing a corporeal experience to generate empathy.

As part of a team teaching in higher education, Hurtado has constructed a workshop that invites participants to experience cow being. As a moving meditation, the workshop evokes emotive and visceral experiences that make use of the neurological principles of empathy and are focused on conveying the happy and peaceful life of a cow. This chapter goes into detail about the theory behind this idea and sketches out how this workshop comes to life, combining the imagination of the mind and the physicality of the body, which is something that is rarely made use of in Eurocentric capitalist curricula and campaigns.

To equip us with a liberation vocabulary that will make it easier for us to coherently create and communicate emancipatory knowledge for animals that is not harmful, but indeed empowering for humans as well, you will also find a glossary at the back of the book, with terms used by the authors.

Before moving on to these chapters, let me express my gratitude to all the contributors for their committed work on their chapters. I appreciate their gentle approach and the kindness that permeates their texts, even as they accentuate the force and urgency within them. I hope you remain with us through the challenging and, at times, discomforting parts of *Teaching Liberation*, and perhaps even find ways to honor the unease and mild anguish you might experience. These are the feelings of change and progress, of shedding our old speciesist skins and learning another way to dismantle that within us that oppresses others and ourselves.

1

Dismantling the Human/Animal Divide in Education

The Case for Critical Humane Education

Sarah Rose Olson

Western education systems are often based on neo-colonial, patriarchal, and humanist ideologies. In response to this, critical scholars and educators have developed innovative educational approaches that challenge Western education's problematic practices. The goal in doing so is to open schools to the possibilities of empowerment and social justice through education. Inspired by these efforts, I am proposing the adoption of a framework I call Critical Humane Education.[1]

Critical Humane Education (CHE) is a proposed educational praxis born from the merging of two important fields of schooling: Humane Education (HE) and Critical Pedagogy (CP). Humane Education encourages students to think critically about their relationships with animals, other people, and the environment, whereas Critical Pedagogy pushes students to note the political nature of education and to seek social justice through education. Thus, as a combination of these two, Critical Humane Education would, in practice, serve as a political means of confronting the patriarchal, colonial, anthropocentric systems currently informing formal education. It is time to move away from these systems that have dominated Westernized classrooms since the Enlightenment and which stand in the way of all students' success. When left undeterred, these patterns in education allow for racism, sexism, and other forms of oppression to work their way into classrooms.

Such barriers restrict students' academic success, their career opportunities, and their own ideas of self-worth and community. Critical Humane Education, I argue, would provide the tools needed to transform students into political actors able to dismantle the patriarchal-colonial human/animal divide upon which much of Western education is based. Disrupting this divide and Western conceptions of humanity would aid students in liberating themselves and their communities from the oppressive systems that keep them from fully thriving in the classroom and beyond.

The Critical Humane Education framework I propose places animal studies in conversation with other fields of critical scholarship and puts forth an educational praxis through which interspecies justice can be sought. Animal studies is strengthened and enriched when it engages with other disciplines, as proven by the widely popular merging of feminism and Critical Animal Studies in Carol J. Adams' work on the sexism connected to animal exploitation, and A. Breeze Harper's outstanding work on the racialization of food spaces. Critical Humane Education aims to bring these advances in animal studies into classrooms so that students become exposed to animal studies reaching its full potential through interdisciplinary exploration.

Critical Humane Education is intended to be multi-dimensional and interdisciplinary in practice. It not only aims to address the speciesist human/animal divide itself but also the specific struggles that stem from a society-wide adherence to this notion. CHE recognizes that although combating speciesism is a necessary *step* in seeking social justice, dismantling speciesism alone will not bring about liberation for all. Racism will not end with the dying of speciesism, and so combined with curricula working to erode speciesism must come curricula addressing the lived realities of racism and other oppressions.

Despite its roots in Humane Education, CHE would not place only the liberation of "the animal" at the forefront of its goals and lesson plans. Instead, it would allow students to come to know "the animal" in new ways that are oppositional to the very systems of power that hold hostage the progressive possibilities of educational systems, students, and animals alike. The notion of "the animal" exists outside a simple species definition, creating a *human* ideal. These ideals are governed by racism, sexism, classism, speciesism, ableism, and queerphobia. Such power systems work to define who is humanized and who is animalized. Thus, whether overtly or covertly, Eurocentric society at large and the education that takes place within it works to dehumanize students of marginalized identities by pushing them towards the concept of "the animal." In turn, animals are held firmly as an oppressed group: they represent the ultimate idea of "lesser than" allowing unchecked violence towards animals. In coming to know "the animal" as something other than a category of "lesser than," students can begin to dismantle the process by which dehumanization and oppression across species lines is made possible.

UNDERSTANDING PATRIARCHAL-COLONIAL BINARIES AND THOUGHT

To implement a resistance to oppressive structures into teaching practices, it must be understood how these systems emerge and how they sustain themselves. Re-conceptualizing both the animal and education means breaking away from the dualistic norms to which most Western formal education systems are currently bound. These dualisms—human/animal, man/woman, white/people of color (POC), civilization/nature—keep students from reaching their full potential when their education does not allow them to see the world and their place within it holistically, but rather as binary. Teachers and their curricula are often informed by these dualisms, causing the binaries to be reproduced and reinforced by formal education systems. In turn students, their parents, and the worlds we all navigate, are steeped in these dualisms as well. When these binaries become fixed within the minds of young students, they are taught which side of the binaries they fall on, and of equal importance, who falls on the *other* side and why. This is a dangerous process that neglects the complexities of identity as well as the relationships we create based on these identities.

Ecofeminist scholar Karen Warren attributes the process of othering to oppressive conceptual frameworks. "A conceptual framework," explains Warren, "is a set of basic beliefs, values, attitudes and assumptions which shape how one views oneself and one's world." A conceptual framework is a "socially constructed lens through which we perceive ourselves and others. It is affected by such factors as race, class, age, affectional orientation, nationality and religious background." A conceptual framework becomes oppressive when it "explains, justifies and maintains" unequal power structures.[2] Oppressive conceptual frameworks are not merely a set of *individual* beliefs, but are rather systematically constructed views through which we come to learn our world. Challenging an oppressive *conceptual* framework must mean challenging a *systemic* framework, not simply sets of beliefs and ideas as they trickle down to individuals.

Warren argues that oppressive conceptual frameworks are based on—among other elements—value dualisms: "disjunctive pairs seen as oppositional rather than complementary and exclusive rather than inclusive."[3] Greta Gaard expands upon Warren's work on value dualisms to illustrate how "the many systems of oppression are mutually reinforcing."[4] Here, Gaard stresses the similarities between interconnected forms of human oppression (racism, classism, sexism) and animal oppression (speciesism and naturism). Gaard notes that just as Western culture devalues certain genders, races, classes, and other identities, it too devalues nature and animals. Furthermore, Gaard argues that these devaluations mutually reinforce one another.[5] Gaard draws upon the work of Val Plumwood to further illustrate the value dualisms that constitute much of Western patriarchal-colonial thought. Introducing Plumwood's "master model," Gaard defines the latter as "the identity that is at the core of Western culture and that has initiated, perpetuated, and benefited from Western culture's alienation from and domination of nature."[6] According to Plumwood the master model continuously reproduces "dualized structures of otherness and negation"[7] which consist of the following binaries:

culture/nature
male/female
master/slave
rationality/animality (nature)
universal/particular
civilized/primitive (nature)
public/private

reason/nature
mind/body (nature)
reason/matter (physicality)
reason/emotion (nature)
human/nature (nonhuman)
production/reproduction (nature)
subject/object
self/other[8]

To this list Gaard adds white/nonwhite, financially empowered/impoverished and heterosexual/queer,[9] in order to further decolonize critical thought.

The dualisms serve two purposes, as Gaard explains. First, they create difference between both elements in a dualism so as to establish one's superiority over the other based on "the full humanity and reason that the self possesses but the *other* supposedly lacks."[10] Secondly, the superior category of each pair is linked to the superior category of every other pair. We see "associations between reason and heterosexuality, for example, or between reason and whiteness as defined in opposition to emotions and nonwhite persons; or associations between women, nonwhite persons, animals and the erotic."[11] The dualisms thus mutually reinforce power on one side, and devaluation and subjugation on the other.

Such an understanding of oppressive conceptual frameworks, with their reliance on binaries, is crucial in critiquing the formal Western education system. Whether intentionally or not, these structures work their way into curricula, ultimately molding students' minds to see the world through a binary lens. Such a lens inhibits students from critically thinking about processes of Othering that lead to many of the inequalities and injustices that occur both in the classroom and society at large. Of particular concern here is the fact that "each of these oppressed identity groups, each characteristic of the other, is seen as 'closer to nature' in the dualism and ideologies of Western culture."[12] This system represents a measure of humanity through which power and privilege is granted within Western society; therefore, educational systems must move away from oppressive definitions of humanity itself. Otherwise, certain actors, including students of marginalized identities, will inevitably continue to be left out of the equation.

EUROCENTRIC STANDARDS OF HUMANITY AND EDUCATION

Critical animal studies scholar Maneesha Deckha argues: "One of the organizing narratives of Western thought and the institutions it has shaped is humanism and the idea that human beings are at the core of the social and cultural order."[13] Given the oppressive conceptual frameworks that Western thought and its related institutions exist within, one must be critical of how far the idea of the "human" extends. To whom does Western thought grant humanity? As one learns to see the world through a lens of Western thought, one comes to learn who is allowed to exist as central to society and who is pushed to the margins.

"Although there have been countless ways of expressing human activity throughout history," Aph and Syl Ko argue, "the *model* we take for humankind is that devised by colonial Western Europe." This model of the human centers the Western, white male and his "ideal female counterpart: the white, Western female."[14] Developed throughout the Enlightenment period, this Eurocentric notion of humanity laid the foundation upon which modern education and European identity have been built. As the Western white male centered himself as the marker of humanity, he, too, centered his way of knowing. "This particular ethno-cultural way of knowing the world was universalized as the only way of being," argues Michael Baker. "Consequentially," notes Baker, "knowledges and experiences of all those who are *not* White, heterosexual, European men were and are excluded, unless they are willing and able to acculturate."[15] Baker argues that in centering his way of knowing, the Western white man justified marking all other ways of knowing as inferior.

Furthermore, "the ways in which the West has learned to understand itself are tied to systems of knowledge and disciplinary practices of which modern education [. . .] is a central institution."[16] If students come to learn about themselves through modern education grounded in Western thought, how are they coming to view the world? Students learn to see the world through an oppressive binary lens, in which certain actors are granted humanity and central interest in society, while others are marginalized. The world becomes categorized by those who are deemed human and those deemed sub-human/nonhuman. Linda Tuhiwai Smith explains that our concepts of "what counts as human" inform violent hierarchies, such as those of race.[17] It, therefore, becomes clear that these structural binaries have real implications for those individuals who find themselves on the dehumanized side of the binary.

In education then, these conceptualizations of who counts as "human" reproduce this oppressive binary model of humanity through Eurocentric curricula. Through such curricula, students are given little context as to the power structures and violent histories from which such narratives about humanity emerge. Westernized concepts of what it means to be civilized and progressive are taken for granted, becoming an unchallenged norm when taught in the classroom, especially in a teacher–student constellation that grants the teacher an authority over their students when it comes to passing down knowledge. Little is done to critique the violent colonial history in which these notions lie, or who loses within these definitions of civilized humanity. Many students then lack the critical awareness necessary to challenge an education that inherently bolsters certain actors, while pushing others towards subhuman status.[18] This has a significant impact on their lives outside the classroom, in a world where it is important for students to be able to recognize and challenge unjust power dynamics sufficiently.

If we educate our students through a dualistic worldview that places the human on the high end of the spectrum and those less like "the human" on the other, then to whom do those "less human" individuals fall closer conceptually? The animal. It is this mutually reinforcing oppressive system, with speciesist assumptions at its roots, that always allows us to come to learn that the Western white male is most human and subsequently most important. Thus, we are teaching the human/animal divide, which in turn further divides humans.

The human/animal divide does not merely act as a species divide, but as a sliding scale upon which all persons/beings are measured. "What separates 'human Others' from the Ideal Human and what distinguishes the human Others from each other is their ranking on the human–animal scale," argue Aph and Syl Ko.[19] On this scale, what is human comes to be defined just as much by what it is—supposedly Western, white men—as it is by what it is not: the animal.[20] Thus, on the scale of humanity, opposite the human and opposite of whiteness sits "the (necessarily) nebulous notion of 'the animal.'"[21] The power of this "nebulous" positioning of the animal lies in its ability to apply across species boundaries. It, therefore, serves as a violent label that Western thought can place upon anyone who the white male benefits from oppressing/conquering.

This label extends across all aspects of identity to create a "massive domain of subhumans." Here, humanity isn't simply measured by physically *having* white skin or *Homo sapiens* species status but *how* you are white and *how* you are *Homo sapiens*.[22] Therefore, if you are unable to exist in a state of being in which whiteness is *simultaneously paired* with cisgender maleness, heterosexuality, able-bodiedness, "legal citizenship" status, Christianity, and high socio-economic status then you do not meet the qualifications of the ideally constructed form of humanity. This status pushes disabled, POC, queer, trans and/or non-binary, undocumented, non-Christian, and low-income individuals and communities further from humanity and closer to conceptual animality.[23]

This process of dehumanization perpetuates the deeply oppressive injustices that plague our classrooms and societies. Not directly tackling this divide allows all forms of marginalization and oppression to continue. Precisely because teachers are also part of the human–animal sliding scale, the knowledge that educators accumulate often reflects unjust power relations. In teaching, this translates into educators pushing certain ways of knowing aside in the classroom in favor of Eurocentric knowledge. This not only teaches students to come to know themselves and the world around them in a very narrow way, but also acts as a form of epistemological violence.[24]

Discrediting these other ways of knowing through Eurocentric standards of teaching also discredits marginalized students and their communities. That discrediting teaches white students that it is permissible to perpetuate the human/animal divide and that world history is centered upon them. This undoubtedly shapes the ways in which students come to know the world and how they treat others, with teachers acting not only as bystanders but as active participants in this process. Thus, it is an educator's responsibility to undo human-centered learning facilitation by conveying knowledges produced by those who are animalized. Let us now explore to what extent principles from Humane Education as well as Critical Pedagogy can help us do this.

Merging Humane Education and Critical Pedagogy: Critical Humane Education

Drawing from the existing fields of Humane Education and Critical Pedagogy lets educators promote a teaching and learning practice through which the patriarchal-colonial binaries plaguing formal education can be challenged. In order to understand the importance of merging these two fields, they must first be explored individually.

Humane Education serves to provide students with the tools needed to actively participate in society through a holistic, empathy-based education. The focus is on what the individual can do to better their community and relationships with people, animals, and the environment. The Institute for Humane Education (IHE) views Humane Education as encompassing four main elements:

> (1) Providing accurate information about the issues of our time so that people have the information they need to understand the consequences of their decisions as citizens; (2) fostering curiosity, creativity, and critical thinking so that people can evaluate information and solve problems; (3) instilling reverence, respect, and responsibility so that people have the motivation to face challenges and act with integrity; (4) offering positive choices that benefit oneself, other people, the animals, and the earth so that people are empowered to create a more humane world.[25]

The Institute hopes to inspire young people to recognize their power as informed global citizens and to equip students with the knowledge necessary to become critical problem solvers. Helena Pedersen describes Humane Education's goals in similar terms to those of IHE: as an "innovative teaching and learning process that supports students in their development of empathy, responsibility, critical thinking and active citizenship." Pedersen stresses the role that education plays in fostering respect for "the other" in order to challenge violence and oppression among all beings.[26] Humane Education allows students to draw connections between all kinds of social justice movements in such a way that inspires "creative solutions" and "individual action, so that their life choices can improve the world."[27]

Critical Pedagogy emerged with a similarly socially conscious goal: to address the political nature of education. CP makes explicit that "education is not a natural, ahistorical phenomenon but that it should be understood in its sociohistorical and political context." The goal of CP is to influence society in "the interest of justice, equality, democracy and human freedom."[28] Critical Pedagogy equips students with politically relevant knowledge that allows them to become responsible citizens and activists.[29] According to Gert Biesta, "Critical pedagogy starts from a dissatisfaction with 'what is' and wants to bring education into action against injustice."[30] Critical Pedagogy, therefore, is an educational practice meant to produce social change. It inspires critical reflexivity, a means through which students can begin to understand their own situations and the larger systems of injustice that shape their lives. Critical Pedagogy is also critical of the role that education itself plays in (re)producing oppressive and marginalizing social structures.[31] It is critical of classroom narratives that uphold systems of oppression. It operates as a means of exposure; an educational praxis through which students can begin to uncover the social fabrics by which they are held.

Both Humane Education and Critical Pedagogy aim to create active citizenship and combat violence, though how they do so differs: Humane Education is more focused on *individualistic* attempts to foster sustainable, equitable, and compassionate relationships. In contrast, Critical Pedagogy has a more *systematic* outlook through which students are encouraged to challenge oppressive systems of power.

In order to truly critique and begin to dismantle the human/animal divide through education, students must be educated through a holistic, political, non-anthropocentric schooling that is critical of not only violent relationships but also the oppressive systems that enable them. Here, Humane Education offers a comprehensive worldview in which all actors are considered and compassionate living is encouraged. Critical Pedagogy offers an education that dismantles structural violence and is dedicated to social justice and liberation. Both support active citizenship, which is imperative to challenging patriarchal-colonial binaries outside of the classroom as well as in it.

Humane Education is committed to "independent research and investigation, so that students may determine for themselves what is or is not humane, rather than accepting at face value the information that is given to them."³² Critical Pedagogy insists that education should be understood within its socio-historical and political context. Combined, the two produce an education in which students are given the tools to look at the historical context from which problematic notions of humanity arise. Where HE is too individualistic in scale to truly inspire students to opt for systemic change, CP makes up for this in its critiques of larger networks of injustice. Where CP is too human-centric to promote a holistic ethic of interspecies justice, HE brings a more inclusive education to the table. Combined to create *critical humane education*, the two allow students to engage in compassionate, dignified relationships with "the other" while simultaneously stripping away the systems that enable othering in the first place.

Thus, the goal of Critical Humane Education is to ultimately combine the commitment to liberation from oppressive social structures that Critical Pedagogy promotes with the crucial understanding of the interconnectedness of all forms of life that is taught through Humane Education. Both focus heavily on the role that students play as informed citizens. Critical Humane Education would foster this focus in an attempt to encourage politically engaged scholarship and citizenship among its students and educators. A combination of both approaches would have to aim to move away from problematic methods of seeking social justice that rely on extending the reach of humanity in order to extend the reach of justice.

In other words, instead of moving those on the far end of the human–animal scale increasingly further to the left, thus granting them more "humanity," Critical Humane Education should acknowledge and do away with this often-practiced attempt at fostering social justice. It is a proposed educational philosophy suited to do away with toxic notions of Eurocentric humanity altogether and to reimagine the human in such a way that is not separate from or opposite to the animal and thus less likely to (re)produce the category of "less-than," while acknowledging and even promoting difference over assimilation.

Aph and Syl Ko provide important insight as to why social justice efforts centered on expanding the boundaries of humanity cannot produce true liberation. They argue that when activists do so, they fail to recognize "that the basic building blocks they have used to structure their campaigns are actually products of the very same system they are trying to fight." Ko and Ko claim that such activist frameworks inherit the "conceptual tools and activist theories from the Eurocentric system"[33] that they are attempting to dismantle. Furthermore, they argue that even attempts by social justice movements to "begin to disrupt the modern, imperialistic understanding of humanity" are bound to fail because they leave "the *foundation* untouched," and thus "the dismantling can never be complete." They continue by arguing that we must go beyond the racialized categorization of marginalized people and "subvert their anchor: the human/animal divide."[34]

Inspired by, and convinced of the urgency of, these arguments, the Critical Humane Education framework does not accept the commonly held notion that granting the label of humanity to a greater set of humans will bring about more equitable treatment of all people. Instead, in practice, CHE would help students recognize that a social justice plan rooted in oppressive logic cannot produce a just outcome. CHE curricula would aid students in disrupting the human/animal divide. Any attempts by politically engaged citizens to do away with systemic injustices must be rooted in the dismantling of this divide. If the basis of the problem is left intact, then vulnerable groups will remain vulnerable, as those in power can go back to this foundation at their leisure as it best suits them.

Critical Humane Education curricula would enable students to recognize the human/animal divide as the epistemological foundation for all oppressions. An adaptation of the CHE framework within curricula design is necessary because neither HE nor CP alone is suited to tackle this speciesist divide. CP is still very much rooted in the idea that "the humanizing practice is a practice of liberation that puts persons in possession of their original freedom."[35] Given its preoccupation with "the humanizing practice" of cultural assimilation and striving for equality rather than difference and emancipation, CP alone is not prepared to move away from humanist anti-violence discourses. However, paired with HE's anti-violence discourses that center a reconceptualization of the animal and an interconnectedness of life, CP is able to erode the Eurocentric standards of humanity it engages with.

A combination of both approaches can draw on HE's task of coming to (re)learn about animals and the environment in ways that exist outside the monolithic, theoretical category of "the animal." A Critical Humane Education curriculum would stress both the individual agency and interconnected dynamics of all animals. Through CHE practices, students would come to learn about animals not as a broad category of otherness, but as actors and communities with their own needs, preferences, and lived realities. Coming to learn about animals in this way works to re-conceptualize the notion of "animality" in a positive light that is not seen as being in opposition to humanity, but rather its own diverse phenomenon. CHE teaches students that (re)learning animality and moving away from reliance on problematic humanist discourses must extend beyond individual action. Students are taught to look at not only how current conceptions of humanity/animality play out in systemic power structures, but also how re-conceptions of these notions could play out (positively) on a larger structural level.

Deckha cautions us that a move away from humanist anti-violence discourses may cause discomfort, especially among marginalized groups and individuals. "Obviously, it can be very unsettling for vulnerable human groups to destabilize the boundary and the corollary belief in human specialness that is said to be at the root of Western knowledge systems," Deckha explains. "[T]his is especially so for human groups whose humanity has been historically denied."[36] Despite the fact that Deckha argues that "this might be precisely what is required (if insufficient) to alter the dynamics of violence that amplify vulnerabilities," educators engaging with CHE, especially those on the "ideally human" end of the human–animal scale, must be respectful and cognizant of the given discomfort. Although a move away from humanist social justice discourse is absolutely necessary, educators engaging with CHE must be aware of their own positionality and how this may affect the way students of both similar and different identities receive such information.

For instance, it is the duty of white educators to actively attempt to dismantle the human/animal divide within their classrooms, as they have a duty as citizens of privilege to disrupt the systems that afford them disproportionate power. This means being aware of the fact that it may be easier/less painful to immediately re-conceptualize animality and humanity from the position of whiteness given that animality has never been used to disempower white people on a basis of race alone. There are ways in which educators of all backgrounds can and should engage with the project of disrupting the human/animal divide within their classrooms, but this should be done differently, depending on the composition of the classroom and the educator's background. This is the type of contextual approach to education that Critical Humane Education aims to promote.

Ultimately, this approach not only liberates us as teachers and our individual students but more so impacts our complete social networks with a variety of other humans and animals navigating them. As Deckha argues, this must be done in order to put an end to Eurocentric logics of domination and the process of subhumanization and related violences. Doing so in a compassionate, contextual, critical, and self-reflective way will be the challenge for educators engaging with CHE. Nonetheless, I believe this process of beginning to dismantle the human/animal divide in the classroom can and must be encouraged.

Avoiding Harmful Comparisons

Among the most harmful practices that privileged vegan educators are guilty of is that of insensitive comparisons between human and animal suffering. Many vegan campaigns, classroom curricula, and conference talks include a comparison between situations of human and animal suffering. The most widespread examples of problematic comparisons include mentions of sexual violence, the holocaust, and chattel slavery as tools to explain animal cruelty. These comparisons become problematic when they are used insensitively and perhaps even casually, often purely utilizing human suffering to evoke a shock response (often through spectacle and controversy) with a pretense of inspiring empathy for the animal. Approaching comparisons in such a way often results in (re)traumatizing the audience and possibly counteracts the actual goal of including animals in an anti-speciesist ethics.

A commitment to destabilizing the framework upon which oppression is based does not entitle educators—or anyone else—to make inappropriate and triggering comparisons between different forms of oppression. Whereas we can agree that oppression stems from the Eurocentric conceptualization of the human/animal divide, this in no way gives us license to make comparisons between the *experiences* of human and animal oppression. What must be made clear is that CHE is proposed as a means of tackling the *logic* of domination that upholds the human/animal divide—a logic that is rooted in virulent notions of humanity in which the Western white man and his counterparts will always win.

We regularly see such disrespectful comparisons arise among the predominantly white mainstream animal rights community. Activists openly compare animal agriculture and abuse to human rights atrocities. Appropriating violent histories is not only problematic because it re-traumatizes affected individuals when mentioning them, but also because in drawing such comparisons we further use the human victims of these crimes as props to bolster an animal rights agenda.[37] Furthermore, when white vegan educators make comparisons between the way we use animals and chattel slavery when speaking to a black audience, it is, argues Christopher Sebastian McJetters, "nothing short of emotional blackmail. And emotional blackmail is one of 'the master's tools', as Audre Lorde is famously quoted as saying." McJetters further argues that this becomes "a pattern whereby blackness is used and commodified at different times and by different groups to further an agenda without offering any type of real solidarity on black issues."[38]

Aph and Syl Ko argue that "not only are these types of comparisons or connections absurd—even worse, these simplistic characterizations miss the ways in which these struggles and these wounded subjectivities relate to one another." Ko and Ko argue that when making connections between human and animal oppressions we should move away from comparisons that center "the *literal, physical* bodies of the oppressed" and instead tackle "the root of these oppressions conceptually." Instead of making comparisons, Ko and Ko say, they encourage us to note the common source that holds oppressions intact. They argue that when we do the opposite we miss the point, that "what makes the physical violation of these bodies possible is their citizenship of the space of the other or the 'sub-human.'"[39] Ko and Ko claim that if we rely on physical comparisons rather than getting to the conceptual base of oppressive behavior "we risk reproducing the oppressive framework in our own liberation movements."[40]

In dismantling the oppressive conceptual linkages between Western notions of animality and various forms of oppression, Critical Humane Education should act as a tool through which students can begin to understand the different aspects of their identities. Although CHE should not make disingenuous comparisons between experiences of oppression, the rejection of Eurocentric binary logic can act as a tool for students struggling to make sense of their oppressed identities. At the same time, CHE should encourage students to reflect upon their own identity aspects that make them powerful in certain situations. Thus, CHE fosters confidence, courage, and solidarity that not only includes the liberation of oppressed humans but also that of animals and the environment.

Real Life Applications for Critical Humane Education

Critical Humane Education should then actively work to reimagine how animals are portrayed in the classroom in ways that are beneficial to disrupting the human/animal divide. It should ensure that the way animals are represented in the classroom does not allow them to become reproduced as a category of justified violence and subordination outside the classroom. This means rejecting practices of dissection, resource management, and anthropocentric narratives of animals that rely on animals being positioned as resources, as disposable, and as background to human life.

Concretely, this includes that schools reject the use of animals (dead or alive) or their body parts for educational purposes in science classes. This also includes a rejection of "class pets" trapped in cages at the mercy of children who are supposedly learning a lesson in responsibility, care, and empathy. Rejecting the idea of animals as resources then also includes a vegan cafeteria, and class trips that refrain from visiting places that imprison animals, such as circuses, aquaria and zoos. Learning materials should also not promote the exploitation of animals, especially in children's education, where many stories and fairy tales, other media and even toys include speciesist themes, when critical engagement with these might not always be possible.

Further, animals should be taught as having their own individual agencies, collective power, and importance rather than as a monolithic category. By re-conceptualizing animals in schools, students learn to see them as important actors in their own right, and move away from viewing "the animal" as a category of insult, degradation, and subjugation that human individuals and communities can be pushed into.

Discussions of animality and human-based oppressions can easily fall into the same oppressive logic that CHE stands in opposition to. Educators must be thoughtful and deliberate in the ways in which they address these topics. Being open to critique and feedback from students is immensely important. Educators should always learn and grow alongside their students. Dismantling the human/animal divide means dismantling hierarchies of knowledge; all knowledge brought to the table, whether student or teacher based, should be considered and taken seriously in the classroom.

I believe that a Critical Humane Education will look different in different educational institutions. The CHE framework is deeply committed to ecofeminist tenets of contextuality, positionality, and subjective knowledge. Depending on the composure of the classroom space and the positionality of the educator, CHE practices would likely manifest themselves in different ways. And this is encouraged. Lesson plans inspired by CHE that have both global but also specifically local applications are bound to be most productive to the goal of inspiring politically engaged students. A Critical Humane Education should be taught in such a way that students see themselves represented in the curricula and can relate to the subject matter on a personal level. There can be no one specific curriculum or lesson plan implemented across school districts. At the educators' discretion, CHE should be molded to represent the specific classroom setting in which it is being taught, making it applicable across disciplines and age groups.

I do not expect Critical Humane Education to act as a solution to the human/animal divide or the political issues that stem from it. Rather, education should be used to address the ideologies in which our society is rooted and it should address these ideologies as they pertain to education. My hope is that, through CHE, education will continue to evoke new ideologies, hopefully those that are more fair and just on the broadest possible scale.

I do expect Critical Humane Education to act as a tool for liberation in the hands of students as they go about their inherently political lives. Given that education is inherently political, we need to equip students with an education committed to the politics of liberation, re-conceptualization, holistic worldviews, and representation of the intrinsic agency of all beings. With such an education in hand, students can begin to see the world outside the narrow and oppressive Eurocentric lens through which it is too often sculpted, and begin to recognize and critically address oppressive Western binaries and logic as they appear in their everyday lives.

Although there is no strict curriculum for Critical Humane Education, lesson plans should be structured around the following goals of an education: 1) that looks at the world systematically; 2) is able to identify and be critical of oppressive pedagogy; 3) that promotes a holistic worldview in which the individual and collective agency of all species is recognized; 4) that encourages politically engaged citizenship; 5) that represents all students and their communities; 6) that is rooted in postcolonial and queer feminist theory and practice; and 7) is always open to reassessment, critique, and self-reflection. In abiding by these guidelines, I believe Critical Humane Education has the power to liberate students in and out of the classroom, and promote a world in which interspecies justice might be possible.

2

OUR BODIES, COMPLEX AND CONNECTED

ANALYZING INTERCONNECTED OPPRESSIONS AS A METHODOLOGICAL BASIS FOR A LIBERATING PEDAGOGY

Beti Scott Brown

This chapter outlines how educators, artists, activists and anyone else communicating for liberation can explore anti-speciesism through the lenses of other forms of social justice, connecting resistance to power. Specifically, this is an exploration of the intersections between the liberation of two marginalized groups: disabled humans and nonhuman animals. As a member of the disabled community my writing and my pedagogical practice are informed by disability theory but I also hope to contribute to the growing body of existing work in the field of feminist vegan studies to address the relationships and intrinsic connections between the origins of human and nonhuman animal oppressions.[1] Further, this chapter shows to what extent such an understanding of the relation between human emancipation and the animal movement is needed when approaching a pedagogical setting. I offer an insight into how this interconnectedness can be pointed out in an educational context with the example of eugenics and the pathologizing of the disabled community as a possible topic of interdisciplinary interest. I also provide a general toolkit that can guide our lesson planning and our pedagogical dialogues. My suggestions are embedded in a description of my own artistic teaching practice.

It is my aim to provide an accessible piece, which refers to academic work and form, but which will still be useful for non-academic readers. As socially engaged academics and teachers—whether formal or informal—it is vital that we work towards making our fields of study more widely available, and to make our knowledge transferable to as many people as possible, so it can be developed and disseminated. People of marginalized identities are systematically excluded from academic spaces;[2] classism, racism, misogyny and other systems of oppression impose barriers to education (formal and informal), whether these barriers are financial, cultural, or—in the case of people with disabilities—physical.

Barriers do not only apply to the physical spaces of learning: there is also the inaccessibility of knowledge and the transfer of knowledge itself. Some people simply do not take information in very well from papers dense with academic language. There are many ways to share and take in information: you can learn by reading, learn by doing, learn by teaching; some learn visually, some aurally; and still the majority of teaching at a higher education level is done through detailed readings of texts. Academic forms and language do serve a purpose; however, when they become overly academized and exclusive, they serve to maintain the systems which exclude people from both academic institutions and sometimes non-institutional personal learning.

When I was an art and art history student I did a semester long course on Socially Engaged Art Practice. This should have been the dream course for me, as I make socially engaged art, I research socially engaged art—socially engaged art is definitely *my thing*. However, many of the required readings for this course were prohibitively complex; theories which could be explained in simpler terms were given complicated—and often convoluted—explanations which were more confusing than they were enlightening. I found this most egregious in this particular course because so much of the content concerned social justice, yet so much of the literature seemed to prop up systems of power and privilege which the works they were addressing were trying to dismantle. In writing their criticism and theory in such a way, the authors almost ensured that their positions in an academic or cultural elite would not be threatened by those outside the elite or those who are not able to "speak that language." Tendencies towards over-academizing in both disability theory and animal studies render many of the works particularly difficult for many people to truly engage with. This is something we all should bear in mind when constructing and delivering our lesson plans.

I hope that this piece will serve as a bridge between the academic and the activist. But first you should know a bit about where I'm coming from; my experiences and identities have shaped each letter in this work, just as yours will shape the way you read them. I strongly believe that recognizing our own positionalities and how they differ from others' is vital in all fights for liberation, so here is mine: I am an artist (although forever fighting imposter syndrome and feeling that this is too grandiose a term to use about myself). I use fiber arts practices to explore themes of healing, survival and resistance. Teaching is also part of my practice, though I prefer to think of this work as facilitation. For me, thinking of my work as facilitation allows myself and those I am working with to interact as a collective body, exploring a subject and moving beyond any of our individual understandings. When I facilitate a group discussion, the knowledge which is being shared is fluid, I am not simply a teacher and the information is not simply static, I am also a learner, working with others to develop our ever changing collective and individual understandings. I predominantly work with people who experience different forms of marginalization and oppression, often people with additional support needs, mental health challenges and disabilities.

I see my art practice (and possibly all forms of art?) as a form of exchange similar to teaching or facilitation. My work relates to social justice issues, it is highly textual, and I struggle to maintain a healthy middle point between politically didactic and static work and opaque and politically vapid work. Throughout my Fine Art degree I received constant feedback warning me to step away from the polemical,[3] but I also had the feeling that the social issues I wished to address were too important and urgent to be dampened down by "art speak," abstraction or symbolism. Being largely text based, it seems obvious to me that through my work I aim to impart feelings, knowledge and concepts in some kind of pedagogical exchange. I want people to experience a feeling, know a thing, think about something from a different perspective; so rather than standing in front of a class and speaking, I stitch. (See images on pages 23 and 27). The objects I create serve as an opportunity for exploration, an expression of a specific point in a process of critical engagement or as a site of affirmation and healing in and of itself.

As well as having a teaching/facilitation practice with disabled people, I am myself disabled. I have a connective tissue disorder which manifests itself in chronic pain, fatigue and limited mobility. The position from which I write is one of simultaneous privilege and non-privilege; I am a white European human, I have a UK passport, I am verbal and literate and have access to a multitude of resources; I also live with mental health challenges which largely stem from the trauma of being a survivor of gendered forms of abuse and violence, relating to my identity(ies) as a queer woman. I feel the weight of existing in a world which devalues bodies and minds like mine; I feel it viscerally as if my body was literally straining under its pressure, as if my back was physically bearing the weight.[4]

I am also a vegan and my approach to pedagogy is significantly shaped by what veganism means to me. After many failed attempts at going and staying vegetarian, a conversation with a good friend and hugely important sister in struggle made it click in my mind. Through a gentle pedagogical process, based on our shared experiences as women of similar backgrounds and our bond as friends and sisters, she made me see the inconsistencies of my non-vegan feminist politics, the curtain was lifted, and I suddenly felt what I would later read in *Defiant Daughters*, that "Feminists who eat meat may be fighting for their own liberation, but as long as they participate in animal exploitation [...] they are propping up the very system they are fighting against."[5] Though the struggle to live ethically or non-oppressively in an unethical and oppressive world is hard and ultimately impossible, this is a conversation which has shaped my life, and for which I am always grateful. As well as this sister, and others whose actions and beliefs have shaped my own, I owe my politics to the wisdom of writers, including A. Breeze Harper and the contributors to *Sistah Vegan*,[6] to Marjorie Spiegel,[7] to the women who shared their stories in *Defiant Daughters* and Carol J. Adams[8] (to name just a few; all of which contain fabulous interdisciplinary, accessible and pedagogically valuable texts). I understand if this all is a bit touchy-feely, get-to-know-each-other, but teaching, learning and pedagogical exchange are social and interpersonal processes. We should work against the de-personalization of the role of "the teacher," which manifests itself in that feeling we experienced as children: if we saw our class teacher in the supermarket we would feel a weird sense of embarrassment and intrigue, because "this person who teaches me math only exists in school and definitely isn't a full and complete being outside of that!" Why should we continue reproducing this?

UNDERSTANDING INTERCONNECTED OPPRESSIONS

My journey towards animal liberation and vegan feminism began at a young age. I remember being acutely aware of the effects of the foot-and-mouth crisis on the animals who shared with me the fields and hills of rural Herefordshire. I remember in primary school how, every playtime, groups of boys would head straight to an ant hill in the corner of the playground, for the sole purpose of stamping on as many ants as they could. I also remember my first act of resistance against such violence, myself and my girl friends would stand together, arms linked, forming a human barrier—as I would years later, at protests against austerity, militarism and other forms of violence against both human and nonhuman animals alike.

At sixteen, I was in a strange city with a group of older friends. I was a vegetarian and at the beginning of my feminist awakening. Drunk, we bought food at a burger van; I only ordered chips, which prompted the usual vegetarian baiting. The usual pattern escalated, until I found my mouth full of another friend's burger, as he shoved more and more into my face with instructions to "take my meat." With the benefit of hindsight and a vegan feminist theoretical framework, I now understand why that experience stuck with me in such a specific way: this "joke" combined sexual violence and carnist violence, shoving both in my face. What I have learned from experiences such as these is that oppressions are often overlapping and that our struggle against them thus needs to be multifaceted.

In this section of my chapter, I offer some topics and starting points that can be helpful when teaching a holistic approach to liberation politics. Although it might not be perceived as relevant to animal liberation at first glance, I ask you to bear with me throughout this part, as I delve into the basics of identity and emancipation as a basis for a holistic approach to anti-speciesism. Further, when we interact with our students, it is important for us to bear in mind the complexities of our identities as teachers and those of our students themselves. This helps us to improve our own liberatory practice and gives us a great opening to include animals in our teaching.

My understanding of identity has been primarily informed by intersectional feminist politics. Legal scholar Kimberlé W. Crenshaw coined the term *intersectionality* in the 1980s to give a language to the experience of black working-class and poor women. In essence, Crenshaw critiqued the view that before the law you could only ever be seen as either black or poor or a woman, but never as a complete person with an identity whose parts are simply not detachable from one another. Of course, these values and practices appeared in many social movements far before this realization. Sojourner Truth's "Ain't I a woman?" speech demonstrates the existence of what we would now call intersectional practice in the movement to abolish slavery. Later, we also see terms like "triple oppression," "double jeopardy," and "multiple jeopardy" arise (coined by Claudia Jones in 1949, Frances Beale in 1969, and Deborah K. King in 1988, respectively).[9]

These theories arose out of black women's radical thought. For Crenshaw and others, the white-dominated feminist movements and theories of the 70s and 80s did not address the racialized oppression black women experienced. The civil rights and black liberation movements did little to examine their gendered experiences, and the working class, socialist, and communist movements were (and can still be today) openly hostile to considering any analysis not exclusively class-based. Through her 1989 work "De-marginalizing the Intersections of Race and Sex," Crenshaw defined the theory and brought it to the attention of academics and activists spanning multiple disciplines. Essentially, intersectional analysis sees all systems of oppression as connected, and as such, states that they cannot be examined on their own.

It's a theory that seems obvious to anyone who experiences oppression on multiple fronts. As a woman who is disabled, my experiences are shaped by both ableism and sexism/misogyny. For example, my interactions with medical institutions have often been traumatic. I have experienced gaslighting and other abusive behaviors, as well as outright denial of my symptoms and experiences. These experiences arise out of the intersection of patriarchal and ableist oppressions. They are not limited to disabled women, but they appear consistently in academic and non-academic literature and accounts of our lived experience.[10]

Intersectional theory is also helpful for anti-racist feminists interested in including a vegan practice in their teaching. Traditionally, theories on multiple identity markers creating a complex person have been concerned with systems of power and privilege relating to humans (racism, classism, sexism, transphobia, homophobia, xenophobia etc.). Recently, however, they have also been expanded beyond human-centered species boundaries.

Animals' experiences of speciesist violence are, like those of humans, shaped by their multiple identity markers. For example, different forms of violence are perpetrated against animals dependent on their assigned sex. A female-assigned animal will be used for their reproductive abilities; they lay eggs, provide milk, and create offspring, who go on to continue the cycle. A male-assigned animal will be used primarily for meat and studding.

Although different in form and expression, human and nonhuman oppressions are linked by ideology, mechanism, and outcome. As Sarah Rose Olson describes in Chapter One, the underlying source that stifles and exploits all is the dominant *ideal*: a human, white, cisgender, non-disabled man. The closer a being is to this ideal, the more privilege, power, and value they are ascribed. Exploitation and oppression are enabled through the mechanisms of othering, objectifying, and dehumanizing. The oppression a being will experience is based on their proximity to this ideal.

The ideal is socially constructed, created in the image of those in power and reinforcing their privileged positions in the hierarchy. Those who fit into the "ideal" understand themselves to be the standard: people of color, queer people and other marginalized groups are defined entirely by their difference to *him*. In deviating from this socially constructed ideal, by being a different gender, different race, differently abled, or indeed a different species, they become *other*, they are objectified and commodified, and it is through these processes that their oppression is justified. Understanding this complex construct should be the basis of our pedagogical methods in any field.

Historically, both racialized and gendered oppressions have been justified by the perpetrators as natural, because of the oppressed groups' perceived proximity to (or distance from) humanity—as it was then defined—and the ideal as we might now see it. For much of human history, women were understood to be a deviant form of the man. This classification has justified everything from sexual violence to political disenfranchisement to exclusion from public life.

Similarly, the exploitation and oppression of people of color have been justified by their perceived distance from humanity and proximity to animality. In the case of (human) disabled experience, difference to and distance from the ideal justify oppression and ascribe worth (and worthlessness). Difference in terms of ability, physicality, appearance, mental capability, etc. are used to "other" the bearers of difference. The impairments and differences are seen under oppressive social systems as inferiorities, and this leads to the social and political disablement of people with impairments. Disabled people are dehumanized and animalized to varying degrees, dependent on social and cultural values at the time, their impairment(s), their proximity to "normalcy," and their ability to assimilate to non-disabled standards and behaviors.

It's worth mentioning that the words *dehumanize* and *animalize* are tricky to come to terms with as an anti-speciesist disabled feminist. To my mind, these words actually serve to perpetuate and legitimize species-based oppression. When we use this discourse, we unintentionally buy into the idea that "humanity" is the ideal and that the reason we should not face oppression is our humanity rather than the fact that no one and no being should face it. Similarly, women often describe being "treated like a piece of meat": this is a feeling that many, including myself, can identify with, and may be a useful rhetorical device (see image below). However, it is ultimately damaging. By using phrases like this, we assert that, as women, it is wrong for us to be objectified, commodified, and subjected to a gaze that consumes us. We fail to address the fact that nobody and *no body* should be treated this way; that no body is meat, and should not be seen or treated as such. We also actively participate in the objectification and symbolic consumption of animal bodies. By using their violated bodies and body parts as a proxy for our own, we erase the animal, the *being* that the "meat" once was.

The language we use in conversation with our students is at the basis of our anti-speciesist teaching practice. Undoing how we learn to speak about animals is part of actively undoing common sources of oppressions in the classroom. Analyzing the way we intertwine oppressions through language and action opens our learning facilitation to a wide array of vegan-feminist topics that, at first glance, might not seem relevant.

How to Didactically Illustrate Interconnected Oppressions

To teach emancipatory practice we need to show our students that the origins and expressions of human and nonhuman oppression are often the same or similar.

Let us use eugenics as an example of similarities between speciesism and human forms of oppression. Eugenics, far from only being a historical atrocity limited to the Third Reich, existed prior to it and continues to this day in many forms.[11] A set of lessons could be developed around the topic and materials could be presented on how different identity groups are affected by it. With some background knowledge provided by the course facilitator, groups of students could be asked to prepare presentations on "how the theory and practice of eugenics affects disabled people/people of color/animals/people with wombs."

The teacher's role is to provide impulses for the students to interact with the subject, to analyze it, and to explore parallels across chronologies, cultures, and species. Many avenues for potential new discussion across a range of disciplines (e.g., biology, history, political science, linguistics, philosophy, and ethics) will appear with this subject. Some of the knowledge exchanged might look like this:

For example, oppressed groups are often subjected to various forms of incarceration. For disabled people, this can mean incarceration in "correctional" or medical facilities, under the medical industrial complex; for people of color in particular this would mean the disproportionate incarceration in the prison-industrial complex; for nonhuman animals, it is incarceration in the industrial farming or agricultural complex as well as in the zoo and medical-experimentation industries.[12]

Reproductive control is also a thread that runs through both human and nonhuman oppression. People with wombs have, throughout history, been denied the right to control their own body, fertility, and future. This continues today, as people across the world fight for bodily autonomy in the form of abortion rights and wider reproductive justice. Specifically, people of color have also had their reproductive rights taken away from them through many means, including the sterilization of African American, Native American, and Puerto Rican women in the U.S. in recent decades.[13] Non-human animals incarcerated in the industry have little to no control over their own reproduction, as human "owners" are in total control of their reproduction, and in the case of female-assigned animals, this is where they are given their value. The industry itself knows that it is sexually violent: the apparatus used in the artificial insemination of dairy cows, for example, is known colloquially as "the rape rack." From the breeding of pets to the breeding of animals for consumption, animals' reproduction is controlled in order to benefit humans and industry.

Countless examples exist of nation-states and other bodies, including medical institutions, using sterilization and reproductive control to eugenicist ends in the last century, not only in Nazi Germany but throughout Europe and in America.[14] Today, that control is rarely as explicit as non-consensual sterilization. Now disabled sexuality, for instance, is both erased and policed structurally. For people with learning difficulties and cognitive impairments, advice and information on sexual health are often withheld by care providers. In denying disabled people information about sex, as well as sexual and romantic relationships, non-disabled society strips them of their sexuality. It denies them their ability to make informed decisions and take ownership of their own bodies and reproductive capabilities (and equip them with understanding of consent and empower them against all-too-common abuse).

Even a basic knowledge of human oppression and liberation movements can help us articulate the importance and urgency of animal liberation. With the example of eugenics programs, for instance, we can easily show our students how oppressive mechanisms work to hurt humans and animals alike. Eugenics is openly practiced in the farming industry, under the euphemistic terms *husbandry* or *selective breeding*. A key difference between the human and nonhuman experiences of eugenics is that when it is applied to humans, one often seeks to remove what is understood as an impairment from the gene pool. For nonhuman animals, however, impairments in animals are often encouraged in order to increase profitability. Chickens, for example, have been bred to develop much faster and possess more of the "popular meats," like breast. This results in numerous medical conditions, discomfort, pain, and death, as their bodies strain under the pressure.

When addressing these topics with your students or audience, it is essential to be sensitive and careful. We must not only be respectful towards the truths we speak but (perhaps more importantly) towards those with whom we speak. As educators, we must consider the trauma our students may be carrying and we must create spaces in which facilitating difficult and often personal discussions feels safe. We must recognize that many of the participants of our classes and conversations may live with inherited trauma of the events and attitudes discussed above. Many will have had firsthand experiences of the present-day effects of this historical context.[15]

Letting students explore identity allows them to work with their own vulnerability. They will get to know themselves and their world better by identifying their own position in society and exploring their options for navigating it. Further enhancing their awareness of difference, struggle, and power will evoke care and compassion for others experiencing different forms of oppression. This will in turn open their minds to considering animals ethically.

In order to be able to make our knowledge of eugenics relevant to animal liberation, in the classroom and beyond, let us return once more to the medical-industrial complex, specifically the practice of animal testing. In nonhuman animals, proximity to "human-ness" defines how animals are seen and used by humans under speciesist social ordering. In this social order, the human is at the top and, as such, nonhuman animals that are considered to be close to humans in terms of genetics, brain function, and appearance, for instance, are spared *some* of the violence that others are subjected to.

For example, it is generally accepted by people who are pro-animal testing that medical tests should not be carried out on any of the Great Apes ("higher primates"). It is, however, deemed acceptable to use "lower primates" in both specific medical testing and general research testing. John Stein of the Oxford Functional Neurosurgery Group discussed his work on an episode of the debate show *The Big Questions* and explained that he had qualms about the use of "higher primates" in medical testing because he must consider the intelligence of the animal when considering *its* suffering.[16] Measures of cognitive function and intelligence are, however, socially constructed under speciesist, hetero-patriarchal, ableist, and white supremacist social ordering. These human-centric standards serve to maintain positions of power and dominance, which make exploitation possible.

An examination of the human/animal binary from a disability or *crip* perspective[17] is necessary when exploring this issue with your students or audience. It is at least accepted in scientific terms that humans are indeed animals, that we are one specific species in a world full of them. The binary of animal and human has been socially constructed in order to exclude nonhuman animals, as well as humans of marginalized identities from the dominant group at a time when "man" has dominion on Earth, the Anthropocene. This dominance has been developed through everything from biblical scripture and manifest destiny to children's nursery rhymes. Despite being so ingrained in the fabric of Eurocentric society, few justifying arguments actually stand up to scrutiny.

This socially constructed binary is often defined along capability lines: language acquisition—that humans as a species have developed thousands of verbal and written languages—is frequently cited as a significant differentiating factor. It is argued that nonhuman animals have not developed languages and therefore are different. This is where we run into problems. First, our understanding of ways of communicating or definition of language has (once again) been socially constructed by humans; therefore, the ideal is defined as *human* and such a standard is unattainable for nonhumans. Secondly, animals absolutely do have ways and means of communicating; they do not always fit our human construction of language, but they exist. Thirdly, there are human and nonhuman beings that transgress this binary; various species of Great Apes have been taught forms of sign language, which is of course a form of communication created by humans. What happens when an animal acquires a skill that is seen as central to our identity as humans? Or, perhaps more pertinent to disabled activists, what about people who have sensory and/or communication challenges? What of people who cannot use any standardized form of language? We shudder at the idea that someone who is not traditionally communicative could be seen as an animal (as they were in historical cases of "wild children"), because it implies they have a lesser value. But this is only because we assume that humans are valuable and animals are less so.

The implication of the utilitarian argument for animal testing is that only the suffering of an "intelligent" being matters. This is especially troubling for the disabled community considering the fact that intelligence and cognitive function are socially constructed to non-disabled, neurotypical standards. If we are to accept violence against animals who do not "measure up" to these standards, where do we stop? At what point might someone be deemed so intellectually impaired that we find their suffering does not matter? When analyzing this with our students and supporting them in cripping the human/animal binary, we will notice how they will actively rupture and abandon this social construct.

In order to address the universal liberation that is needed, false binaries like these must be torn down and replaced with an understanding of a being's inherent worth, regardless of their proximity to, or distance from, an ideal. This is why it is not only logical but necessary for our pedagogies to present a holistic approach to liberation: one that includes animals in our moral understanding of emancipation, autonomy, and freedom.

As Crenshaw and many others point out, to approach different oppressions individually and without an understanding of the complexities of identity is to limit our grasp on the multifaceted matrix of oppressive structures and systems that animals are also part of. For this reason, I believe it is our role as activists, artists, teachers, protesters, and facilitators to foster solidarity and connectedness through inclusive pedagogies. This is how we learn, together with our audiences, to resist the logic of othering through which systems of oppression are maintained.

A Toolkit for Vegan Artists, Educators, and Activists

To effectively communicate difficult topics such as animal liberation, we must internalize a few principles that should guide our attitudes towards our pedagogical practice. The following eight points should be applied when planning and facilitating a lesson:

1. Understand Intersectionality
Know the theory and why it's important. Know the theory's roots. Know why it is necessary and how to practice it.

2. Expand Your Audience
Don't privilege knowledge and information. Don't limit your ability to access others by limiting their ability to access you. Understand that a diverse audience is desirable and necessary when it comes to creating meaningful change at a societal level.

3. Expand Your Sources
Have diverse groups of people to source. Have diverse means of exchange. Use podcasts, documentaries, art, comic strips, blogs, and other non-traditionally academic sources to explore and share knowledge.

4. Understand Positionalities
Understand how every person's positions within society inform their experiences. Work out ways to use this understanding of positionalities to break down barriers to cohesive relationships and movements.

5. Understand the Power of Language
Know the harm you can do by using certain language or certain metaphors. Arbitrarily using examples of human suffering when explaining animal suffering relativizes both. Do not do so to evoke an emotional reaction from your audience but ensure critical engagement.

6. Listen
Listen to other people. Listen to yourself. When people (particularly people who face oppressions that you don't experience) raise issues, listen. If you are white, and a person of color tells you that your behavior turns them away from veganism, listen. If you are non-disabled and a disabled person tells you that your vegan potluck is in an inaccessible space, or your health advice is unwanted and oppressive, listen. Do not see issues raised as an excuse or justification for that person's own political or personal failings; see them as opportunities for personal and movement growth. Listen

to the small part of your brain that thinks maybe an aspect of your work is problematic: explore that possibility and listen to yourself.

7. Be Gentle

Be gentle with yourself. Be gentle with others. Understand that we are all at different stages of the journey. Be aware of the experiences that people may have had that could shape the way they respond to you and what you're saying. Build movements and communities, in your classrooms and beyond, which are inwardly nurturing as well as outwardly revolutionary. Model your fight against oppression on how you imagine life without oppression. Reject the logic of "just a means to an end." Do not push yourself or others too far. Remember that social justice work is hard, that burnout is real, and that you do yourself and the movement a disservice when you fail to take care of yourself.

8. Be Critical and Accountable

Be critical of yourself. Be critical of others. Be critical of people you agree with. Be critical of people you don't agree with. Constantly be critiquing structures, tactics, means, goals, theories, and movements. Cultivate critique as a political practice. At the same time, be accountable and responsible for your actions and incorporate critiques you face into your vegan practice.

BLURRING THE HUMAN/ANIMAL BINARY WITH ART

It is possible and necessary to create pedagogical material, media, and art that address animal oppression without exploiting human oppression; it's even possible to make work that addresses both animal *and* human oppression! I look to the work of many artists and activists for inspiration on how to do veganism without being oppressive. The best place to start is with the women artists whose works make up *The Art of the Animal*, a wonderful exploration of themes from Carol Adams' *The Sexual Politics of Meat* by women in art.[18]

In her contribution to that volume, "Beautiful Little Dead Things," Lynn Mowson effectively illustrates the concepts of *The Sexual Politics of*

Meat with her sculptural work, which is simultaneously dead but sexualized. In *Slink*, the female-presenting form is hinted at, made out of latex and suspended by wires; it is grotesque in all of its grizzly reality. The figure is both human and nonhuman animal, speaking to the oppressions experienced by both, neither privileging nor exploiting one in favor of the other.

In my own work, I have often struggled with how to make art about oppression without replicating oppression or its images. For example, a project that has been marinating for years began with still images from hardcore pornography combined with images of abattoirs. I was never happy with the ethics of this; while trying to call out the objectification in patriarchal and speciesist oppression, I had actively participated in it myself. What I wanted to address was distaste at the dinner table joke, "Are you a breast or a leg/thigh man?" I have long found this a sinister confirmation of the link between gender- and species-based oppressions, and the need for integrated vegan and feminist movements. I've remade and remade this work and it's taken many forms, including a sculpture hybrid of a blow-up doll and a Christmas turkey costume. The most recent version of it is included below. I hope this gives you a good example of how my own pedagogy and vegan practice is informed by all the things discussed in this chapter.

In its present form, I use patchwork techniques juxtaposed against objectifying stock photographs and the text "A sinister Sunday lunch joke; are you a breast or a leg man?" to demonstrate the perverse undertones of what is, at first glance, a jovial family occasion—sitting together and sharing food. The fabric I had printed to make up the patchwork consists of stock photographs of a dead chicken's uncooked body, a white woman's legs, and "chicken fillet," breast-"enhancing" bra inserts, which are made to look like conventionally attractive white woman's breasts. Aesthetically, I thought it was important to connect the three images through similar coloring, to underscore the cohesion between human and nonhuman animal objectification. However, I was also aware of my use of white bodies (or prosthetics). This was a conscious choice to avoid speaking to an oppression that I do not face and accidentally participating in oppressive behaviors and re-creating objectification. Though it was not an informing factor, this choice led to a subtle exploration of white-centered beauty standards.

The work and I are not finished growing together. Every new version raises new ethical and political questions and displays some new problematic element. I feel that as long as I remain open to being told (and to telling myself) where my work has hit and where it has missed, I will keep developing and growing. Each issue raised is an opportunity to become better. This is also how I conduct my pedagogy when addressing students or any audience. I remain open, flexible, and accountable.

The conclusion to this chapter is simply written but will take our collective lifetimes to put into practice: be inclusive, be reflective, be humble, be brave, be what your human and nonhuman family deserve. Base your vegan practice and vegan pedagogy on radical compassion, for those you are advocating for, those you are advocating to, and for yourself.

3

MODELING DISSENT

TEACHERS AS PROTECTORS, ACTIVISTS, AND PUBLIC INTELLECTUALS

Jacqueline Adamescu

[T]he more radical the person is, the more fully [they] enter into reality so that, knowing it better, he or she [or they] can better transform it. This individual is not afraid to confront, to listen, to see the world unveiled. This person is not afraid to meet the people or to enter into dialogue with them. This person does not consider [themselves] the proprietor of history or of all people, or the liberator of the oppressed; but [they do] commit [themselves], within history, to fight at their side.—**Paulo Freire**[1]

When I was little, my father would often tell me that he wished he'd have had a son instead of a first-born daughter. This mantra underscores all memories of my childhood. Each tear I shed, each scraped knee or wad of gum stuck in my tumbleweed of hair, this was his response. "I should have had a son," he'd tell me, massaging paint-thinner in my hair to let the gum loose, pouring iodine on my open wounds. "Quit crying," he would often add. "What do you have to cry about?"

Midwestern exurbia was my first home: conservative, middle-class, and white. My survival as a young woman in this context hinged upon two core aspects of my personality: I was a tomboy who loved to read. My tomboyish nature was certainly who I was deep-down, a child who ran around barefoot and constructed stick-forts at the mouth of the woods behind my grandmother's house, rubbing silt from creek-beds on my forearms up to the elbows (armor to protect me from invisible foes).

I played sports not only because I truly enjoyed them, but because I was naturally athletic and loved competing with the same boys who, off the field, would shove my head against the brick walls of our elementary school. Since I wasn't stick-thin, they called me fat, and when in the fifth grade I cut my hair to emulate my favorite music group—The Beatles—they found it ugly and weird, and often whined, "You know you're a girl, right?" I should also mention that my parents sent me to Catholic school for all of elementary, middle, and high school, a context in which it is never safe to be a girl of any sort, much less one that wears her hair short and prefers the company of books to the approval of boys.

That Catholicism functions in and through institutionalized misogyny is unquestionable. My experience growing up in and being educated by an arm of this church convinced me at a young age that my body (my femaleness) defined my worth, and that to question or critique structures of power was a crime punishable by private and public shaming, derision, intimidation, and virtual excommunication from the community of the "saved." Once, during sophomore year, my (male) theology teacher called me a whore for having the top button of my oxford shirt undone. When I brought this up to the (male) assistant principal, demanding an apology and for administrative action to be taken, I was chided for having been "out of dress code" and leaving that teacher "no choice" but to admonish me for baring the skin of my clavicle. In that moment, I wondered whether or not a similar conversation had occurred between the administration and my math teacher, a man who was notorious for making inappropriate comments and physical advances towards young women he deemed the prettiest.

Books were at the heart of my survival in this situation. Through constant reading, I developed the critical reasoning skills that would eventually help me to overcome my repressed, authoritarian upbringing. My sense of self, my language of autonomy, and my empathy I owe all to books and to the few teachers who, throughout my life, taught me to nurture my love of learning as a gardener who weaves her hands deftly through soil. The teachers who impacted me the most, however, did not simply plant the seeds themselves, but placed them in my hands and taught me how to sow.

The whole of my life I've been watering those seeds. As such, successful gardeners develop an intimate knowledge of plants only by working in and among them, with dirt up under their nails, caked in the soles of their work boots. The same goes for learning: one's strength as a reader and, by extension, as a thinker or writer, is measured by the strength of one's commitment to grapple with those texts that test the boundaries of language and understanding. One becomes a skillful, attentive reader much the same way the gardener develops calluses on her hands: she shapes the earth slowly over time, considering the pain brought on by blisters and the drought of fatigue as necessary parts of the struggle for growth.

This is the fecundity of books. This, also, is the bedrock of dissent: possessing the ability to think, speak, write, express, and act in full knowledge and in spite of oppression, along with the understanding that one can and must do all of these things. Certainly, if there is to be any hope of more than just survival for women, people of color, the working poor, immigrants, the non-religious, queer folks, refugees, the otherly abled and disabled, young people, and nonhuman animals chiefly among them, those of us who are able must dissent, always and often. We must identify each and every oppressive force that acts upon and through us, whether in our name or against us, in order to destroy that which destroys us.

If we take this responsibility to heart, and apply it with humility and seriousness, we begin to see the ways in which human liberation intertwines with that of other animals. A commitment to dismantling oppression naturally encourages us to develop the twin senses of empathy and compassion for the other, regardless of whether or not these others share our same plight, speak our same language, or exist in the world as we do. The only holistic approach to achieving total liberation requires the inclusion of *all* marginalized and oppressed groups; considering this, activists must also work against anthropocentrism and speciesism, facing the fight for Earth and animal liberation with the same fire in their bellies that kindles their passion for liberating humankind.

It is incontestable that knowledge is power. However, the way that power is wielded—including what form it takes—depends upon *who* shares that knowledge, and *how*. This is further impacted by the person sharing knowledge or information: his/her/their personal histories, unconscious biases, personality traits, and political affiliations. All of these can shape information and significantly impact how it will be received. Educators must, therefore, provide numerous, diverse opportunities for students to access subject-area content while striving to meet the academic, social-emotional, and behavioral needs of each individual. This is a reliable way to ensure that the knowledge exchange is not compromised by gatekeeping, whether intended or otherwise. Stressing once more what Beti Scott Brown writes in the previous chapter, here are a few of the ways I feel this can be achieved:

1. Purposefully seek out texts and authors that reflect the lived experiences, interests, and culture(s) of students;
2. Incorporate project-based methods, including small group activities and collaborative learning;
3. Model a liberatory, inclusive language that honors the narratives of students while encouraging them to think reflexively about the power of language to shape the world and their understanding;
4. Lay bare the pervasiveness of white supremacist and colonial structures by incorporating outside materials that address, for instance, the whitewashing of history and the rigid exclusivity of the white masculinist canon in literature;
5. Select texts written by and about people of color, the working class, women and other marginalized authors and explain to the students your purposeful inclusion of these authors;
6. Contextualize every unit, text, or lesson within a wider sociopolitical and historical context, to the greatest extent possible;
7. Place deliberate emphasis on a measured, thorough critique and methods of questioning and reasoning, interweaving these skills throughout every lesson regardless of the specific subject area or content standards;

8. Further encourage students' critical thinking by openly discussing the representation of women, gender nonconforming folks, people of color, the working class, and other animals in class texts, the news, on social media, or in daily conversation;
9. Enact transformative and restorative justice techniques when approaching issues of students' academic performance and behavior;
10. Pause to listen to your students' ideas and concerns, and prioritize their academic and social-emotional needs as much as you do your own;
11. Model kindness, curiosity, creativity, work ethic, patience, humility, studiousness, and a growth mindset to the students, for they do not simply view you as their teacher, but as a whole person: quirks, flaws, interests, achievements, and personality.

In light of these general suggestions, reconsider the following: how might the skills of the gardener and the constant reader be adapted as tools of resistance against our oppressors? Further, how might educators model or effectively teach radically liberated subject positions to students, with the goal of helping each one of them to develop an autonomous sense of self apart from (and against) oppressive ideology? To begin, teachers must first adopt the liberatory pedagogical principle that *radicalization of thought leads to liberation*. The fact that I am an atheist, anarcha-feminist, and anti-speciesist directly informs my understanding of the significant role that a just, quality public education system has to play in the liberation of all who are oppressed. Adopting investigative subject positions such as these promotes an always-deepening social awareness, productive self-doubt, and critical reasoning skills—the very qualities I strive to model for my students.

WOMEN WHO TEACH, TRANSGRESS

> I am grateful that I can be a witness, testifying that we can create a feminist theory, a feminist practice, a revolutionary feminist movement that can speak directly to the pain that is within folks, and offer them healing words, healing strategy, healing theory.—**bell hooks**[2]

For bell hooks, a classroom is "the most radical space of possibility"—of healing, of transgression, of "education as the practice of freedom."[3] For girls and women, and for other marginalized groups and nonconforming individuals, classrooms can provide safe, productive spaces in which novel modes of thought and being can be tested with relative freedom. In the same way that, since childhood, I have been comforted and challenged by books, and have found a home in worlds unlike that of any I have inhabited in the physical sense, I have also found sanctuary in the classrooms of those few teachers who treated me with respect and love. Most of these teachers have been women. To my mind, this is no small coincidence.

Women teachers who enact their pedagogical practices in line with an *ethic of care* engage in a subtle form of feminist resistance that undercuts capitalist, patriarchal expectations of supposed rigor and productivity. Approaching our students and content *with empathy* is the first in a series of important steps women educators can take in order to dismantle oppressive structures that inform our lives and the lives of our students. To be clear, I am not suggesting that women who teach must be meek or endlessly forgiving, or that they adopt a "caretaking" attitude. In the most literal sense, I advocate for women educators knowingly and purposefully to engage with an ethic of care as a means for establishing authentic, non-antagonistic relationships with students. Once established, this type of learning environment can open up discussions around race, class, gender, ability, culture, species, language, and other differences, effectively creating what bell hooks describes as "a context where we can engage in open critical dialogue with one another, where we can debate and discuss without fear of emotional collapse, where we can hear and know one another in the difference and complexities of our experience."[4]

There need to be more women in all educational positions at every level; but there also needs to be a greater number of women historians, engineers, scientists, and mathematicians who publish in their respective disciplines and are hired to influential teaching positions at competitive rates with those of men. The further lack of representation and visibility of women of color and working-class women must form the center of any discussion of transgressive women educators. Transgressive women who teach have a unique responsibility to model alternative modes of being, particularly for girls, young women, and gender non-conforming youths. Through the ways in which we conduct our classes, construct the language and format of our lessons, approach literature and writing, and in our everyday interactions with students, we have opportunities to work against sexist, racist, classist, and speciesist stereotypes while ensuring that all students are provided a curriculum that is critical, relatable, and of high interest to them.

In my classroom, I am consistent in my language and tone with the students, and establish high standards of thoroughness and personal accountability from the start. My effectiveness and impact on students depend upon my transparency as much as it depends on follow-through. Young people have come to expect that adults in positions of power will let them down or, at the very least, be inconsistent in their words and actions. This is the oppressive logic at the heart of ageism: that young people have inherently less value and ability as agents for change, whether in their own lives, the lives of their friends and relatives, or in the community at large. The impact of ageist stereotypes on students is too often underestimated or completely left out of conversations about the current state of public education.

We also must elaborate upon how our socialization as women has contributed to our politics and reasons for teaching. For instance, I, an able-bodied, cisgender woman of white European ancestry, having been raised in a large, middle class, Catholic family from the Midwestern United States, was for the first fifteen years of my life oblivious to the myriad struggles faced by students in public schools. It was not until I attended college that I even began to cultivate a liberatory language for myself. I spent the latter part of my teens and early twenties unlearning the posture that feminism was a dangerous stance for any *truly* enlightened young woman to take. Once I self-identified as a feminist, I further developed my lazy questioning of organized religion into agnosticism, eventually fully embracing atheism. My perception of society shifted from something of a loose affiliation with corporate capitalist humanism to incorporating Marxist, post-colonial, deconstructionist, anti-racist, and anarchist critiques.

I became vegan at twenty-two, but did not encounter Kimberlé Crenshaw's work[5] until my first year of graduate school, at which point my sapling political self grew, bolt upright, into a tree with many grasping branches, each radiating upwards and outwards, gathering photons full to bursting with information to feed every part of me, from my leaf-veins to my wooden roots. This, I feel, is an adequate picture of the process of learning that I strive to model for my students. What is chiefly emphasized is the unending process of grasping, gathering, and effectively judging information, and incorporating all that we read or hear or otherwise experience into our evolving self-perception, including our morals and methods for making choices.

Too often, I have had teachers in the past who deliberately walled themselves off from students, refusing to engage in any line of questioning or thought that strayed, however wildly, from the topic at hand towards the more outrightly personal or political. As a student I never understood this. Why, if I am asked to share my whole mind and self through multiple subjects and modes, must I never interact with my teachers as persons of interest, as fellow citizens with personal histories and ideas that are of obvious import to me? Any perpetuation of an immovable divide between teachers and students is a perpetuation of hierarchical, authoritarian thinking. Again, it is ageist to presume that my life as a teacher is somehow more important or worthy of protection than that of my students. They are young, yes, but they teach me about myself and my subject and my profession all the time. I am always learning from them, arguably more than they will ever learn from me. Truly transgressive classrooms foster a learning environment in which both teachers and students can be vulnerable enough to ask questions. This is another way to create accountability for one's own learning—which, in the current sociopolitical context, very often means asserting authority over one's own self while remaining humble to all that remains to be learned.

Safe, critical classrooms allow students and teachers to begin taking responsibility for our beliefs, attitudes, and behaviors. The more we participate actively in the learning community, the more likely it becomes that we develop empathy towards one another and begin to consider the experiences and well-being of our peers. The development of critical-thinking skills often coincides with the consciousness-raising that occurs in such learning environments. Also of interest is the way in which radical open-minded curiosity opens up conversations around transgressive politics that liberates both humans and other animals.

It often starts with students inquiring deeper about my own veganism. I explain that I am boycotting the use, exploitation, and killing of other animals in all its forms; when students inevitably ask *Why?*, I add that it is unethical to treat other animals the way that humans have treated them, and that it is unnecessary for us to consume animal products when we in fact do not need to do so in order to survive.[6] I make explicit connections between veganism, feminism, and my reasons for teaching, emphasizing the interconnectedness of these multiple struggles (while acknowledging the singularity of each). The minds of young people are amazingly plastic and readily make room for such challenging concepts. Young people also tend to be more emotionally open. They have not yet had their empathic nature completely ruined by adults, society, or circumstance.

Brazilian educator and philosopher Paulo Freire addresses the need for educators to grant more power of authority to students in engaging with, and shaping, their own learning. This student-centered approach is required for any authentic liberatory model of teaching to exist. Freire insists that teachers should consider themselves as teacher-students, and that they must consider their students as student-teachers. He cautions: "If students are not able to transform their lived experience into knowledge and to use the already acquired knowledge as a process to unveil new knowledge, they will never be able to participate rigorously in a dialogue as a process of learning and knowing."[7] This is why transgressive educators must purposefully and transparently center the needs and lived experiences of students. In Freire's understanding, if students are kept from actively and authentically engaging in their own processes of learning—if they are prevented from making contributions or levying critiques—both their intellectual and social-emotional development will be grossly undermined, if not stunted.

To teach transgressively is to know that the personal is political. Our lives are not made or unmade in secret; we cannot unglue ourselves from society's all-encompassing web. These entailments are the measure of our lives. To deny this is either the result of ignorance or privilege. In *Teaching to Transgress: Education as the Practice of Freedom*, bell hooks emphasizes that teachers have a moral responsibility to confront, vigorously and honestly, the political structures that shape our lives and the lives of our students. This practice lays the groundwork for cultivating true solidarity with and among students, which hooks proclaims "must be affirmed by shared belief in a spirit of intellectual openness that celebrates diversity, welcomes dissent, and rejoices in collective dedication to truth."[8] Educators who hope to affect positive change for students in the current educational context must therefore be committed to treating the practice of teaching as a revolutionary act. We must each see ourselves as equal partners with our students in an accumulative and multifaceted movement for social justice that is intimately tied to all individual, familial, communal, national, and global liberation struggles.

What socially progressive teachers must keep in mind is that participating in corporate capitalist school politics as "business as usual" spells the death of critical thought and inquiry for all students currently caught up in the public education system in the United States. The advent of No Child Left Behind (NCLB) in the early 2000s hastened the corporatization of schools, the results of which are as numerous as they are corrosive. Consider the following:

1. Standardized tests do not measure any authentic academic or social-emotional outcomes and are easily passable only by certain subsets of students, chiefly white middle- or upper-middle-class youth who come from families that place significant emphasis on academic achievement and who are enrolled in well-funded school districts with smaller class sizes and more equal teacher-to-student ratios.
2. NCLB fast-tracked the corporatization of public education. School districts, boards, and administrative bodies have scapegoated teachers for students' poor performance on standardized tests, sometimes docking teacher pay, withholding pay raises, or threatening to fire educators. In this context, what teachers are really being blamed for is not their purported lack of ability to teach but

for the loss of monies allocated to public schools and districts based on student performance and/or improvement on any number of state-issued standardized tests.⁹

3. It is also problematic that standardized tests do not fully or authentically measure core curricular standards or learning outcomes. Even when (or if) they do, can they accurately encompass the societal, intellectual, or academic values we desire? Most public school districts have adopted (i.e. purchased from textbook or testing companies) increasingly restrictive, pre-designed curricula that teachers are mandated to use in their planning and instruction. Unsurprisingly, these curricula focus on skills and norms directly aligned to state and national standardized testing. This requires that teachers effectively "teach to the test," forcing us to teach in a regimented, one-size-fits-all fashion that de-emphasizes critical-thinking skills, reading and in-depth analysis of literary texts, interdisciplinarity, project-based learning, etc.

4. This ultimately not only limits possibilities for critical engagement with systems of oppression that we both struggle with and reproduce (such as racism or speciesism), but it can prevent us from authentically engaging with them in the first place. Further, teachers—myself included—are discouraged from incorporating any "external" texts or lessons. This is especially true for probationary teachers who have not yet earned tenure. The overarching message: teachers must teach pre-designed curriculum, as purchased by boards of administrators at the school or district level, *or else*.

One way to unpack these observations is by considering what Paulo Freire refers to as the "banking concept of education."¹⁰ Adherents of this hierarchical approach consider students as passive receivers of clandestine knowledge, kept safe and administered by teachers who place *themselves* at the center of their pedagogy. In this scenario, teachers are the primary holders and distributors of knowledge, keeping students in a perpetual receiving mode (which, proponents of the "banking model" would argue, is sufficient, since in their view students enter classrooms in ignorance and leave them not having done enough to achieve *intellectual greatness*). Again, this is no secret. How many times has each of us sat in a class with such a teacher? Their lessons are stiff, driven by lecture and note-taking, and rely chiefly upon the rote memorization of canonical facts and figures with little to no room for student inquiry into the innerworkings of the texts, models, modes, or figures under consideration.

Women in education have an increasingly important role to play in the protection of our students, especially those under direct threat during this time of social upheaval in the United States and abroad. Neofascism and white supremacist patriarchy have renewed platforms due to nationalist and populist backlash. The election of Donald Trump as the forty-fifth President of the United States, in addition to the appointment of Betsy DeVos as Education Secretary, Steve Bannon as Chief Advisor to the President (to 2017), Jeff Sessions as U.S. Attorney General (to 2018), Mike Pompeo as Secretary of State, and Scott Pruitt as the head of the Environmental Protection Agency (to 2018), all serve as proof of a new era of authoritarian rule: one of an absolute concentration of power in the hands of white masculinist supremacists, autocrats, religious kleptocrats, crony capitalists, the egregiously wealthy, and those whose definition of truth is more dependent on their greed and vanity than it is on logic, empathy, or objective reasoning skills.

Conclusion

> Skepticism must be a component of the explorer's toolkit, or we will lose our way.—**Carl Sagan**[11]

Carl Sagan often spoke of the duality of the public intellectual. The intent to behave in a morally upright fashion and moral acts themselves are not one and the same, and those charged with the responsibility of educating the public can perilously toe the line between self-interested sermonizing and teaching with humility. Commenting on the responsibility of scientists to uphold democratized scientific ideals, Sagan affirms that "it is the job of the scientist to recognize our weaknesses, to examine the widest range of opinions, to be ruthlessly self-critical."[12] This ruthless self-critique can help to establish a truly liberatory pedagogy, one in which all participants are seen as equal actors with an inalienable right to contribute to the accumulation of knowledge while being held to account for their own biases.

Unlearning is hard work. Asking questions of ourselves and the world can be even more difficult a task than this. Evolving out of attitudes mandated by oppressive environments, at home and school and society at large, is painstaking work that can fill years or decades. The cultivation of my own revolutionary consciousness reflects a growth process that has taken years of reading and exposure to unfamiliar experiences and ideas. As I look back through time, sifting through the dustier, more thickly cobwebbed corners of my memory warehouse, I easily find examples of early empathy in myself: my compassion towards other animals, my love of books and deep feeling for the characters within them, and the unrest I have felt in the face of aggressive assaults against otherness—*my* otherness. I find comfort in the core aspects of my personality that have been there from the beginning and am thankful for every opportunity to continue evolving alongside my students, whose resilience is only matched in intensity and depth by their desire for learning. In these and many other ways they are trees who never cease to grow: their roots reach ever deeper as their branches and leaves grasp for the universe.

4

Including an Anti-speciesist Practice in My Work with Neurodiverse Youth

Riley J. Taylor

To me, anti-speciesism is an ongoing, everyday resistance to living in a world that gives value to some lives over others. Anti-speciesism is more than a moral and ethical stand against using animals for food, clothing, and entertainment. It is political. Whereas anti-speciesist activists don't always advocate for total liberation—which includes the liberation of oppressed humans—I believe that the only way for anti-speciesist practice to work is to engage critically with the capitalist, patriarchal, heteronormative system that allows speciesism to exist. That same system creates and authorizes countless types of discrimination, such as racism, sexism, and ableism. Speciesism does not exist in a vacuum, so opposing speciesism cannot be successful if we ignore the foundations it grew from. On a more compassionate level, extending moral consideration to animals feels hypocritical without acknowledging the daily struggles some of our fellow humans endure to survive. We need to support each other. I understand that this probably feels vague and difficult to put into practice, so I want to tell you about myself and how I involve anti-speciesism in the work I do with students.

I'm a neurotypical adult working in an autism base at a predominantly allistic (that is, non-autistic) UK secondary school for students aged eleven to sixteen years. Obviously, I can only describe the relationships with the students I work with and the experiences that we have shared from my (neurotypical) perspective.

For those who are unfamiliar with or have limited knowledge of autism, I will briefly summarize my knowledge here. (I wish to note that all individuals are different and much more complex than a few sentences written by a neurotypical person.) Autistic people[1] interact with and understand the world in different ways to allistic, neurodiverse, and neurotypical people. Sensory differences can mean that some individuals can be hyper- or hyposensitive to light, sound, smell, and touch. For example, particular colors or materials can cause feelings that range from discomfort to physical pain. Our society, built *by* and *for* the neurotypical and able-bodied, is largely unaccommodating to autistic people. This means that autistic people use huge amounts of energy blocking out triggers. Ultimately, autistic people are expected to learn how to conform to a neurotypical world that has little interest in understanding and accepting difference.

Many mainstream secondary schools, for example, have been built with tight corridors due to space constraints. Students are expected to travel to classes at the same time, resulting in large groups of young people blocking stairwells and room entrances waiting for permission to enter their class. Maneuvering loud, busy corridors is incredibly difficult for the autistic students I work with. Instead of agreeing to devise a system that resolves this for the entirety of the student body, schools expect autistic students to either conform or find ways to cope with the noise themselves.

I work in the south of England, in a predominantly white and middle-class area. Pockets of poverty exist between the lines of well-ironed uniforms and designer-brand trainers (sneakers), and the widening chasm between the "haves" and "have-nots" will continue to grow as the current Conservative government slashes education budgets.[2] I work as a support assistant with six students, one of whom is part of a free school-meals plan. Young people who are autistic experience ableist oppression (discrimination or prejudice towards people who are disabled, which includes disregarding accessibility needs). Young people who are poor experience class-based oppression—they may have more responsibilities at home and are less likely to continue to university for economic reasons.[3]

Young people who are autistic and poor exist in a system that disempowers them for their economic standing and their neurodiversity separately, not recognizing that their *complete* lives and identities are affected by both. To critically reflect upon this fragmented perception of young, autistic, poor people it is helpful to consider Kimberlé Crenshaw's concept of intersectionality.[4] As we have seen in the previous two chapters, this theory highlights that black women could only be considered in law either as black or as a woman: legally, these parts of their identity were regarded separately when they should instead be thought of as overlapping. Crenshaw's theory points to a flaw that exists in systems of power, whereby individuals are categorized by one aspect rather than the entirety of their being. It provides us with a framework for identifying oppression.

For example, students who are entitled to free school meals have a daily allowance which restricts them to purchasing specific food. Some autistic people eat particular food because of sensory differences: one child, for instance, could only eat chips (French fries) and bread for a period of time because all other food had an uncomfortable texture which made the child ill. Therefore, being limited to certain meals is distressing and has an impact on the overall well-being of the students. This in turn has consequences for their social relations and educational performance. The food on offer typically contains animal flesh or dairy. Students with limited food options are thus forced to accept the exploitation, murder, and consumption of animals as normal, as choices are in fact limited.

As vegan educators we usually try very hard to portray veganism as easy and accessible, and for the most part we are probably right in doing so. However, it is easy to forget that there are people, including many of our students, who in fact do not have a choice, and who are even stripped of their autonomy when it comes to picking a meal. If we are following a total liberation approach, one not solely concerned with animals but also with the emancipation of our fellow humans, it is clear that much more needs to be done in our pedagogies than simply making visible the abundance of cheap vegan food options.

At our school, as in most speciesist institutions, there are no ethical discussions about the use of living beings as food. There is no information about where the flesh served up at lunch has come from, or what conditions the animals were living in before they were killed. In an ideal world, we want young people to grow into critical thinkers. Yet, children and young adults are denied the knowledge to make their own informed choices. Withholding information leaves room for animals to be treated like objects and be denied the right to live as sentient beings with the expectation that their offspring and flesh are naturally owned by humans.

Speciesism, as a system, relies on existing power hierarchies. Humans, as the dominant species on Earth, reinforce power over the environment in various ways (destroying forests, pouring waste into the ocean, farming animals, etc.). Having power over animals and the environment leads to the perception that animals are property: objects for humans to use and control however they wish. These behaviors are normal for the majority of society and seen as essential for the continuation of human life. It is easy for these practices to go unquestioned because we exist within a hierarchical structure where white, able-bodied, neurotypical property-owning cis men are wielders and retainers of power. The pinnacle of the hierarchy is regarded as a standard to aim for (or else, be controlled by). Thus, traditional values protecting the structure are repeated to the masses through media and education. As the school curriculum is created and directly influenced by people who maintain power and require the continuation of the status quo to keep power, it is important to recognize that schools are organized to replicate the wider environment so that young people are familiar with the systems that privilege some over others (including humans over animals).

As a support assistant, I am not supposed to undermine, call out, or correct teaching staff. This is an uncomfortable position to be in when witnessing oppressive language or behavior: not calling it out conveys the message that harmful views can be expressed and will go unchallenged. However, with my adult privileges, I am able to maneuver between limits of power because I am allowed an amount of authority. Sometimes, I wonder if I am breaching that power by discussing animal liberation openly with students. The young people I work with are already disadvantaged by the school system and expected to attend six lessons a day, constantly receiving both educational and sensory information during their time at school. Many students tell me that just existing within the school system is exhausting.

My priority at work is the well-being of the young people I work with. Once, a fifteen-year-old student asked me why I don't drink milk. I paused before I responded, trying to weigh up the information I felt was necessary with the information I felt he could process. I explained that cows only produce milk when they are pregnant, and that our demand for cow milk means that cows are kept in a constant state of pregnancy induced by humans. I told him I felt that this was unfair because cows also bond with their children and that they are deprived of this experience. He was silent. After a few moments, he said "okay." I asked him if he was all right, and he responded affirmatively. He changed the topic, and we didn't return to the milk discussion. I think we were both slightly uncomfortable afterward. I mostly felt as if I had made a mistake by discussing my personal beliefs before opening the topic up as an ethical question to him. I'm sure he would have felt more comfortable to talk about his own opinion if I had given him the facts and asked for his thoughts before deeming removing cows' babies as "unfair." This was a learning opportunity for both of us, and I am very careful now to create a non-judgmental atmosphere for discussions.

Veganism often comes up as a topic, particularly during break and at lunchtime. Other members of staff often bring in non-vegan food to share, which I am left out of. My explanations are usually short ("I am vegan, so I don't eat animals or anything taken from animals including eggs and milk") and almost always evoke defensive responses from my colleagues ("I only eat *this* animal," "I don't eat cheese," "I like the taste of this and that animal," and so forth).

Some colleagues have misunderstood and have made comments about my weight, wrongly assuming that veganism is a form of dieting. I am often drawn into group discussions where I am the only vegan in the room and the only person expected to explain my ethical and political beliefs. The pressure to form cohesive and compelling arguments to a room full of people usually puts me in a low mood for the rest of the day and sets me apart from the rest of my work team. I often worry that any discussions around veganism and animal ethics are detrimental to my role: we experience many high-stress situations, and it is crucial that we can effectively work together as a team. However, after two years of working with them, my colleagues are generally accepting of veganism and make fewer divisive comments.

It is also important to me to remain aware of my identity dimensions at work, as my teaching is informed by my own education and experiences. I am white British. I am a woman. I grew up on a council estate, but was privileged enough to attend university and to be surrounded by supportive family members along my journey. I am a feminist. I am bisexual. I am an anti-speciesist vegan. These labels can operate as stereotypes, allowing strangers to form opinions about my personality or political and ethical beliefs. For me, however, these signposts have been useful starting points to exploring my identity and privileges. (For example, I am white, so will not experience institutionalized discrimination due to my skin color; but I am not heterosexual, and have experienced prejudice, hate, and alienation surrounding my queerness.)

Navigating sections of my identity at work can be challenging. Most of my colleagues and students are carnists; many have traditional and harmful opinions about binary gender roles; some have expressed homophobic remarks. Education does not exist in a vacuum, and our individual learning is shaped by our experiences within the society that we live in. For example, my own work is directly influenced by my identity and my belief that power needs to be redistributed. I try to reflect this by promoting the voice of students, in an effort to shift the balance towards pupil-led learning, and supporting the autonomy of autistic people within a neurotypical infrastructure and also with my work to dismantle the perception of animals as human property.

When I decided to stop eating animal flesh, milk, eggs, and honey, I had done extensive research into the horrors of the animal industry. I watched endless videos and documentaries about the mistreatment of farmed animals and those experimented on for vivisection purposes. I was heartbroken for days after realizing my complicity in animal abuse, and intensely angry about being lied to by media and businesses that treat animals as property to be owned and used for profit and human entertainment. I could not expose the animal industry to the students I work with in this way. People come to veganism differently and at various ages. Claiming that everyone should "go vegan" immediately upon discovering the way animals are used and abused comes from a privileged position that uses classist and ableist rhetoric without considering individuals (replicating power systems that serve some humans but not all humans).

Educating about animal liberation is not my priority at work, but ensuring that young people receive honest information about the world in order to form their own opinions is crucial. Food and cookery lessons taught in schools reinforce to young people that flesh is a standard, and often healthy addition to meals, teaching pupils to learn the protein and calorie content of flesh while failing to teach the benefits of a plant-based diet. I am able to organize a space for small groups of students to attend lessons on alternative food skills. In the past, I have run these with one or two autistic students, where we have discussed, planned, and prepared food using plant-based ingredients, including how best to budget when buying ingredients. Taking this further, it would be ideal to facilitate a small group of students who run these skill sessions together as a group, rather than relying on adult direction.

All the students that I work with at the autism base know that I am vegan. Many of the students I come into contact with in the wider school also know that I am vegan. I always offer an explanation with the word *vegan*, because there are many misconceptions and stereotypes about what being vegan means. Allowing as much discussion space as students require to ask questions and share their opinions is an important part of learning about veganism. Reactions are always varied: some students enjoy discussing or debating the ethical side of veganism; some leave the topic but ask questions days later; and some are completely incredulous. One child had only encountered veganism through anti-vegan memes online and repeated stereotypes about vegans ("they only eat water," "they smell because they don't use deodorant") until we talked through the root of those beliefs and why people on the Internet might make such memes. Young people are used to adults not engaging in a dialogue with them, or not being given a platform for their speech. Yet, space to talk allows for an exchange of ideas that help all people involved change or expand their opinions.

I have found that the most natural way of introducing anti-speciesist thought to the students I work with is through the language I use. Language is a powerful tool that shapes the way we interact with others and forms the foundation of our beliefs. Humans highlight their dominance by referring to animals with the term *it*. Animals are sentient beings, not objects. Referring to an animal as "it" (even unintentionally) perpetuates the idea that animals are less-than and do not deserve to be respected as living beings. This seems a small point, but is an important start. I often talk about companion animals with the students I work with, and the majority live with dogs or cats. Other people mirror our language choices, so asking someone else how a dog or cat is without using the term *it* is likely to be reflected back after a few conversations (e.g. "the dog is called Spike," "Oh, what color is he/she/they?"). The same can be done with the term "companion animal" over "my pet," which conveys ownership and dominance. Granted, this is much easier with companion animals, as people can recognize that the animals they spend time with have personalities and experience emotions. The same strategy, however, can be used when discussing any animal.

Usually, I wait for students to bring up the topic of animals with me. In my experience, students are unlikely to speak defensively if the communication happens on their terms. When people feel defensive or guilty, it is difficult to have an exchange that is useful, and both parties usually leave feeling frustrated. This is not helpful when students have to attend classes afterward and focus on other topics. If young people are directing, the discussion is also less likely to enter places that are distressing for them. It's not as if I wait around for a student to ask me a question; sometimes discussions around the status of animals happen at unexpected times.

During my first few months as a support assistant, I worked with an eleven-year-old in an art class. We once discussed how Pokémon characters are confined in small balls. Completely unprompted by me, the student remarked that it was unfair to keep living beings in such a small space. This led to an open discussion with a few other students about the way animals are shut into spaces for human entertainment in the form of zoos. Exploring how individual interests can be problematic is a significant step in thinking critically about the information that we consume.

Another student I worked with had an interest in the environment and nature, and was researching environmental politics in his spare time. We talked often about what he had learned, and sometimes I would suggest areas for him to research. One morning, he told me that animal agriculture is responsible for a large amount of deforestation because trees are cleared for farming purposes. We spoke about the damage that this practice had on the surrounding animals, plants, and people in areas where rainforests are cleared. A week later, he told me he had decided to stop eating meat. We discussed protein alternatives and foods we enjoy to eat that don't contain animal flesh. Months later, he is still vegetarian. In this instance, having someone to talk to about what he had learned was incredibly helpful for this student's journey, and culminated in him making the autonomous choice to remove himself from a system that harms the environment.

These examples illustrate only a few of my interactions with students about the way society treats animals. For the most part, I can say that our interactions are student-led, flexible, and that the end is determined by the student. All humans have a different threshold for what information we can process at any one time. Recognizing that every person responds differently to stimuli and allowing them to process the information in their own way is not only crucial when working with autistic young people, but also should be applied to the general public when making others aware of animal suffering. Anyone who works to educate others about animal suffering should take this into account. Most people are indoctrinated to consume dairy, eggs, and animal flesh from birth, and untangling such an ingrained norm is a difficult and complex process. Additionally, individuals are not free from social and economic constraints, and not everyone can access a vegan lifestyle—especially children, who are dependent on their parents to provide food, clothes, and toiletries. For young people who are from impoverished families—like those on the free school-meals plan—food choices are further restricted.

The mainstream animal liberation movement is often criticized for using ableist rhetoric. Like society as a whole, the movement is dominated by able-bodied, neurotypical people; so it is no surprise that disabled people feel alienated from the cause. This will only change if we (able-bodied, neurotypical people) give up some space and work collaboratively to share ideas with disabled people. I am attempting to create a collaborative environment with the students I work with, where we can explore ideas about human and animal oppression together. This is, at times, incredibly challenging considering the power structure that my role as a support assistant contributes to.

I don't have the tools to provide a framework for the best approach for teaching animal liberation truths in my role as an educator because there is no one approach that works for everyone. My work as an antispeciesist educator operates by ensuring that there are vegan food options available for students and facilitating student-led discussions about animal issues. In the future, I would like to build on these practical food-making and critical-thinking skills the young people I have been working with have learned, by supporting students to create a space or group to continue to educate others. Pupil-led learning is an important part of education, and to facilitate this, adults need to make space for young people to explore their own learning.

5

LEARNING ABOUT ANIMALS

How We Are Taught to Ignore Animal Oppression

Susan M. Roberts

I have been giving talks about animals and animal rights for around ten years. The age of the audiences I have addressed has been as young as five, and as old as seventy-five and beyond. As might be expected, the receptions I have received have differed widely. More memorable than particular responses from individuals agreeing or disagreeing, however, has been the varied tenor of the audiences as a whole, which has tended to reflect the age of the listeners and the reason for the talk.

Most notable in this regard was the level of engagement and joy expressed by very young children when talking about animals. It is impossible to convey just how intoxicated with excitement a class of five-year-olds can become when listening to a talk about foxes. How twenty-five small wriggling bodies can be stilled and silenced (almost!) by the image of a vixen with her cubs. What was most extraordinary—and, for me entirely unexpected—was that their passionate engagement did not fade after a few minutes, or lapse when the film-show ended, but continued for the entire length of the lesson. In fact, so interested were these little children in all things foxy that when I left them at the end of the session they were sitting in their reading corner, huddled over the wildlife newsletters I had handed out for their parents, like miniature commuters engrossed in the daily news.

In this chapter I propose to consider the ways in which three distinct audiences discuss animals. My hope is that sharing my experiences will help other pedagogues and open up a dialogue about different teaching strategies that concern the often-controversial topic of animal rights. In looking at how very young pupils (primary school), secondary school youths, and finally adults engage with the topic, I will consider the language they use, the questions they raise, the stories or information they share, and the level of emotional engagement they express. I am mindful of the fact that, whereas the adult listener will have volunteered and probably paid for their attendance at the animal rights lecture or discussion (albeit often as part of a longer course concerned with moral philosophy generally), the children will have been compelled to attend as part of their compulsory general education.

This can, and has, raised issues concerning what I deem to be excessive levels of supervision, as pupils have been rebuked by their teachers for bringing up ethical issues and asking questions that were entirely appropriate and sensible but were deemed cheeky or too challenging by their teachers. For example, a question that has gotten at least one pupil a telling off is "What would happen to pigs if we didn't eat bacon?" The answer, of course, is that there would be no more pigs. A few might survive in animal sanctuaries, but domesticated pigs would no longer be bred if people stopped eating them. It is interesting to observe how readily children accept this rather obvious answer, whereas adults generally seem more resistant to its stark logic, and often struggle to articulate some measurable loss on the part of the pigs. However, when most pigs are sent for slaughter at just a few months of age, having spent the entirety of their short life in cramped confinement without sunlight or fresh air, it is hard to see how their extinction could represent any sort of loss for them. What is most noteworthy here, however, is not the insubstantial nature of the arguments raised, but why it is felt necessary to make any argument at all.

The purpose of carrying out this analysis is to show—in a somewhat rudimentary fashion to be sure—how through the process of enculturation, the views children entertain regarding animals change (certainly those in mainstream education, at least). In essence, I have noticed while teaching different age groups that the older we get, the more animals lose their identity. They cease to be kin and are reduced to materials available for rational use. It is my contention that children have an affinity with animals that is stronger than in most adults, who have been integrated into the world of social constructs (which includes a division between the human and other animal species). I believe this to be self-evident. It is my further contention that through the pedagogical process, this affinity becomes attenuated if it is not rooted out altogether. The reason is that such an affinity serves no functional purpose and if left unchecked could be politically destabilizing.

Pedagogy is concerned with far more than simply imparting information; it is about forming identities and shaping human agency. It determines how new members of society engage with one another and with the wider world. It shows them what they need to know and, more importantly, how they need to think. In shaping the modern subject, the pedagogical process—under Eurocentric, neoliberal standardization—seeks to draw out and cultivate traits congruent with the dominant paradigm, or at least doesn't run counter to it. Allowing children to retain their natural connection with animals certainly increases the likelihood of future conflictual situations in wider society; more importantly, however, it leaves intact an inner resource capable of nourishing an alternative, self-reliant citizenry. Such a citizenry would have no desire to set itself up against the rest of the animal kingdom. Nor would it see the need to continue constructing a surrogate world, feeling perfectly at ease in this one. Whatever goals it pursued would be framed around the natural constraints of sustainability and species biodiversity, just as Plato counseled more than two thousand years ago.[1] It is difficult to overstate the significance of so reoriented a citizenry: comfortable with its animal nature and at home in the world.

Primary School

I began the wildlife talk to the five-year-olds with a film show. I had about fifteen slides of foxes in various settings. Many of them were of cubs playing and all of them were beautiful (it is difficult to find an unphotogenic fox). It is, therefore, not surprising that my young audience "oohed" and "aahed" to every single one, which got the event off to a promising start.

I then proceeded to find out what the children knew about foxes with a short factual talk. This is when the most fascinating exchanges occurred. I should point out that although the children were glued to their seats during the film show, that excitement did not abate when the lights went back on. Their attention simply transferred to the blackboard—the new source of fox wonders. One little boy asked whether foxes could fly. The question is not as silly as it may sound, because the whole tenor of the conversation thus far had been quite magical. The children couldn't have been more animated if I had been telling them about dragons or unicorns.

I didn't want to bring the talk crashing down to all things mundane, nor did I want to disappoint the little boy. So, I told him that, given the extraordinary nature of these creatures, one could easily imagine that they would fly. But in fact, foxes were such fast runners they didn't need to. Another, equally enchanted child asked whether they ate butterflies. What else would such magical creatures eat? Although the children clearly regarded foxes as very special animals, that did not mean that they considered them to be rare or even uncommon. Most of the children had seen foxes in their own gardens or those of relatives. And one little boy boasted that "his" fox was such a frequent visitor, they had become engaged to his cat!

I also had worksheets for the children to complete: dot-to-dot pictures of a fox to join up and color in. They all pounced on these and started hastily joining the dots, some with more mathematical acumen than others. Their teacher had moved a numbers poster to the front of the classroom for them to check their counting, as the dots were numbered to well over one hundred. But many appeared not to feel numerically constrained; they knew what a fox looked like. Anyway, since many foxes turned out blue or stripy, and even rainbow-colored, a missing tail was neither here nor there. (Adding a coloring segment to the talk was an excellent idea—not mine, I should point out.) Coloring together gave the children not only a creative outlet for all their energy, it also gave them the opportunity to chat with their neighbors about what they had heard about foxes and what they thought.

The session concluded with the whole class sitting on the carpet in the reading corner, as I handed out newsletters. As I pointed out above, their intense interest in these leaflets was, perhaps, the most noteworthy feature of the whole talk. Their appetite for all things foxy had clearly not been sated and they were eager to learn more. Even though they knew that the news sheets in their hands were far too difficult for them to read, they held on to them and studied them for any more precious information they might glean.

SECONDARY SCHOOL

The education department at Animal Aid[2] has spent years establishing good relations with schools all over the United Kingdom and has a supply of trained volunteers keen to speak to children about animal rights. Being familiar with the national curriculum has enabled Animal Aid to produce a wide range of worksheets and PowerPoint talks, tailored to fit subjects as diverse as English Literature, PSHE (Personal, Social, Health, and Economic education), Science, General Studies, Religion, Citizenship, and Cookery. It is under the aegis of Animal Aid's school-speaker project that I have delivered talks on animal rights in secondary schools, covering subjects such as hunting, vivisection, and factory farming. I have also given vegan cookery demonstrations.

Although the age range of pupils attending secondary school is wide, and children are obviously changing a great deal over this period, a common factor in just about every talk I have given has been the curiosity of the students. Generally speaking, they have very little idea about where their food comes from. They are unfailingly shocked when they hear just how many "farmed" animals are killed in the UK each year (one billion), and are even more shocked when they hear about the cruel practices inflicted on those animals as a normal part of industrialized animal agriculture. Piglets having their teeth trimmed and tails cut off, because in the stress of their crowded conditions they could bite each other; male animals castrated without anesthetic; cows separated from their young within hours of birth; and those calves then sent abroad to become veal, ending their short, sad lives constrained and alone in the dark: these are just a few of the examples I mention.

It is very easy to entertain and inform younger pupils, say ages eleven to thirteen, with the aid of worksheets and quizzes. Simply asking questions about the natural length of animals' lives (always dramatically cut short by factory farming) or how to eat healthily (many children have no idea that it is possible to survive, let alone thrive, without meat) is an excellent way to get across some basic facts. Taking in samples of plant-based food, like meat-free sausage rolls or dairy-free chocolate buttons is also very popular. Making a vegan dish in a cookery demonstration, usually something simple and cheap like a chili, is another informal way of introducing the topic of animal rights.

Generally speaking, secondary school students are not as animated or as emotionally engaged as younger pupils when talking about animals, which isn't surprising. They certainly don't entertain magical notions about them. However, since many students have pets, they do regard these animals as members of their own family, and have stories to tell that clearly indicate they place enormous value on these special relationships. As it is a common, and convenient, misconception that companion animals are more intelligent than those in factory farms, I find it a useful exercise to draw comparisons between the intelligence of dogs and pigs. The idea of this comparison is to dispel ableist myths that uphold the idea that intelligence determines someone's value: in film clips showing both animals trying to solve a computer puzzle, it is the pigs who emerge triumphant. This alerts students to the fact that the maimed piglets, cramped together in pens and separated from their mother, who are sent off for slaughter when they are still only a few months old, are just as intelligent and sensitive as their pet dogs.

The material shown to secondary school students differs from that shown to primary school children, as might be expected. Unsurprisingly, the images of incarcerated animals, whether they be victims of intensive animal agriculture or bred for vivisection in the laboratory, are uniformly upsetting. However, what is shown to these older children is still more suggestive of animal abuse than a graphic depiction of it. The aim of the talks is not to distress or traumatize students but to make them aware of how animals are treated and to encourage them to engage their developing critical faculties to think about this, so they can draw their own conclusions. For many teens it is a lot to take in, especially when there is so much else going on in their young lives.

We know that young people are under a lot of pressure, with studying for exams, achieving good grades, and competing for university places, as well as the desire to fit in and be popular.[3] One thing that has struck me, going into schools to give talks, is how omnipresent that pressure to perform and succeed really is. Just about every wall in every corridor of every school I have been in seems to be shouting out accomplishments. Whether it is winning a prize, getting good grades, or taking part in some charitable event, the whole emphasis seems to be on enjoining the passing student into achieving some goal. Although it is wonderful to celebrate a child's, or indeed anyone's, successes, it is surely also important to appreciate there is an essential un-achieving dimension to life that likewise needs to be honored. This relates to what we are as human beings: to our inherent qualities and to the relationships we have with one another and the wider world.

This is particularly pertinent to the question of how we treat animals. It is because we view animals solely in functional terms that enables us to reduce them to a material resource. This mindset is at the root of all forms of exploitation. And it is difficult to extirpate that root in a world where so much has been reduced to mere function. When the driving force of the education system you are speaking from is shaped by that same functionality, it is particularly difficult to point to the deleterious effects of such reductive thinking. The problem, of course, is that functional thinking has become normal; it is the predominant vocabulary we now use. But, although technical terms are obviously useful for precision and clarity, they can only relate to what is measurable. What that means, as Herbert Marcuse warned, is that not only does the world "out there" have to be shrunk to fit within the narrow, artificial parameters that functionalism demands, but that we also lose our ability to think and speak critically.[4]

Not everything can be reduced to technical jargon, and nothing of any importance can be addressed in such simple, reductive terms. Difficult questions should be challenging, which is why the language used to discuss them is so often opaque and imprecise. In such debates, clarity, if attainable at all, is only reached through a long process of deliberation. The premature clarity offered by the technician has nothing to contribute to philosophical questions about how we should live.

What particularly pained Marcuse was the realization that as pedagogy became increasingly infected with the empty functionalism of the technocrat, the students' ability to reflect and deliberate would become irredeemably impaired. What would be lost when the thinking process had been hijacked to serve so mechanical an agenda would be not only the ability to articulate profound and difficult questions, but, more worryingly, the ability to contemplate, or even recognize, them.

Forty-five minutes isn't long enough to discuss anything much, let alone a subject as significant as how we treat animals. When a class arrives and departs in squadrons of six or eight, each headed by a teaching assistant to ensure good behavior, there is even less time, and far less attention. I am not suggesting that discipline doesn't have a place in school, but some of the demands made of children that I have witnessed (like queuing up in strict alphabetical order) seem incredibly petty. The difficulty that follows is that having had impressed upon the young audience the importance of the trivial, it becomes harder to elevate their minds to consider something really important.

At times like this, I am often reminded of Martin Heidegger's self-reflective question, "What calls us to speak?"[5] It is my recognition of the importance of this question that persuades me to eschew the ubiquitous "housekeeping" preamble whenever I give a talk. It has always seemed to me that instructing an audience on the meaning of self-evident signs is a sure way to diminish any emancipatory expectations they may have. In just a few short meaningless sentences about fire drills, washrooms, and muster points, what is most efficiently dispelled is the hope that anything different will, or indeed, can ever be said.

What Heidegger recognized, as would later Marcuse, is that the most effective forms of social control don't involve violence, or indeed any kind of compulsion. Rather, it is through the inculcation of certain social norms and practices that "appropriate behavior," i.e., behavior that is passive, predictable, and uncritical, is most reliably achieved. Ensuring that all public discourse reproduces an identical regulatory rubric, however unnecessary or inappropriate (indeed, particularly when it is unnecessary and inappropriate), conveys a powerful message to the audience. It tells them that the speaker and the address to follow are also part of the same regulatory regime that dominates their lives. Delivering a talk on those terms amounts to nothing less than collusion with an oppressive status quo.

Of course, it would be preferable to discuss these matters with children in a neutral space outside of school, where they might feel less constrained and more open to ideas that challenge the dominant paradigm. Nevertheless, it is reassuring to know that the vegan population is growing, particularly among young adults. I often point this out to the older students, on the verge of leaving for university. I tell them about how the planet is suffering under the burden of meat production; how clearing land for cattle is responsible for so much of the destruction of the Amazon rainforest. I tell them about the amount of water it takes to produce a single burger—an extraordinary 660 gallons (more than a week's supply for a family of four)!—and about how the waste from industrially "farmed" animals contributes more to global warming than all the transportation systems put together. It all seems so staggering. They haven't heard any of this before and I am not sure they entirely believe me.

Although it seems like a good idea to respond positively to requests from schools to provide talks on animals, it can sometimes feel like you are just filling a gap in the timetable. My concern is that by fitting the exploitation of animals in to a morning's lessons—somewhere between, say, geography and lunch—the impression given is that nothing fundamental is being relayed. Having said that, I am very much aware that schools are being offered teaching resources from a wide array of interest groups, many of which are directly involved in the exploitation of animals. Consequently, just turning up to say something that challenges the status quo must be worthwhile. Schools can hardly be blamed for taking advantage of free resources.

Adults

For an animal rights talk with adults, I chose an article written by James Rachels entitled, "The Moral Argument for Vegetarianism."[6] Rachels is not known for his advocacy for animals, which is largely why I chose his essay—that and the fact that the essay on vegetarianism was just one of a diverse range of essays raising very different ethical questions, from abortion to euthanasia. I was mindful of the fact that this adult class might not consider the imperative of vegetarianism a worthy topic to discuss; that some might even think it extreme. It was for that reason that I felt it important to show that the essay we were discussing was very much "mainstream."

My fears were well founded. The general consensus was that eating animals was not an ethical issue. Only one person (out of thirteen) begged to differ; unsurprisingly, she was vegetarian. The others were not hostile to the proposal; they simply didn't give it any weight. As I recall, the only time emotions became at all raised was at somebody's suggestion that we were all in debt to British farmers. Whether this was nostalgia for some imagined pastoral idyll, a nod to rosy childhoods and simpler times, I have no idea. Such a bucolic vision is obviously what food producers would like us to retain; hence the use of fake farm labels to persuade us to buy their produce. But with fewer and fewer animals seeing daylight or even being free to roam, the continued use of the word *farm* is little more than a fetish. Concentrated Animal Feeding Operations, or CAFOs, as they are known in the U.S., is the distressingly more accurate term for many animal agriculture plants.[7]

Although perhaps a bit dated, Rachels' article asserts that eating animals is, indeed, a moral matter, and one that we ignore through our normalization of animal abuse. He goes on to describe a number of cruel practices to which animals are routinely subjected and then poses the question whether our enjoyment of the way they taste is sufficient justification for mistreating them. The argument is well made, because once it has been established that we don't need to consume animal products in order to survive, it becomes impossible to distinguish consuming them from other trivial uses to which animals are put, such as forcing them to perform in circuses or hunting them for sport. This is a crucial point and one on which those who consume animals, as well as the corporate interests that produce them, refuse to give way. This is because once they do so, the masquerade is over and the abuse can no longer be ignored. Hence the vociferous insistence by animal agriculture lobbyists, preaching to the classroom as well as to the wider populace, that consuming animals is essential for our health.

Rachels blames our lack of discomfiture at abusing animals on Immanuel Kant and his "categorical imperative," which was of pivotal significance in the development of Western moral thinking. "Act so that you treat humanity, whether in your own person or that of another, always as an end and never as a means only,"[8] instructs Kant, which essentially means that people should never be regarded merely as resources or tools available for use. This is a sentiment I also saw reflected among my adults.

So far so good. But what about animals? "But so far as animals are concerned, we have no direct duties. Animals are not self-conscious, and are there merely as a means to an end. That end is man."[9] Kant does add the following proviso, however: "He who is cruel to animals becomes hard also in his dealings with men."[10] The proviso often gets ignored, but it is important, particularly here, in a discussion on pedagogy. This is because what we as a society understand by cruelty, and how we differentiate between "the acceptable cruelty" meted out by the state and the "unacceptable cruelty" of random individuals, is largely the result of the enculturation of societal norms. In many instances of the most egregious cruelty, society does not respond at all. For example, it is well known from the mountain of evidence on vivisection that animals experimented on in laboratories have been treated with unimaginable cruelty, and still are. The perpetrators of those pitiless actions have never been challenged or even exposed. On the contrary, many are the recipients of awards and accolades, congratulated on "the service they have offered humanity."

Conclusion

Thus, what we mean when we talk about cruelty or violence or exploitation generally, is largely shaped by the pedagogical practices to which we have been subjected. It is through pedagogy that we are assimilated to a particular worldview. Working with different age groups made this very clear to me. And, although a proper understanding of all these issues is essential if the mistreatment of animals is ever going to be addressed, it is also fundamental to the establishment of an informed and effective citizenry. However, if through the educational process the cruelty and violence inflicted at the state's behest is merely airbrushed from the picture, then what is produced are simply generations of pliant consumers inured to state-sponsored cruelty and devoid of any political power.

On a more subtle level, though, Kant is correct. It is not possible to divorce our treatment of animals from our attitudes towards each other. The functionalism that underscores our relationship with animals and the wider environment increasingly shapes most of our human relationships, too. Even the youngest children are now measured and assessed against a rubric better suited to products on the factory floor than students in the classroom. But then, the purpose of education is not to elevate young minds or to imbue in children a love for learning. Rather, its primary aim is political: to manufacture and reproduce an ideal social personality—compliant and consumerist.

Like the good Aristotelians they are, young children instinctively know that they are animals. They also recognize their kin. They haven't yet been inculcated into a divisive taxonomy that sets them apart from the rest of the animal kingdom and consequently feel an innate relatedness to the natural world that we have long forgotten. Before being constrained by the pedagogical demands of uniformity and conformity, young children are able to see and to articulate a conjoined world of interconnecting relationships and mutual dependencies. They see animals much like themselves, with families to care for and friends to play with, and as having similar needs like food and shelter. This precious vision is one we should seek to retain at all costs; and not just retain, but encourage and nurture. It is children who lead the way in reconnecting us with the planet and reacquainting us with the animals with whom we share it.

6

WHAT ZOOS TEACH US

SPECIESISM, COLONIALISM, RACISM, AND CAPITALISM IN THE CAPTIVE ANIMAL INDUSTRY

Liz Tyson and Nicola O'Brien

The focus of this chapter is to better understand the role of zoos in education and, importantly, examine whether the educational claims of zoos and their supporters are accurate. Furthermore, we seek to consider other, potentially unintentional educational messages disseminated by zoos; including those which speak to colonialism, capitalism, the perpetuation of xenophobia, and a failure to value and respect individual animals as rights-holders with value outside of their biological role as members of their species. Ultimately, we put forward an argument that advocates for the dismantling of the zoo industry not just on grounds of animal liberation, but as a direct challenge to the damaging educational messages disseminated by zoos, which, in our view, support and perpetuate wider systems of oppression.

Our analysis will also hopefully prepare fellow educators, parents, and critical thinkers for the sometimes-inevitable zoo visit our children and students undertake and ensure they are indeed provided with an educational experience when confronted with captive animals. The chapter will hopefully encourage other educators to challenge parents, head teachers, or deans who insist on continuing the longstanding tradition of exploiting captive animals for supposedly educational purposes by giving you all a repertoire of arguments to use in difficult conversations. If a trip to the zoo or a live animal in captivity on campus, for instance, is unavoidable, this chapter will at the very least give you an indication of how to approach the issue critically with your audience.

The role of zoos in education and conservation has long been promoted by the zoo industry itself, governments around the world, and some conservationists. Although there have always been vocal opponents to the holding of animals captive in zoological parks—notably Freedom for Animals (formerly known as Captive Animals' Protection Society)[1] and the Born Free Foundation,[2] whose work is largely focused on challenging the captivity of wild animals—zoos remain on the periphery of discussion surrounding animal rights and ethics. In our own experience of working in organizing, campaigning, and lobbying on the issue of animals in captivity, it appears there is a spectrum of opinions on the role and value of zoos, to which a large part of the public and indeed members of the animal liberation movement subscribe.

On one end of this spectrum can be found those who believe that there is no moral, ethical, educational, or conservational justification for holding animals captive for their lifetime in zoos—a position we ourselves represent. At the other end of the spectrum is the assertion, which is commonly played out in public dialogue, that zoos are not only necessary to "save species"[3] but are also in fact providing the animals with a "better" environment than they could hope for if they were living in their natural home. Justification for this view is often focused on the trope of the animal's natural habitat being a dangerous place for animals (almost exclusively as a result of human actions such as hunting or deforestation) or the assertion that animals who suffer from ailments in zoos can be treated by vets, whereas animals in their natural habitat may suffer and die in varying circumstances that would not (or perhaps should not) occur in a zoo. The following claim was made, for example, in a 2016 article in *Time* magazine: "Animals in zoos and aquariums today can live longer, healthier, and richer lives than their forbearers [*sic*] ever did in the wild."[4]

More nuanced opinions can be found between these two endpoints on the spectrum. Some argue that zoos are a "necessary evil," citing the need to conserve species or protect endangered animals from hunters. This differs from the "the wild is a dangerous place" view in that those who hold this view do not argue that the zoo is better than the animals' natural habitat. Rather, they implicitly accept that zoos are not the right place for these animals to be, but believe zoos are necessary to keep them safe (either on an individual level or on a species level).[5]

Others argue that zoos are not ideal but are necessary for educational purposes, as "not everyone can afford a safari to Africa."[6] This is a phrase that often references children from inner-city areas or low-income families and is a common response leveled at those who express opposition to zoos. The implied belief in this view is that children either have a "right" to see these animals in real life, and that it is discriminatory (and specifically classist, as it is seen to discriminate against poorer children) to suggest otherwise. It also assumes that seeing animals in the flesh provides a far superior learning experience for young people than learning about them in other ways. Interestingly, seeing the animals in the flesh is often linked with the suggestion that such an "affective connection with animals greatly helps conservation."[7]

Also interestingly, and despite education being one of the major selling points employed by the zoo industry, there is very little evidence available to demonstrate educational contribution. Indeed, in 2010 the zoo industry in the United Kingdom was examined as part of an independent study carried out by ADAS, the UK's biggest independent consultancy for environmental and agricultural issues. The study, entitled *Review of Zoos' Conservation and Education Contribution*, states: "It was found that the review of available literature reported considerable evidence of the wide range of conservation and education projects conducted by zoos. Concerns remain, however, with regard to the lack of available evidence about the effectiveness of these projects."[8] In effect, the report concluded that although educational projects and initiatives were clearly in existence in zoos, whether they achieved their purpose remained largely unknown.

A paper published in 2014 in the journal *Conservation Biology* appeared to further question the veracity of claims made by the zoo industry as to its impact on education. The study considered learning outcomes for over 2,800 pupils visiting London Zoo. The children were part of either visits guided by a member of educational staff from the zoo or unguided visits. Only 38 percent of children could demonstrate positive learning outcomes, said the paper's author. In comparison, most children (62 percent) were deemed to show no change in learning or, worse, experienced negative learning[9] during their trip to the zoo.

In addition, despite zoos claiming that they inspire children to become proactive conservationists, it was concluded in the same research report that the zoo's impact on children's belief in their ability to actively do something about conservation was "weak." The author, Eric Jensen, went on to conclude that his findings suggested that pupils did not feel empowered to believe that they could take "effective ameliorative action"[10] on matters relating to conservation after their zoo experience. In contrast to the findings, London Zoo claims on its website that its site offers "the perfect education choice" and boasts "a diverse and highly skilled Education Team, provid[ing] unique learning sessions for all ages and abilities."[11]

This cursory exploration of available evidence about the educational impact of zoos would suggest that it might not be wise simply to take at face value the claims that zoos perform a positive educational function. In addition, we strongly believe that, not only is little if any positive learning achieved in a zoo environment, but negative learning outcomes are in fact more likely to be the result of a visit to the zoo. These ideas will be explored in the sections below.

Learning about Animals

In seeing an animal in a zoo, visitors are receiving a distorted image of who and what that animal is. Little, if any, re-creation of a natural habitat can be demonstrated in a zoo. Thus, animals are neither able to carry out many of their most innate behaviors when held captive nor can they be observed within their natural environmental context. Add to this the tendency of animals held captive to engage in a recurring set of behaviors found across species and zoos. These are repetitive behaviors that appear to serve no useful outward purpose (such as pacing, bar-biting, self-harm, head-twisting, and regurgitating food): so-called stereotypies.

Zoo visitors are witnessing an animal out of place, out of context, and exhibiting signs of mental distress or illness. Importantly, these stereotypical behaviors have not been observed occurring in animals in their natural habitat. As such, confinement in the zoo has arguably created these behaviors: a pacing tiger or a swaying elephant in a zoo has literally been forced to repress their natural behaviors and has developed coping mechanisms, which manifest as disturbing behaviors, as a direct result of being in the zoo.

Not only are these disturbing behaviors rife in the zoo (and wider captive wild-animal industries), but they are regularly dismissed, explained away, or misunderstood by zoo visitors. For example, a sign addressing the persistent head-weaving of an elephant in the UK's Chester Zoo, which was on display when one of us visited during 2014, read: "Why is that elephant moving her head from side to side? A bad habit. Do you bite your fingernails or smoke? These are bad habits. An elephant moving its head from side to side is a bad habit. As everyone knows, bad habits are hard to stop." Repetitive, compulsive behavior or stereotypies are recognized in both human and nonhuman animals and can be indicative of serious mental trauma or distress. Whereas it is unarguable that bad habits can be both difficult to stop and, like smoking, can threaten our health, describing a recognized mental health issue in animals as a "bad habit" is misleading, offensive, and ableist—particularly when the true explanation behind stereotypical behavior in animals in zoos has been accepted for many years, even by some parts of the zoo industry.

In numerous public responses to concerns over big cats pacing in zoos—widespread across the industry—the latter will generally say that the animals knew they were about to be fed, had seen their keepers, and were excited, or that they would naturally patrol their territory in the wild and were thus pacing, which in and of itself is not problematic. When two lions were witnessed pacing for long periods of time at an after-hours music event held at Bristol Zoo in the UK, where they were subjected to loud music from a live band and a DJ and exposed to visitors for an increased number of hours late into the night, the zoo responded:

> The lions were hand-reared by our keepers after being abandoned by their mother at thirteen days old. As such, these keepers became their "mother" figures and they still have that association. The pacing seen in the footage was in anticipation of seeing someone they knew and the association with food, and not as a result of sound levels.[12]

This statement was released by the zoo after the event and after footage of the pacing lions had been released to the public by an animal protection organization, footage in which a member of staff could be heard stating that the lions were pacing due to the noise and the presence of visitors being on site in the evening.[13]

During a visit to Dublin Zoo in the Republic of Ireland in 2014, one of us witnessed a (human) mother with her young child observing a chimpanzee in her indoor enclosure. The mother said to her child: "Look at the funny monkey; he's playing on the swing." In fact, the chimpanzee was rocking backward and forward in a hammock in her indoor enclosure and repeatedly regurgitating and re-ingesting her food—a stereotypy noted regularly in captive chimps but not seen in free-living groups.[14] In effect, what we were looking at was a distressed animal obsessively carrying out a very disturbing stereotypic behavior. What the public witnessed was a happy (although additionally misidentified) animal playing. Nothing could have been further from the truth.

Stereotypic behaviors aside, the way in which animals are presented in zoos as isolated or carefully curated "exhibits" fails to communicate the complexity of ecosystems and the interdependence of species—both animal and plant—that exist within them. What can be learned is simply the size, shape, sound, and smell of the animal when viewed in a zoo: information that could undoubtedly be learned (with the exception of smell) through other means. Indeed, a well-produced wildlife documentary will demonstrate far more in terms of education on the way in which animals live naturally, behave naturally, and interact with their environment than a zoo possibly could.

Finally, under the mantle of "essential conservation work," zoos also present a very disturbing message about the animals under their care. When living in their natural environment these animals have autonomy over their own lives and choices. They can choose a mate, choose how and when to move through their territory, and choose when to eat and when to rest. They can choose their companions. In zoos, every element of the lives of these animals is controlled. Animals in zoos eat when fed, spend their lives confined in the space designated to them by the zoo managers, spend time with the individual animals that the zoo has chosen as their companions, are often forcibly impregnated, and subsequently have their young removed from them.

This all-encompassing dominion and complete denial of agency and autonomy that the human captors exert over the animals has the effect of communicating to visitors that not only is it acceptable to treat animals in this way, but that we as humans are in fact doing something good for the animals by holding them captive for their entire lives in order to "save them." This feeds into the view that humans are placed hierarchically above other animals; that we "know better" and, therefore, have the right to make these decisions on their behalf.

Perhaps the most blatant example of this "dominion disguised as saving a species" trope in recent years is that of the pandas held in Edinburgh Zoo in the UK. Tian Tian and Yang Guang failed to mate through choice for the first year that they were held at the zoo. For the next three years, Tian Tian was artificially inseminated using the sperm from Yang Guang (a panda she had rejected) and another panda (a panda she had never met). Research has shown that pandas, like all mammals, have preferences when it comes to choosing their mate.[15] Therefore, Tian Tian's rejection of Yang Guang as the father of her children is reasonably interpreted as a choice she made. Going ahead and repeatedly artificially inseminating her with the sperm of Yang Guang and that of a panda she had never even had the opportunity to meet, is therefore not only a physical violation but also a complete disregard for the very little autonomy that Tian Tian had left to her: to choose whether she wanted to mate and with whom.

For some, the questions over whether zoos enhance or compromise learning do not arise. For many, zoos are simply where wild animals live. As people see familiar species in zoo collections around the world (elephants, hippos, lions, giraffes, for example), it reinforces the belief that these animals belong in zoos and erases questions surrounding how they got there and whether they should be there. In effect, for many there is no need to argue whether animals are better off in the zoo or in the wild as their presence in the zoo has become so normalized that it is simply no longer questioned.

This is particularly evident in children's entertainment and literature where we see "zoo animals" living in the zoo and being cared for by the zookeeper. Similar conditioning of public opinion and narratives can be found in the use of the term "farm animals," where the animal is literally defined by the means of exploitation they are subjected to without question. Of all of the damaging educational messages highlighted above, this normalization of wild-animal captivity is perhaps one of the most concerning of the ways in which zoos mis-educate the public.

Learning about Conservation

Oft-cited by zoos is the purported impact that seeing the animals has on visitors' learning—not about the animals themselves, but about vital conservation issues. Aside from the statistics outlined above that suggest that zoos are ineffective at achieving meaningful educational impact on their visitors, there are a number of more nuanced and, in our view, hugely damaging impacts on conservation. In some part, these are a result of the way in which zoos present their work.

In the first instance, the way in which zoos focus on the "charismatic megafauna" (elephants, lions, tigers, rhinos, gorillas, orangutans, etc.) as the targets for conservation efforts is misleading. Conservation is only effective when entire ecosystems and habitats are protected. With the best will in the world, keeping animals "safe" in zoos while failing to tackle very real conservation threats[16] in the animals' natural habitat is pointless. Even more misleading is the suggestion that the zoo's breeding of these animals will protect them from habitat degradation and threat of extinction in the wild. These arguments are simply not based on evidence. Few, if any, animals are introduced into the wild as a result of zoo-breeding programs, yet zoo visitors are told that visiting the zoo in and of itself is a conservation action. This is exemplified in the following claim by UK zoo trade body, BIAZA: "By visiting BIAZA zoos and aquariums you are helping to safeguard the future of vulnerable, threatened and endangered species."[17]

Research has shown that the vast majority of animals in zoos are in fact not threatened in the wild, from a conservation perspective, begging the question of why they are being held captive. The globally recognized IUCN Red List categorizes species based on the level of conservation threat they face in the wild, using scientific data to determine population numbers.[18] Using this classification, numerous separate studies have concluded that around five percent of species held in zoos in England and Wales are endangered in the wild and just 17 percent of species are threatened in the wild.[19] We would reasonably expect, when making claims about their conservation value, that zoos would hold more endangered species captive to be able to "educate" visitors, breed more of those species, and "protect" them by holding them in cages. Yet we see this is not the case.

Recent results of a public survey on public perception of zoos show just how misled the public are over the conservation status of species held in zoos. Over three-quarters of respondents to the survey, carried out by travel company "Responsible Travel," estimated that at least one fifth or more of the species kept in captivity by zoos would be endangered species—far higher than the reality.[20] This distorted view of the role of zoos in conservation may also lead to negative learning by zoo visitors, who, thanks to zoo propaganda, may believe some species are endangered when in fact they are not. For example, most zoos in the UK seem to hold meerkats captive, animals popularized by appearances on TV programs and adverts in recent years. Yet these animals are classed as "Least Concern" from a conservation perspective. As such, there is no feasible conservation benefit to keeping these animals in captivity and they are there simply as profit-generating visitor attractions because people like to see them. During discussions with the public when campaigning on zoos, it is striking how often we hear comments about zoos "only housing endangered species." When questioned, members of the public have stated that they believe meerkats are endangered by virtue of being held in a zoo.

Some zoos may even display incorrect conservation information on the animals they hold, despite the fact that the conservation status of the animals held by the zoo is information that must be accurately communicated to visitors under EU law. Drusillas Zoo in the UK appeared to have assigned conservation statuses to animals arbitrarily, telling visitors that some animals considered to be of "Least Concern" by the formal IUCN standards were in fact endangered, and some animals at genuine risk in the wild were "common" (a term with no scientific meaning). Of the sixty-three species of animals exhibited by Drusillas, all but two had the wrong conservation status attributed to them.[21]

In its somewhat bizarre statement, the zoo claimed that its visitors simply could not understand the globally recognized classification system used by the IUCN to gauge the conservation threat and so had made up their own system. Unfortunately for visitors to Drusillas, the system appears to follow no rationale and bears little to no relation to the true conservation status of the animals held by the zoo.

Beyond any potential learning about the animals held captive by zoos, the industry does little to encourage conservation and animal protection action outside the zoo. Once visitors have gone home, the result their zoo-learning has on their behavior towards the environment and animals is questionable. Visiting zoos is a very popular activity with schools and other educational establishments; the majority of children (and particularly those in affluent countries of the so-called global North) will have visited a zoo at some point in their lives. Yet the world's ecosystems remain in a dire situation and animals continue to be exploited and destroyed. Just 12 percent of zoo visitors who responded to the survey carried out by *Responsible Travel* said they had participated in some form of conservation volunteering in the last twelve months and, returning to Jensen's study, we must remember that pupils did not feel empowered to believe that they could take "effective ameliorative action" on matters relating to conservation after their zoo experience. This would suggest that visits to zoos have little impact on creating meaningful behaviors or consideration for animals in visitors.

Implicit Racism and the White Savior Complex at London Zoo

A rarely cited but often-observed tendency within the zoo industry is its often appalling representation of local people in conservation efforts. A clear example can be found in the grounds of London Zoo, where the institution's "Pygmy Hippo Conservation" project is promoted.

On the side of the pygmy hippo enclosure in London is a brightly colored sign entitled "Check in with Chief," which can be seen below. On first glance, it looks like the zoo might be giving local people's contribution to conservation in their own area the credit it is due. On closer inspection, it becomes clear that this is not the case. The sign purportedly sets out "important steps for successful fieldwork," telling budding hippo conservationists how to engage with local communities:

1. Arrive in forest village. Head straight for a chat with the chief.
2. Slip chief a small gift to move things in the right direction.
3. Chief bangs his drum to summon villagers to his house.
4. Introduce ZSL [London Zoo] and our mission. Ask for assistance.
5. If the Chief says yes, we can ask villagers if they've seen fresh hippo tracks and employ guides to lead us to the spots. The guides know the forest paths like London taxi drivers know London.

In just five short sentences, the local people in the western African communities that pygmy hippos are native to have been fetishized (the image of the primitivized chief "banging his drum" to call villagers). They have been tarred with the implication of only responding to conservation concerns if paid/bribed. And, if the chief agrees to ZSL's "mission" (note that there is no suggestion of discussing local conservation needs or input requested from the local people), then villagers can be employed as "guides" for the "conservation scientists." This racist and reductionist view of the local people is further perpetuated in the zoo's formal education pack used with school children.[22] In the pack, role-play activities give the children the option of playing a conservation scientist, a villager, a farmer, or a poacher.

Without exception, local people are presented as primitive, uninterested in conservation for conservation's sake, motivated by money, lazy, unknowledgeable, poor, and useful only to the extent that they can lead the conservation scientists to the relevant sites where the animals might be found. The "conservation scientists" on the other hand are portrayed as motivated by their passion for conserving this unique animal and representing the belief that the local people need to be "educated" about the importance of the pygmy hippos by the conservation scientists. Yet there appears to be no recognized need for dialogue with the local community about what they might be able to offer, or what they might need or want.

The Pygmy Hippo Conservation project is not the only one that exploits this "primitive natives" trope; elements of it can be found in zoos around the world. In addition to similar narratives surrounding the Western zoo "scientists" being required to save animals from the implied barbarity of the locals, the fetishizing of local people in zoos is rife. "African Villages"—or rather misrepresentations thereof—are common in zoos around the world, with zoos claiming to have created "authentic tribal villages" for visitors to view as exhibits alongside the captive animals.[23] A more realistic and evidence-based view on the contribution of local people to conservation efforts (and the reason that it serves the zoo industry to demonize local people under capitalism) is explored in the next section of this chapter.

CAPITALISM AND CONSERVATION

The capitalist and colonialist mindset promoted by the zoo industry is further compounded by the repeated narrative of the need for monetary contributions to support conservation. A common narrative surrounding zoos and conservation is focused on the financial support that has purportedly been offered by the zoo industry to conservation efforts. These conservation efforts may include support for *in situ* efforts to preserve species and the environment. Importantly, because breeding animals in captivity is considered by the industry to be in and of itself a conservation effort, money invested in running the zoo is also promoted as support for conservation of biodiversity.[24] This positions the zoo industry as both indispensable to conservation efforts via the implication that conservation is not possible without significant financial investment and further reinforces the narratives surrounding the "poor" locals in range-states who need the rich Western zoos to solve their conservation problems.

Although there is no doubt that effective conservation efforts can and do require financial investment, the message provided by the zoo industry on this issue is misleading in a number of ways. Zoos are seen to act as a necessary conduit for conservation funding on the basis that people do not generally give to conservation directly but do so through the zoo. This is demonstrably not the case and was proved in a 2010 article commissioned by the World Association of Zoos and Aquariums (WAZA).[25] The results, which were widely publicized by the zoo industry, were that WAZA zoos (made up of some 300 members) were (collectively) the world's third largest financial contributor to conservation efforts.

This may appear impressive on first glance. However, the research concluded that the two largest contributors to conservation efforts worldwide were two not-for-profit organizations (World Wildlife Fund and the Nature Conservancy, respectively). To clarify: two charitable organizations give more independently of one another than the entire global association of zoos. To suggest that the general public is uninterested in conservation for conservation's sake and that zoos are necessary to act as a conduit for conservation simply isn't supported by evidence.

It is important to note, too, that not only is the zoo industry failing to play a leading role in financial support of the conservation of species, but we do not seek to laud without question the efforts of major NGOs from affluent countries in the global North. Although large conservation NGOs may not hold animals captive, that certainly doesn't mean that they don't perpetuate capitalist, colonialist, and xenophobic attitudes. Community conservationists such as Dr. Noga Shanee seek to dismantle the prevalent negative view of local people's involvement and motivation in conservation efforts, so as to rebuild a movement around more radical, community-led organizing.

In an article published in 2014, Dr. Shanee said: "In order to capture funding, [big conservation groups] need to create a spectacle presenting themselves as conservation heroes fighting against 'bad,' illicit destroyers."[26] By contrast, Dr. Shanee's experience of working on the front line of conservation efforts in the Peruvian Amazon for over a decade has shown that "rural people in Northeastern Peru find nature and biodiversity conservation attractive for their intrinsic, social, aesthetic, and moral values, as well as a measure to ensure their own future. In most cases the prospects of economic benefits are perceived as an obviously welcome, but secondary outcome."[27]

Conclusion

In the preceding discussion, we sought to provide neither concrete conclusions nor empirical data to categorically prove or disprove the educational impact of zoos. Instead, we sought to explore the wider impact that these institutions have on the animals they hold captive, those who visit and interact with them, and those living in areas where the zoos claim to operate under their *in situ* conservation efforts.

Damaging educational messages might be unintended and even unwanted by the zoo industry. It would be cynical to suggest that the zoo industry actively seeks to teach young people that animals should be treated as little more than commodities, nor do we claim that individual zoo workers hold and actively seek to perpetuate damaging stereotypes of local people in conservation efforts. Our conclusion, from combined experience in this field of over two decades, is that zoos form part of wider, overarching systems of control and oppression—not just of animals, but of people and the environment.

When we fail to question the holding of animals captive for their lifetimes, when we fail to challenge colonialist views of people considered "other" to our privileged, largely white, Western gaze, and when we continue to, albeit uncomfortably, accept zoos as a "necessary evil," we are perpetuating these systems of oppression that are actively destroying the environment and the lives of animals and people worldwide.

We propose that there is a vital need to actively unlearn the teachings from zoos, governments, and society that would have us believe that zoos contribute in any positive way to educating about animals (and respect for them), the environment, and the conservation challenges facing animals and people (particularly those in the so-called global South, who have been long subject to racist stereotypes). Instead, we must recognize zoos for what they are: oppressive, speciesist prisons. We need to learn to let go of the (false) positives we may believe the zoo industry will deliver—not just because centuries of their existence have failed to produce meaningful results in terms of conservation, but because it is simply not our right to dominate other animals and take control of every element of their lives in order to pursue our own ends.

As animal advocates, we want to create a world where humans no longer control and oppress other animals. To achieve this, we need to build a societal view that rejects speciesism and promotes ultimate respect for animals and their freedom. Zoos can never be a part of such a world and to support or promote zoos not only muddies the water of our anti-speciesist message, it hinders progress significantly.

7

ECOCRITICISM IN THE CLASSROOM AND AT HOME

GENERATING A NEW ETHICAL AND ECOLOGICAL CONSCIOUSNESS THROUGH FAIRY TALES

Tanja Badalič

In the last few decades, the environmental crisis has affected the entire world, and its consequences can be perceived everywhere. However, the human relationship with the nonhuman world—the natural environment and nonhuman beings—not only suffers from environmental degradation but also faces an ethical challenge. It seems that humans have lost their ability to relate to the nonhuman world, continuously trying to dominate it.

For this reason, a new discipline in the humanities—ecocriticism—has emerged that tries to contribute to the restoration of Western, neoliberal peoples' connection to Earth and other beings by rethinking the relationship between humans and nature, particularly through literature. Literature and its study can help with an understanding of the environmental crisis and can thus encourage a new ethical and ecological consciousness in readers, which could also greatly contribute to Earth and animal liberation. Therefore, the reading of literary texts—a crucial part of Critical Pedagogy—that incorporate ecological and ethical questions should be particularly recommended for children from early childhood, on towards primary and secondary education.

In fact, a new consciousness oriented towards a more sustainable way of life and kindness to other living beings would allow future generations to potentially remedy the damage that past and modern generations have failed to solve. The role of teachers of literature is thus pivotal in generating this new consciousness, which will undoubtedly stimulate a more responsible relationship between humans, the natural environment, and animals in particular. Moreover, ecocriticism can begin at home, when reading bedtime stories to our children.

In this chapter, five representative fairy tales have been chosen from the Slovenian-English anthology *Svetlana's Fairytales* by the Slovenian author and proponent of animal rights Svetlana Makarovič. These case studies are useful since they encompass several ecological and ethical topics that will be analyzed in order to propose some possible ecocritical interpretations that teachers of literature can later apply in their classes. At the same time, parents, grandparents, and all guardians might find inspiration to engage their children in a conversation about these, and similar, stories.

Ecocriticism represents "the study of the relationship between literature and the physical environment," which takes "an earth-centered approach to literary studies."[1] The subject of ecocriticism is thus the interconnection between nature and culture. Cheryll Glotfelty explains: "As a critical stance, [ecocriticism] has one foot in literature and the other on land; as a theoretical discourse, it negotiates between the human and the nonhuman."[2] This discipline was first limited to the study of representations of nature, to ecological themes and genres about nature, but later its thematic area broadened to include various theoretical questions, such as the criticism of anthropocentrism[3] and relations between culture and nature, as well as humans and the environment. Thus, it contributes "significantly to the realization that man [sic] is defined not only by social relations, but to the same extent by the natural environment."[4]

Timothy Clark[5] states that in the question of the animal, ecocriticism finds perhaps its most striking ethical challenge: animals in our everyday life are exploited for food, materials, experiments, work, entertainment, and so on. Humans in their anthropocentrism want to dominate and take advantage of every living being, which seems to be valuable exclusively according to the point of view of humans. Writing about animals poses a particular challenge, since an animal ethics often concerns itself with "the animal as an individual existence, more in a way in which a person is considered," while also bringing with it the question of anthropomorphism: "How to represent animal lives in human language and culture without illusion or injustice?"[6] Moreover, representations of nonhuman animals in literature can be considered as a strong criticism of anthropocentrism.

Nevertheless, the basic premise of ecological criticism is that "human culture is connected to the physical world, affecting it and being affected by it."[7] The role of ecocriticism as a discipline in the humanities is to help understand the consequences of human actions for the planet. Glotfelty links ecocriticism to Barry Commoner's first law of ecology—"Everything is connected to everything else"—concluding that, "literature does not float above the material world in some aesthetic ether, but, rather, plays a part in an immensely complex global system, in which energy, matter, *and ideas* interact."[8] Moreover, Glotfelty states that most ecocritical work shares a common motivation: "The troubling awareness that we have reached the age of environmental limits, a time when the consequences of human actions are damaging the planet's basic life support systems."[9] As a possible answer to how professors of literature can contribute to environmental restoration, Glotfelty quotes the historian Donald Worster:

> We are facing a global crisis today, not because of how ecosystems function but rather because of how our ethical systems function. Getting through the crisis requires understanding our impact on nature as precisely as possible, but even more, it requires understanding those ethical systems and using that understanding to reform them. Historians, along with literary scholars, anthropologists, and philosophers, cannot do the reforming, of course, but they can help with the understanding.[10]

The role of educators in the humanities is thus to pose ecological and ethical questions to other people, helping them to understand environmental problems. Serpil Oppermann states that the ecological turn has brought an awareness of the natural world into literary studies, "reorienting the humanities towards a more biocentric worldview," and drawing attention to "the role of literature in influencing our knowledge of the world":[11]

> Literature is one of the most effective "signifying practices" (producing and receiving experience), and conceptual frameworks (what we think and know about the world) find their best expression in it. Its influence upon our conceptions of ecological systems produces culture-specific discursive practices (acts of reading and writing the earth) that profoundly affect the state of human and nonhuman communities.[12]

Therefore, literature and its study can contribute to restoring our connection to Earth: in fact, literature "generates knowledge, because it involves inferences about the world which influence our perceptions."[13] Oppermann continues that knowledge is "the prime instrumental tool for the desired change from anthropocentrism to more holistic ecological thought in our biotic relations."[14] The anthropocentric discourse has affected all segments of a human life (culture, ideology, art, economy etc.), which results in devastating consequences to the natural environment. According to Oppermann, ecocriticism can help to "change the conceptual frameworks that have shaped our present way of thinking and are largely responsible for the ecological crisis."[15] This change in consciousness can be performed through literature.

When discussing the importance of ecocriticism for environmental restoration, ecocritics usually refer to scholars who work and teach at universities, but this approach can also be applied to teachers working in early childhood education as well as primary and secondary education. By means of youth literature and children's literature (especially fairy tales), teachers can show their pupils how nature is represented in literature as well as how the relationship between humans and their natural environment—nonhuman beings in particular—is depicted. In doing so, children might be stimulated to develop an ethical and ecological consciousness from a young age.

An Ecocritical Approach to Svetlana Makarovič's Literature

Svetlana Makarovič (born in 1939) is a Slovenian multifaceted artist: a singer, illustrator, actress, and writer of prose, poetry, and children's books, as well as periodical columns. She is regarded as the First Lady of Slovenian poetry, but is also renowned as an author of youth literature. Her bibliography comprises more than three hundred entries.[16] She has received considerable recognition in Slovenia and internationally, and many awards, for her literary works.[17] Her writing for children and youths is extensive and varied; however, she mainly writes fairy tales. Since 1972, she has published more than fifty collections of fairy tales and poems or picture books.[18]

Makarovič has also dramatized many of her tales for theater and radio. Many have been translated into foreign languages, such as English, German, Croatian, Italian, and Slovakian. The author herself does not recognize the difference between "children's" and "youth" literature. The stories she writes are for children as well as for adults: "We, who are adults, need fairy tales in order that, in the anxiety of this world in which we live, we might more easily retain our belief in the beautiful. I think I do not know how to write only for children; I write for children and for adults at the same time."[19] This explains why most of her fairy tales include a subversive message with regard to modern society and particularly speciesist culture, as the author is also a proponent of animal rights.

Makarovič's literary works, particularly her poetry, have been the subject of research on several occasions. Among other areas, the thematization of nature, or rather the thematization of nonhuman subjectivity, has been focused on. The author includes her standpoint of the world in most of her work. By means of strong, suggestive images in her poetry, she shows the problematic relation of people towards the natural environment and animals. Marjetka Golež Kaučič classes Makarovič's poetry in so-called literary ecology, after Joseph W. Meeker.[20] Kaučič states that Makarovič is "undoubtedly on the side of the animals and has wrapped all her stories in her ethical view that animals are equal to humans and often even surpass them.[21] Nevertheless, Kaučič continues,

Makarovič in her poetry has a "Sartrean attitude" towards the other: "To her, the world she lives in seems dark and full of (human) evil. [. . .] In [nature] the human is the one that destroys other beings and devours the animals' children. Otherness is stigmatized and an individual that stands out from the crowd faces nothing but ridicule and isolation."[22] On the other hand, Makarovič's fairy tales represent the lighter side of her work:

> In them [. . .] she comes close to children's emotional and perceptual world, and to their manner of expression. At the same time, however, her tales as a whole are so complex and communicatively rich that we readers of different ages can also delight in them. We also understand them depending on our maturity, sensitivity and breadth of vision.[23]

The animals in Makarovič's tales incorporate the animal and the human. She often stresses the need of co-existence between humans and animals[24] and encourages kindness to all other living beings: "[B]e kind to animals and flowers [. . .] . Think and imagine for yourself, not in a group."[25]

To illustrate these themes, let us have a closer look at the Slovenian–English anthology of sixty fairy tales written by Makarovič and published under the title of *Svetlanine pravljice (Svetlana's Fairytales)*. In this anthology, the best and the most representative of Makarovič's fairy tales are collected. For the purposes of this chapter, let us consider only five of the fairy tales from an ecocritical perspective. For each tale, a short summary will be presented, followed by an ecocritical analysis. Special emphasis will be given to the (ethical) treatment of animals.

Before diving into this case study, we should answer the following question: How do we read a text through the lens of ecocriticism? In fact, when we engage with stories about nature, animals in particular, we have the tendency to understand them from our point of view, i.e. from an anthropocentric perspective. The literary analysis is thus centered on our perception of the world, our thoughts, needs, actions, etc. We do not really ask ourselves what the point of view of an animal or a plant is in a story. For this reason, ecocriticism encourages us to take a step back from our self-centered position in order to identify anthropocentrism, as well as the connections to embodiment and physicality that is outside of the human, and the importance of recognizing that literature influences our realities and that our realities influence literature. Therefore, while reading a literary text, we should be able to address questions such as:

1. What do we mean by "nature" and how is it represented in a literary text?
2. How do we interact with the nonhuman world, animals in particular, and how is this interaction mediated by our cultural, historical, social, geographical, and political background? How is this represented in the text?
3. Can we change our perspective to a more biocentric point of view, and if yes, how? How can this change in perspective be perceived in the text?
4. What are the consequences of our actions for the natural world and how could this be reflected in literature?
5. What does the anthropomorphized nonhuman world teach us about our human nature?

Let us now turn to the selection of fairy tales and offer some examples of an ecocritical approach that can be useful in conversations with children at home as well as for teachers across texts, disciplines, and their students' age groups.

EMILY HEN

Emily Hen is the smallest but at the same time the smartest among thirteen hens, all good egg layers, living in a large henhouse. Their human eats some of their eggs every day and sells the remaining eggs to neighbors. Emily, however, soon realizes that the housewife comes to the henhouse every day, collects the eggs, and leaves without being grateful.

Most of the chickens are unconcerned, but every morning Emily is left contemplating long after the housewife leaves, grumbling that she could at least say "thank you" for the eggs they give her: "W-what w-would it c-cost her to be a little g-grateful? She p-probably thinks that laying eggs is q-quite simple. Just let her try it herself!"[26]

Other chickens, however, take no notice of Emily's words, since they are convinced that this is their fate. One day, Emily starts eating her own eggs, making the housewife angry with all the hens, since she cannot discover why there are only twelve eggs instead of thirteen. Emily, however, becomes stronger each day due to eating her own eggs. The housewife resolves to take revenge on the hen that is mocking her by slaughtering and eating her. Before doing so, however, she tries to give the hens more food. This time, Emily, satiated with so much food, leaves her egg untouched, making her human overjoyed. Nevertheless, the housewife continues to be ungrateful for the eggs, so Emily again starts eating her own eggs and this time the other hens join the protest. When the housewife realizes there are no eggs in the nests, she gets angry, letting out a shriek that summons even the firemen to help her. Realizing the problem, one of the firemen guesses that the hens perhaps need more kindness. The housewife follows his advice, and the hens, surprised by their human's kindness, start saving the eggs for her. Since that day, the housewife gives them the best food and says "thank you" to each hen individually.

The tale "Emily Hen" is a strong criticism of the exploitation of (domesticated) animals[27] for the needs of humans, particularly food. It is also a condemnation of human domination over animals in general. The animals—in this case, hens—are treated as objects by their human mistress: she only takes from them what she wants and she perceives the hens' effort in laying eggs as self-evident, without acknowledging their hard work and even their intrinsic value, i.e. the value that the animals possess in their own right: "Every morning the housewife came to the henhouse, reached into the warm dark nests with greedy hands, and collected the fresh eggs. She placed all thirteen eggs very gently in her apron and left, without a word."[28]

This behavior of exploiting animals is also stressed when Emily starts saving her eggs for the human once again: "But it simply never occurred to [the mistress] to say a kind word to the hard-working hens."[29] The housewife represents the common human belief that we dominate all other beings and that, therefore, we can exploit them as we wish, since we are convinced that we are entitled to what we call their "products," such as eggs or milk. The author also touches on the topic of resignation to one's destiny when she makes the hens speak about their fate to lay eggs for humans: "That's the way it is in life. That's a hen's fate."[30] Even though the resignation is expressed by the animals themselves, it lets us perceive the idea of turning away from what people do with animals (the concept of deflection),[31] persuading ourselves that this is the animals' fate and that this is how it should be.

The tale also criticizes the common belief that hens, or rather animals in general, are not intelligent, since it stresses several times the outstanding intelligence of Emily and her capacity for reflection: "[S]o don't go thinking that all hens are dumb, not at all!"[32]

The main moral of the story is undoubtedly that kindness and gratitude between all beings make a better world. However, it particularly encourages humans to respect other beings with whom they share the world, or as the fireman suggests: "Perhaps your hens need more kindness? Perhaps you should give them a friendly word from time-to-time?"[33] Nonetheless, it must be noted that although this tale allows us to understand Makarovič's appeal to our ethics, there are limitations to an ecocritical reading of the text from an animal liberation perspective: Instead of making the case for animal rights, the tale conveys animal welfare concerns. It is implied that merely a gesture of gratitude would be a fair price for the hens' labor and possession.

KUZMA THE GREMLIN AND THE ANTS

Kuzma the gremlin[34] lives in the woods and likes to annoy other animals. When he sees a cobweb, he tears it down just to make the spider angry. Afterward, he menaces a snail by smashing their shell and blowing in their face. He stretches out a worm like an elastic band and uses their body as a skipping rope. He also sticks a lump of pine sap on a squirrel's tail. Finally, he finds a big anthill—the home of red ants. He pokes a stick into it to make the ants upset. He takes no notice of the tormented ants' complaints for him to stop. When he finishes and leaves the ants' nest, one of the ants jumps into Kuzma's boot and starts biting him as hard as they can so Kuzma suffers so much that he seems to have contracted rabies. The other animals run away from him. Kuzma sits upon the anthill without giving it a second thought; thus, all the ants begin to bite him all over, leaving him exhausted. The next morning, Kuzma is so sore that he does not notice the new cobweb or the snail. The animals start making fun of him for his madness and filthiness. Since then, Kuzma avoids the path of the anthill.

Kuzma the gremlin in a narrow sense represents a child who likes annoying or even torturing other animals, particularly those who are smaller and weaker than he is, in order to have fun or to express his own frustrations: "Kuzma the gremlin made it his business to put someone in a bad mood every day. If he didn't, it would be a very bad day for him indeed."[35] The more the animals suffer or are terrified, the more Kuzma enjoys himself: "At last [the ants] cried out in despair, 'How long, oh Kuzma, will you torment us?' Kuzma simply answered, 'Ho ho, for as long as I like!' And for a long time, far too long, that's exactly what he did, chuckling wickedly all the while."[36] Kuzma does not respect other animals or the environment in which he lives, since he thinks that he is stronger than those he maltreats, and is thus invincible, allowing him to abuse his strength.

However, sooner or later, nature returns all the harm that it has suffered, step-by-step. In the tale this is represented by the smallest ant, who sneaks into Kuzma's boot and starts their revenge. Soon, the ant is joined by others, and together they teach Kuzma a lesson. The ethical and ecological moral of the tale is that every being should be respected and treated well. Moreover, with regard to wild animals and their nests, they should not be disturbed or touched: "From then on, however, Kuzma took his daily walk along a different path—one that took him in a different direction from the ant-hill. But what do you think would have happened if he had discovered another ant-hill? Well, I'll give you three guesses whether he poked into it again or not."[37]

To deepen an ecocritical analysis of this tale we can call into question what Kuzma might represent. In a broader sense, he could signify humankind in general, destroying the natural environment, which at first sight is at his mercy. In the context of the tale, the animals do indeed resist and fight back when mistreated. In a global context, an ecocritical reading of this tale might draw upon the many ways nature, too, resists, with environmental catastrophes caused by climate change occurring on a regular basis. In an educational setting, this parable can be used easily to show that nature and animals should never be underestimated and always be treated with dignity.

KATHLEEN OF THE SPRING

Kathleen is a green-haired sprite who lives in a spring in the wood. Every morning, the forest animals come down to her spring to drink water. Kathleen takes immense delight in observing them. However, none of them notice her, since she is well concealed by the water algae. One afternoon, Kathleen hears two men approaching, Swiggins and Diggins, and realizes they are hunters—the dread of all forest animals. The hunters talk about their plan to kill animals the next day. Kathleen, miserable, contemplates what she can do to prevent such a terrible act. The next morning she squirts water into the animals' mouths so as to confuse and scare them just enough for them to leave. The day after, when the hunters arrive, there are no animals nearby. On their way home, the hunters slip on the ground and fall in the pool, whereupon Kathleen flings water into their faces. Believing that the place is bedeviled, they never return. The animals come back and find out what has occurred. Since then, Kathleen shows herself without fear.

The tale "Kathleen of the Spring" is clearly a statement against the hunting of wild animals. First, it depicts the peace and symbiosis of the animals who live in the forest. Then, it shows that peace is broken when humans come in order to kill the animals. The hunters are depicted as "bloodthirsty men who could barely wait to put out the light in some living creature!"[38] They are not killing animals for need, but for greed, for their own pleasure, and in order to pride themselves on their acts of power:

> And when the animals came down to drink, each of [the hunters] would knock off at least two rabbits and one doe or roebuck, and more besides. And what a splendid

feast they would have later back at home, and all the people they would invite, and how the roebuck's horns would come in handy as a coat hanger in Mrs Swiggins' entrance hall and as a lamp holder in Mrs Diggins' drawing room.[39]

Furthermore, the tale also touches on the topic of hunting trophies, which are typically used as coat hangers or lamp holders. An ecocritical reading serves to highlight the author's direct condemnation of (Slovenian) traditions that demand the suffering, or even the lives, of other beings. The humans are thus represented once again as destroyers of the natural world whose greediness has to be stopped in order to re-establish natural harmony and peace. In fact, as soon as the hunters disappear from the forest, nature regains its peace and natural order: "The little pool soon recovered its clearness, and all was again in exquisite order."[40]

The Peach Stone

A little bear finds a red peach and eats it, leaving just its stone. He wonders what he can do with the peach stone, and decides to bury it in the forest glade to keep it in a safe place. The bear soon forgets about the stone. Years pass by and the little bear grows up. Whenever he passes by the glade where he has buried the peach stone he is reminded of something, although he does not know what it is. After seven years, in springtime, the bear sees that there is a tiny tree in the glade that is in full bloom; however, he still does not remember that he once buried a peach stone there. Finally, one summer day, the bear sees the peach-tree is full of red fruits and he remembers the peach stone. The bear invites other animals to the feast, and after they have eaten all the fruits, he says that everyone should bury their own stone.

This short tale includes the idea of sustainability or rather Earth-keeping: i.e., taking care of the natural environment in order to maintain balance. What one takes from nature must be given back so that the natural cycle continues. Moreover, everything that we get from nature can be "recycled," even though one may think at first glance that it is useless, just as the peach stone: "What could [the bear] do with it? It seemed a pity to throw it away, but he also couldn't eat it. Then he said to himself: 'All comes right in seven years. I'll bury it so it will be in a safe place.'"[41] The tale also indicates a very specific call for sustainability—namely, the duty of the present generation to take care of the forests and the trees that grow in them in order to provide food for generations to come: just as our grandparents planted trees and fruit trees that give us food today, we should provide for our children and grandchildren. The knowledge of self-sufficiency must be passed forward; if not, it will be lost. The bear does not know, at first, what to do with the peach stone, since nobody has taught him. He learns by chance. However, his newfound knowledge may have been lost had he not passed on his expertise:

> After they had polished off the tree, down to the last peach, the bear assumed a serious expression and said: "Never throw away a peach stone—you, over there!" And each animal scrupulously buried its own stone, only the rabbit did not. "Ooof, who would wait seven long years!" he grimaced, but the bear came back at him: "Silence, rabbit! You always want to be smarter than all the rest!"[42]

This wonderful story is also representative of values of community and sharing, since it teaches us that taking care of each other and sharing the abundance of fruits with our communities—despite different species that live in them—makes a better world.

ALLEYCAT

When night comes, the alley cat, a grey tomcat, steals a steak from an unknown house and eats it. Afterward, he begins to sing. In a neighboring house, a Siamese cat hears the alley cat and steps out onto the terrace. They start a conversation in which the Siamese cat prides himself on being a purebred Siamese who has been given a bath that day. The alley cat laughs at the Siamese cat and asks him why people torture him like that. The Siamese answers that they do so, so that he looks handsome. He suggests that the alley cat's humans must be most negligent for not taking care of him as his humans do. He continues that his humans are rich and that he was an expensive cat. Finally, he asks the stray cat what he has out of life. Before leaving, the alley cat responds that he has freedom.

The tale "Alleycat" is a criticism of the domestication of animals, companion animals, and those we call "pets" in particular, evoking the idea that animals have become dependent on humans and can no longer survive on their own. The byproducts of domestication are stray animals, such as cats and dogs—and they are seen as precisely that, a product, as domestication and breeding have long been industrialized and corporatized. Nonetheless, both cats seem to be satisfied with their own way of life, while also criticizing the other:

> "But why do they torture you like that?" asked the alley cat.
> "So that I look handsome. That is why I also eat fish and oat flakes, to have a sleek coat and clear eyes."
> The grey cat thought it over. Then he said: "For supper today, I had a steak like thaaat!"
> "Oh, but that is not healthy," remarked the Siamese. "My masters would never let me have that. Your masters are really most negligent, you know. Too much food overburdens the stomach."
> "Masters? I have no masters! I'm an alley cat," snapped the grey cat.[43]

The degree of the cats' dependence on humans differs. The Siamese cat seems to depend completely on his humans for shelter and food, but also with regard to his cleanliness: he is treated as human property.[44] In contrast, the alley cat is nobody's property. He has to search for food and shelter by himself. However, the alley cat still depends on humans without even realizing it, since besides living in an urban place he steals food from humans. The alley cat has thus adapted to the human environment, and is left depending upon it. The ethical and ecological questions posed in the tale particularly concern the ownership of animals and the responsibilities it entails: where are the borders of human authority over animals, and to what extent has domestication influenced the possibility of surviving for an animal who might be abandoned?[45] The alley cat's last words make us reflect on the illusion of his freedom: "'My masters are very rich. I was an expensive cat, and my upkeep is not for nothing, if that means anything to you. What, then, do you have out of life?' The grey cat, the alley cat, swirled round ready to go, and said: 'I have freedom.'"[46]

Conclusion

Literary texts that include ecological and ethical issues can stimulate our children and pupils to develop a new consciousness, directing them towards a more sustainable way of life and a more responsible relationship with the natural environment as well as nonhuman beings. The analysis of the fairy tales above proposes some ecocritical interpretations, such as animal well-being and rights, the consequences of domestication, hunting, and Earth-keeping, which can be applied and developed further by teachers of literature in their classes according to the experience of their pupils. I hope that the ecocritical analysis of fairy tales provided in this chapter serves as an example of how teachers can approach other literary texts or even other didactic tools, such as animated films,[47] in order to present the ecological and ethical crisis of the modern world, thus encouraging young readers to consciously and actively engage in ecological issues, such as Earth and animal liberation, from an early age.

8

INCLUDING NON-VEGANS IN DEVELOPING AND DELIVERING AN ANTI-SPECIESIST PEDAGOGY TO CHILDREN

TÂNIA REGINA VIZACHRI, ADRIANA REGINA BRAGA, AND LUÍS PAULO DE CARVALHO PIASSI

In this chapter we present our approach to teaching children (in the period between early childhood to preadolescence) about interspecies ethics, sustainability, and otherness with regards to nonhuman animals. We work as part of DIAN (Debates and Investigations about Animals and Nature), the animal rights and environmental ethics team of Banca da Ciência (Science Stand)[1] at the University of São Paulo—a Brazilian science outreach project focused on socio-scientific activism. Although it does not define itself as a vegan initiative, DIAN does support and encourage conveying and discussing vegan thought within the context of science outreach and science education.

One of DIAN's main goals is to make obvious what impacts our lives and connects us all: kindness, compassion, and respect for all creatures. The project aims to design outreach activities to discuss the human–animal relationship from an ethical, cultural and scientific viewpoint, utilizing playful practices and media, in order to analyze how children reflect upon the human–animal bond and how they form and present their arguments about interspecies ethics. DIAN not only teaches children sensitivity towards animal issues, but at the same time trains the university students within the team in interspecies ethics, despite their different backgrounds (e.g. Environmental Management, Public Policy, Nature Sciences) and their limited knowledge about that subject.

This chapter describes and analyzes the interaction between the DIAN research team and kindergarten children at two public schools in São Paulo during 2016. The interactions were centered on two issues: a visit to children's classes with the movie *Chicken Run* (2000) and discussed knowledge and attitudes towards chickens; and another visit on the issue of the exploitation of bees during the production and consumption of honey by humans. Through playful resources such as theater, music, and games, we sought to raise awareness of animal ethics in children and observed in what ways they developed reflective thoughts about how our culture relates to animals.

In this chapter, we refer to the work of Paulo Freire, who guides us in conveying cultural, often controversial, issues. We learn from Freire that it is necessary to know the cultural conditions of the group of learners.[2] The educator should teach learners to question their reality rather than to find answers to it. To evoke a sense of awareness in learners, it is not enough to become aware of reality; it is necessary to reflect on it in a critical way, in order to make them subjects not only of their own knowledge, but also of their culture: that is, of the way they relate to one another and their environments.[3]

To continuously improve upon our own pedagogical methods in respect to the children we worked with, we maintained communication channels with their class teachers before, during, and after the program. Regarding our pedagogy aimed at the university students who joined DIAN, we were also constantly concerned to improve their (as well as our own) learning experience, which is why we conducted a focus group with them, to better understand the group's impact upon its own members. We'd like to share the experiences we gained through this program here with other vegan educators, as we know how important the exchange of strategies and methods is, especially in a pedagogical field as underrepresented as non-harmful human–animal relations.

DIAN IN ACTION FOR CHICKENS

When we started in 2015, nobody at DIAN, except for the team coordinator, Tânia, was vegan or had any experience of approaching the human–animal relationship through a rights-based lens. Before establishing our working and action group, based on interested university students guided by experienced academics, we found that some who had initially volunteered as participants in our project did not agree with the animal rights approach we took in our discussions, and so wanted to leave the team. Others, however, seemed interested and keen to learn about it.

The undergraduate students who joined our team were mostly drawn to DIAN due to their interest in environmentalism. With the semesters coming and going, our team saw members from different backgrounds participating and leaving, too. Soon, most of our non-vegan members began exploring vegetarianism and veganism for themselves. Further, some even became active for animals through the adoption of companion animals, for example, or caring for the abandoned animals at the university, as well as neutering them and facilitating adoptions.

We met once a week. To begin with, we used our meetings to read and discuss texts about animal rights theory, in order to establish a common ground within the team as well as to inspire ideas for possible activities with the children we were aiming to educate about our relationship to animals. We decided to create content based on the animated movie *Chicken Run* (2000), which Tânia had already formally analyzed from an animal rights point of view.[4] The film encourages viewers to see the chicken on screen as representative of an actual chicken, who is destined to live under human domination and be killed for human consumption. This is in contrast to other animated films, which use animals as metaphors for human experiences.

As Baker states, "The notion that talking-animal narratives are not really about animals—that the worthwhile ones, at least, must surely be about something more important than mere animals—is quite consistent with the far wider cultural trivialization and marginalization of the animal."[5] The film *Chicken Run* was chosen by us because it shows the situation of chickens who are imprisoned to serve human interests. The environment in which the chickens are trapped is extremely poor, so much so that the only possibility for improvement is to live somewhere far from humans. Unlike *Bee Movie* (2007), which seeks to convey the message that the consumption of honey by humans is essential for the balance of nature, *Chicken Run* presents the consumption of eggs by humans as problematic. Thus, we prepared activities based on *Chicken Run*, which were performed in two classes at two public schools in Guarulhos (in the São Paulo area).

The eight-year-olds had watched the movie prior to our workshop. Therefore, we began our activities by reviewing some scenes that we had selected based on Tânia's previous analysis. These were the scenes: The initial scene showing the fowl run and the place where the chickens lived; the chickens trying to escape; the human owner of the fowl run controlling the production of the eggs; the chickens planning to escape; the owner of the fowl run showing the machine that turns the chickens into pies; and the final scene, when the chickens get away from the fowl run to live on a desert island. We chose these scenes because they showed very clearly that chickens do not actually want to become pie or even produce eggs for the farmers.

After they had watched the selected scenes, the children were asked about the story, our main concern being the human–animal relationship:

- "What did the human beings want from the chickens?"
- "Why?"
- "Where did the chickens live?"
- "Is this their natural habitat?"
- "Why did the chickens want to run away from there?"
- "Were the human beings good or bad for the chickens?"

The children obviously realized that the animals were suffering in the fowl run shown in the movie and that the human–chicken relationship was not good. They also started exchanging stories of experiences they had made with relatives who were raising chickens. As a team, we concluded that although animated movies are an interesting resource to discuss animal ethics with eight-year-olds, it is a challenge to connect the animation with their own reality. Yes, we did observe how the children realized immediately that chickens want to live their lives autonomously and not simply serve as products for humans. But at the moment that they remembered their relatives who raised chickens, it was difficult for the children to comprehend that their relatives could be doing a bad thing. It was easier for them to say, in effect, "They are different from the farmers of the movie because we know our relatives to be good people."

During the second part of the workshop, we conducted a quiz with the children about the social and behavioral characteristics of chickens. We based the questions on general knowledge about characteristics chickens and humans have in common. We aimed the questions at encouraging the children to empathize with the animals. As they were closed questions, we distributed green cards to the children to indicate a "yes" and red cards to say "no." The children would indicate their answers by raising either card.

We asked them, for example, "Could the chirping of chicks mean something?" The children were confident with their answers to all of the questions; they only had doubts when it came to thinking about whether chickens could be taught to do complex things like turn off lights. To finalize the workshop, we provided three model-sized locations for chickens to be placed in: a desert island, a machine, and a farm (see below). That activity required the children to model chickens with clay and choose in which mockup space they wanted their chicken to be. We asked the children to put their clay chickens into one of the mockup places and then justify their choices. We saw a clear division between the farm and desert island. Nobody put their chicken in the machine. They justified their choices with statements like: "Nobody deserves to go into the machine"; "I'll put them in the farm because they can play there"; or "On the island they can be free."

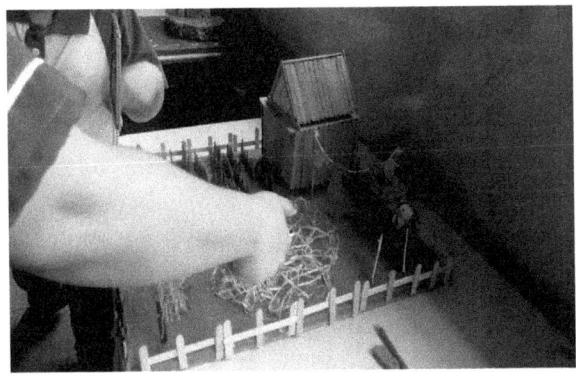

The day after our presence at the children's school, their teacher Rafaela told us that the children were asking her if it was possible to make a cake without eggs. Unfortunately, she told them it was impossible. This might seem like a disappointing and frustrating ending to an overall constructive and challenging day. However, it showed us that our subtle way of introducing animal rights to children encouraged them to approach vegan ethics with an open mind. We also concluded that we should provide the teachers with whom we partner with additional information about topics that might be brought up by the children after we leave, not only related specifically to the animal we discussed in class but also to veganism.

Despite the success in challenging learned speciesism with the eight-year-olds, we encountered very different results with a group of five-year-olds. As soon as we began the workshop, we asked them if they liked chickens. Almost unanimously, they answered, "We like chicken pie." The sequence of activities was almost the same as in the previous class. We simply swapped the quiz from the previous session with a sketch about two women: one a rich farmer who exploited chickens to make pie; the other a sanctuary owner who cared for chickens.

Unexpectedly, the five-years-olds generally preferred the rich farmer, simply because she was rich. During the last exercise, one boy kneaded the clay, saying that he was making chicken mortadella. Most of the children chose the mockup of the machine to put their chicken in. This was our first day discussing interspecies ethics with the five-years-olds. We did not expect to receive such speciesist answers. We assumed that the large difference to the previous group of children occurred because of the age difference.

Our thinking here followed Jean Piaget's cognitive development theory, which states that five-year-old children have not yet developed the needed cognitive abilities to come to similar conclusions as eight-year-olds exposed to the same tasks.[6] This may have hindered their ability to synthesize the presented story. In a study with children aged three to six, Maria McKenna and Elizabeth Ossoff found that the children presented difficulties distinguishing fantasy from reality. They could not, for example, distinguish which content was more or less important and, in comparison to adults, they retained little information about the presented content.[7] We did not see this as a reason to avoid using the movie in our program in the future. Instead, we decided to continue our work, this time with a better understanding of five-year-olds.

Five-year-olds are in what Piaget named the *preoperational stage*. At this stage, egocentrism is characteristic. It means that children have difficulty distinguishing different perspectives from their own.[8] The chosen activity presented a conflict of two values to the children. They had to choose between the chicken's life and the flavor of chicken pie. We believe that the latter was of greater value to the children, not just because of their food preferences but mainly because the taste is what they directly associate with pie.

In Brazil, pie is traditionally made for special occasions, such as celebrations. It is not an everyday meal, especially in working-class families, and is thus probably seen as quite special and valuable by the children. After the workshop, we understood that the young children see the pie as an object of value, which made it easier for them to choose it over a chicken's life.

Nonetheless, we believe that it is important to encourage children to think critically and to put them in contact with other points of view. Thus, we adjusted our questions accordingly: "If you were a chicken would you like to be placed in the machine?" They unanimously answered, "No." We also tried to make them realize that they could make pies with other ingredients, such as apple, chocolate, or vegetables. This experience showed us that speciesism is learned early and that it is essential to engage young children in anti-speciesist thinking and challenge their human-centered behaviors towards animals.

DIAN in Action for Bees

In 2016, one of our members, Carol, was in the process of completing her coursework, which focused on bees, their production of honey, and its consumption by humans. Based on Carol's work we created a second workshop for the five-year-olds. This was an interactive story about bees' lives, their search for nectar, and their joint production of honey as a family. We specifically stressed the importance of the honey to the bees' lives. The idea was to perform the story in an interactive theater setting, with costumes and the involvement of the children. We had a performer dressed as a bee sing a song with the chorus "Abelhinha bonitinha, vou deixar viver," which translates as "cute little bee, I will let you live."

The dedication and excitement in the children were phenomenal (especially compared to their reaction to *Chicken Run*). Some of them spoke very fondly of bee characters from popular media; others completely fell in love with our "bee." The children liked singing and dancing to the song so much that when we asked them whether they liked bees, they said "yes," "I like you," "I love you." The theater got the children's minds so involved in the story that they asked "Are you a real bee?" "Do you really fly?" To finalize this first day of the workshop, the "bee" said she was going back to her house, the hive, to prepare the honey with her family.

Throughout the day, we noticed how the children's attitude towards bees changed with the increasing amount of knowledge they were gaining about the animals. The majority of children agreed that it was not right to eat the honey, as the bees produced it for themselves. One boy even argued that he would not eat honey any longer "because bees have a family." Many children were surprised by how sociable bees are. Nonetheless, some children were still adamant that they could not stop eating honey because they just enjoyed the taste too much.

When we returned to that class the next month the children immediately began to sing the song we had taught them. One child told us she had met a bee but had not killed them; she "let them live," repeating the chorus of that song. For the second day of activities our goal was to show the lifecycle of bees to the children and their importance to the environment. We prepared two games: one was an adaptation of the classic Dominos (see opposite top), the other we aptly named "The Game of Good and Bad" (see opposite bottom). For the domino game, the children had to connect pieces with the same illustration. The pictures referred to the lifecycles of the bees including images of the animal flying to search for pollen and the pollination process.

In The Game of Good and Bad, the children received images of bees with sad and happy faces on them and images of the things that should or shouldn't exist in the environment of the bees, such as garbage, flowers, an apiary, a hive, pure air, smoke, trees, honey, and water with sugar. To represent a healthy environment, we gave the children a green square; a red square was used to signify a harmful environment. If the children felt that the images they saw were good for the bees, they could add these, together with a happy bee to the green square, whereas the images depicting negative circumstances would call for a sad bee to be placed in the red square.

Surprisingly, this game had the most interesting result of that day: The children put all the bees (sad and happy) together in the green square with what they considered to be good for their lives. Thus, they changed the rules to the game and explained their reasoning: "We have to put the sad bees with the good things in the better environment to make them happier."

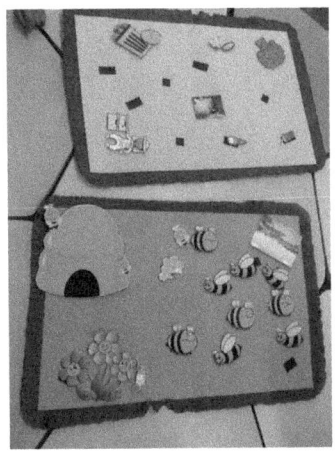

According to the feedback we received from Elen, the children's teacher, a girl told her that she had met a spider in her house and her sister had wanted to kill them. She had explained that the spider was not hurting her, so it was not right to kill them. This was a great example of how children learn to challenge speciesism on a wider scale through our activities: we had not mentioned spiders in our bee workshop; nonetheless, this child made the connection between what she had learned about the complexity and value of bees' lives and those of other animals.

In the second half of the 2016 school year, the DIAN team went into the kindergarten, which, although it is located on the same block as the university, is on the edge of a brook, with lots of trash in the street and unplanned housing. This environment facilitates the proliferation of the dengue mosquito.[9] As a result, the school participates in initiatives to prevent mosquito proliferation. We were given a class of thirty-five five-year-olds whom we'd meet with once a month for four months.

We began the first workshop with the set of activities about bees. Soon, this led to an unexpected issue: the children did indeed very quickly fulfill our aims of developing interspecies awareness and empathy; however, their compassion reached to such an extent that some of the students were unwilling to protect their own lives in order to let the dengue-fever mosquito live. Although in awe of the interspecies compassion demonstrated by these children, we had to incorporate a session into our workshops that would articulate the importance of not harming those who don't threaten us, while explaining at the same time that protecting our own lives always comes first.

Thus, we performed a scene in which two brothers are shown coming back from school, where one had learned about the dengue fever and the other about the lives of bees. We had the brothers have a dialogue with their father and we ended the scene with the father asking: "Why is it acceptable to harm one and not the other?" We invited the students to imagine themselves in the role of the brothers, and give us the answers they would give the father in the scene. They exchanged the strategies they had learned so far to avoid the dengue mosquito, such as, for example, not leaving water standing around. To make clear the difference between the ways we view bees and the ways we approach dengue-fever mosquitos, we guided them towards explicitly pronouncing that the dengue mosquito feeds on our blood, unlike the bees who just eat honey.

DIAN's Impact upon Its Own Members

For a better understanding of the group's impact on its members and their involvement with it, a focus group was carried out at the end of 2016. Before the focus group took place we asked DIAN's eight university-student members to fill out an online form with seven open questions about their motivations for participating in the group, as well as about the changes (mainly in consumption habits) DIAN brought about in their lives. We also asked them about any conflicts during that time. After the eight had filled out the form, the focus group was carried out in order to deepen those themes and for members to develop their opinions while addressing the opinions of the other team members.

We chose an independent person with no opinion about animal rights to guide the focus group. Our team coordinator, Tânia, who was open about being a vegan activist to other DIAN members, also took part. Although she was advised not to express her animal rights opinions in the focus group directly, her presence might have had an affect on the results. We picked up where the questionnaires left off and discussed three categories for analysis: motivation for participation, changes in consumption habits, and impediments to a vegan society. These three categories reflected our goals as a group researching strategies for a vegan pedagogy.

To find out about our student members' motivations to become part of the DIAN team, and since they were given scholarships to become DIAN members, we concretely asked them what they thought about someone joining the team solely to receive the scholarship. Although some of them admitted to have found the group based on the scholarship, all of them agreed that they entered and remained in it due to their affinity with the theme and aims. They voiced their concerns with regards to a team member potentially not sharing their interest in educating children (and themselves) about animal rights, as this type of attitude could damage the dynamics of the group itself.

Although the majority of members did not become vegetarians, we realized in the focus group that they were suffering from a kind of moral pressure to use their consumer choices to cause less harm. For example, Alexandre was a vegetarian when he entered the group because of his religion, ISKCON (more commonly known as Hare Krishna). He said that to join the group "was cool," but, he continued, "it brings the challenge of not eating eggs, drinking milk; but it is a thing that I am working on myself. I am thinking of abandoning this habit altogether and one day being able to be a vegan. I do not know." Kátia also said:

> I think even though not everybody became vegan or anything, it still made a difference, for people's lives, in some sense. For example, Larissa, she takes care of a lot of animals, she is always helping them. [. . .] I adopted two dogs this year by myself. I think everything was because of the group. [. . .] I haven't had meat for seven months. [. . .] I still keep trying.

We could observe that all of them were projecting a positive self-image. They all showed that they were thinking deeply and seriously about speciesism, and that they were trying to change their habits. For example, at first Lucia said: "[When I entered DIAN] I did not care about the question [of animal rights] nor did I pay enough attention to it." But she changed: "When I, for example, talk with my mother, it is perceptible that I am trying to influence her [. . .] to think the same way as me: animals deserve rights like us, they are persons." Pablo, who became a vegetarian a month after joining the group, also said: "I've already influenced a change in habits in my house. People in my family are consuming less meat."

We realized that participation in the group caused the students to experience conflicts within themselves regarding how they should act and how they wanted to act. Developing consciousness is a very conflicting process, mainly because changes can interfere with our comfort zone. However, these conflicts are fundamental for the construction of who we want to be. What we could observe in our team is a growing concern for animals and nature, which means an acknowledgment of their moral value. It is the beginning of an anti-speciesist consciousness. As we learn from psychologist Yves de La Taille, for this awareness to develop further it is necessary to have external opportunities provided for an internal re-evaluation to take place, which results in awareness followed by action.[10] Knowing how one should act comes before wanting to act and the action itself.

With the intention of finding out possible obstacles that might be impeding the students' will and ability to change their actions, we asked them whether they saw the possibility of a vegan future. Only Marina said "yes" with no reservations: "I think that in many years, it will be necessary to have a vegan society, because we are destroying the natural resources little by little, which will contribute to a raising awareness about the planet." Pablo also connected it with environmentalism, saying that veganism is a necessity, although he thought it to be utopian: "I believe in a significant reduction [of animal consumption], but not a total abandonment." Other members said it was a utopia because veganism faces some impediments like "the taste" of meat and dairy, tradition and culture, as well as economic interests, all of which disengage people from making ethical decisions.

In semiotics, a structure that prevents the subject from reaching their desired goal is referred to as the *anti-subject*.[11] Therefore, these factors prohibiting the rise of veganism can be understood as "anti-subjects," as they are the impediments to reaching the ideal of a vegan society. When we understand anti-subjects as something external to us, like the factors mentioned by the students, we will feel that it is impossible to change, because the system does not allow for transformation to happen. We put the action of society above our own attitudes; we consider them more powerful and fixed. We do not consider that the system is made up of individuals who can be changed. Those impediments may raise a feeling of impotence, making the action seem unfeasible. Then, this "utopia" seems difficult to reach, almost impossible. Nevertheless, it is notable that some of the same members who considered external impediments too powerful to be dismantled, became vegetarian, whereas others said they had changed their consumption habits.

The focus group also showed that the team members were concerned with defending the lives of other species. Throughout the session, they used phrases such as, "rights of animals," "right to live," "they deserve rights," "they are like us," "let's think about the animal's point of view," "we are not better than them." Although they did not define what they considered "animal rights," and if and how the concept differed from human rights, they stressed the importance of life, its dignity and integrity. We also realized that some of the students utilized the approximation of animals to human beings as an argument for defending animals—"the animal is like us." This does not necessarily imply the annulment of differences, but the recognition of similar interests, shared by animals and humans.

Identifying the positions of the participants, their particular attitudes towards and perceptions of animal rights and the ethics that go with the topic, as well as the conflicts and doubts that arose within them, was important for the continuity of the group. Now we know where more clarity is needed and which issues and topics need more attention in our future meetings.

FINAL CONSIDERATIONS: WORKING WITH NON-VEGAN PARTNERS

Although the main goal of our group is to discuss vegan issues with children, we had to work to raise awareness among the mediators who go to schools to discuss these issues. A condition for our research group to get funded was the inclusion of students from the university we work at. As we could not find vegan students who were able to participate, we had to partner with non-vegans. This meant that we had to continuously work on raising the students' awareness of interspecies ethics, in preparation for them to work as mediators who would then work with children. The goal we had as animal activists was to educate the students and children (and wider society) so they would make the decision to become vegan. However, education does not produce simple or immediate results. Although it was difficult to stay patient and tolerant of the actions and behaviors we disagreed with, as well as even continuing the dialogue itself (the basis of every educational work), we can highlight two very positive aspects of working with non-vegan partners on this project.

First, if these students had not been able to join our team, they might never have had the opportunity to contemplate and ethically consider their relationship with other species. Their obligation to elaborate and facilitate activities for children, in the context of interspecies ethics, led them to reflect upon their own habits, which in turn constituted a shift in their own praxis.

Paulo Freire confirms that reflection without action is empty of sense, whereas action without reflection is simply empty activism. Action for action's sake, neglecting reflective capacity, "denies a genuine praxis which makes dialogue impossible."[12] Establishing thought without action and action without reflective thought generates inauthentic ways of existing and thinking.[13] Consciousness happens in praxis. That is why our team not only focuses on theory but also develops applicable praxis-based activities. Within our team we put into practice what Freire talks about when he says that through returning to past and present experiences in and with the world, we begin to understand them through living them again, which makes us realize that we are not faced with an insurmountable and overwhelming condition.[14]

The second positive aspect we discovered while working within a non-vegan team is that the dialogue with non-vegan partners made us practice and develop our own tolerance. That was hard work! Often, our personal convictions and political beliefs as educators can lead us to become authoritarian and prohibit any dialogue. Freire and Antonio Faúndez state that the political militant intellectual is always at risk of becoming an authoritarian or intensifying their authoritarianism when they are not able to overcome their messianic conception of social transformation.[15] However, Freire does acknowledge that the educator, as part of a conscientious process, does have a right to express opinions. What they do not have, is the right to *impose* their opinions.[16]

When prescribing your own opinions as an educator, you are manipulating your students by assimilating them into your belief system—a dangerous and harmful process that inhibits critical thinking and reflection. Every dialogue requires faith in the other, their knowledge, as well as tolerance of those who think differently from us. Freire and Faúndez also state that tolerance does not mean denying what we believe, what is fair, what is right.[17] Tolerant individuals do not reject their own dream, their utopia, but they respect those who have a different dream.

We also learn from Freire that in any dialogue it is necessary to respect the other and their culture, to approach them with an understanding and a willingness to learn about the conditions of that group or community, as this allows us, as educators, to identify the ways we can propose change (such as a change to veganism). However, it is very difficult and painful to exercise tolerance and understanding when injustice is so prevalent and obvious to us. It is important here to remember Freire telling us that it is only through dialogue and love that we can act together with the masses to make our dreams come true.

9

"THE THINGS WE CHOOSE TO TEACH ARE POLITICAL DECISIONS. SO, EMBRACE THAT."

NEOLIBERALISM, THE ACADEMY, AND CRITICAL ANIMAL STUDIES EDUCATORS

Heather Fraser and Nik Taylor

The neoliberal academy often tries to stifle dissent and critical pedagogy. Despite this, many educators remain committed to teaching ideas and practices that challenge hegemonic beliefs about power, gender, ethnicity, and, more recently, species. In this chapter, we consider how educators committed to critical animal pedagogies negotiate working in the academy, a place often unwelcoming for those (of us) adopting interconnected and overlapping approaches to problematizing systemic animal abuse. We use the term "critical animal pedagogies" to signal the adoption and teaching of vegan praxis, which we see as a necessary part of a commitment to animal liberation and to challenging the many manifestations of speciesism through integrated and holistic analyses of power.

The impetus for this chapter came from several places. The first stemmed from our interest in the impact of neoliberalism on universities, and on decisions made about the topics and theoretical approaches used to teach and research. In our book *Neoliberalization, Universities and the Public Intellectual: Species, Gender and Class in the Production of Knowledge*, we argue that the commercialization of higher education in public universities is negatively affecting the space and support to teach issues considered controversial, or that engage students with "radical" alternatives to the neoliberal experience.

Another impetus came from personal in-class experiences, working with students hungry for transformative learning experiences. Consider, for instance, an experience one of us (Nik Taylor) had with a student in an Animals and Society class. The student "loved animals" but had never problematized their treatment. After watching a video (shared by other students) that detailed the horrors of life as an animal in the American intensive dairy industry, she welled up with tears and was unable to talk, beyond a couple of words. At the end of the class she stayed behind to talk about the video's impact on her. Among many other things, she was looking into how to become vegan and bring her son up vegan.

Although pleased to hear this, I (Nik Taylor) was concerned about her reaction as she was distraught, to the point of sobbing. After students agreed to discuss it, I asked the class the next week if they found the topic emotionally difficult to deal with. Many said they did. Many reported struggling with the emotions of having "their eyes opened" and "seeing the world differently." However, because animal abuse is normalized to the point of invisibility, the "opening of eyes" for our students can be extremely painful. Put plainly, it can be shocking to learn of the suffering and exploitation of others, especially when they are hidden in plain sight, through conventional marketing and sales of meat and dairy, and associated agribusiness practices.

This stands in contrast to other topics relating to the oppression of humans, where students usually have some prior exposure to and awareness of the issues. For instance, they are often confronted by some of the information we discuss about gender or racial inequalities, for example, as they live in societies that at least nominally discuss and problematize these issues. This is usually not the case for animal abuse. Being forced to think about this from the student's perspective is one of the reasons for the experiences we share here. We realized that if our own students struggle with some of the material we present, then others are likely to have shared experiences. We wanted to tap into the experience of educators in the field of human–animal studies, to find out how they managed teaching controversial animal issues in their fields.

Thus, we conducted a survey. Our data is drawn from fifty-nine (de-identified) responses made to our 2016 online survey taken by current educators teaching animal studies, working in higher education institutions around the world. Ethics approval was given through Flinders University. When asked whether they preferred the term "animal studies," "human–animal studies," or "critical animal studies (CAS)," not all our respondents identified as critical animal studies scholars. This may be because terminology is contested in the field[1] and/or it might reflect particular ideological stance(s) or discomfort with a narrow reading of what CAS entails.

In this chapter then, we focus on the responses by those who deliberately taught contentious human–animal issues/topics; that is, they problematized the relationship between humans and other species as one of asymmetrical power. Our inclusion criteria only required that they teach, or had taught, animal studies modules in tertiary education institutions. So respondents were not limited to full-time, tenured academics, but included part-time, early career, and sessional workers. They also came from a variety of disciplinary backgrounds and taught various aspects of animal studies; some taught full animal studies topics whereas others taught modules or issues relating to animal studies within non–animal studies courses. In this survey, respondents were asked to describe their experiences of academic institutional practices, specifically those that facilitate and/or hinder radical pedagogies. A key theme was how they worked critically and reflexively with the complexities and potential contradictions of classroom scholar-activism.

Our aims for this chapter are threefold. First, we want to open up discussion about the many possibilities and challenges facing animal studies educators who advocate animal liberationism in the classroom. Our second aim is to discuss strategies respondents used to navigate these complexities. Our third, related, aim is to provide some ideas and suggestions to others who highlight vegan praxis and problematize speciesism in their teaching, particularly newcomers to the field of animal studies.

1. Teaching "Controversial Issues": Possibilities and Challenges

Respondents teaching animal studies subjects/courses reported covering a broad sweep of topics, including but not limited to: the possibility of writing animal–human history, representation, agency, change, and culture; animal use, environmental issues, and land use; understanding animal shelter issues; evolving philosophical issues in the human–animal bond and the right to keep animals as companions, and animal-assisted interventions; speciesism, intersectionality, the animal labor and animal rights movements, animals in disasters, wildlife management and laws governing hunting, the medical use of animals, and using animals for food. In response to our question about preferences for terminology of the human–animal field, there was no real standout in terms of preferred terminology regarding Human–Animal Studies (HAS), Animal Studies (AS), Critical Animal Studies (CAS), or Anthrozoology.

The following issues were described as controversial: the ethical implications of animal sentience, including the meat paradox—that is the internal dissonance between caring for animals as well as eating them—and anti-vivisection; the welfare of therapy animals, including concerns about the negative impact of their domestication; and the prevention of human violence against animals. This last included banning dog and horse racing; making it illegal to hunt animals, or to keep them in captivity, force them into industrialized agriculture, or slaughter them for food. Live exports of "farm" animals and government-sanctioned culls (of "feral" cats, bats, kangaroos, and other "pests") were also said to engender a sense of controversy among students. Anti-vivisectionist questions relating to the ethical legitimacy of testing on animals prompted some to pose questions about whether humans have the right to "use" animals at all.

For all their differences in terms of disciplinary background and approaches to teaching, the human–animal studies educators in our survey reported teaching from critical perspectives that promote the fight for animal justice and oppose the idea that animals do not matter within the academy, or are unworthy subjects of concern. One respondent wrote:

There are controversial issues within HAS (e.g. meat consumption), but [when interacting] with the students I do not think of them as a big problem but something that is interesting to work with. More problematic is that the whole issue of animals within academia is controversial and generally not recognized as a worthy issue.

THE NEOLIBERAL ACADEMY

Contemporary educators working from critical perspectives face considerable challenges in the course of their work; challenges intensified through the neoliberalization of the academy. Neoliberalism is a term that refers to the new use of old liberal ideas about individual rights in aggressive, "free market" capitalism that prioritizes private business interests over all others.[2] The rise of neoliberalism and its extension to the higher education sector have led to growing pressures to convert universities from educationally focused institutions to commercial producers of educational exports. This has led to a common pattern across universities in different countries of public management–inspired budget cuts and the casualization of teaching.[3]

One consequence of these economic changes has been the erosion of space for critical pedagogies and research, as universities become single-mindedly focused on the "bottom line" of student numbers (not experience) and a related focus on vocationalism.[4] Encouraged to toe the party line through, for example, tying academic tenure and promotion to the successful application for government grants and/or the publication of research findings in narrow and conservatively focused "top tier" journals, this narrowing becomes a self-fulfilling prophecy as academics scramble to meet (constantly changing) goals.

In the academy, the notion of limiting institutions refers to organizational regimes that may purport to endorse courageous, bold, and unconventional thinking, but in practice marginalize, if not sanction, those emulating these characteristic behaviors. In turn, this can create a treacherous atmosphere of competition and surveillance (through, for example, multiple audits), which can be the antipathy of radical/critical pedagogy. In such an atmosphere, teaching topics and issues deemed controversial can be difficult because they challenge the status quo, at a time when such challenges can be met with disapproval if not hostility.

Respondents indicated that teaching human–animal relations from a critical, vegan perspective left them open to the ravages of a neoliberal administration. Those who refuse to conform—who dare to speak truthfully and refuse to sanitize the content of the subjects they teach and persist with inducing controversial discussions—may be denied institutional support and in turn, can become alienated, marginalized, and disenchanted. As one of our respondents said: "At my university, there used to be a great deal of discussion among colleagues. We have become quite corporate and that personal touch has been lost. No one wants to talk truthfully any more." This is a problem because controversy sits at the heart of (much) animal studies. To quote one of our respondents: "Animal studies are borne in controversy. [. . .] It is a necessary aspect of working within the subject matter." Critical animal scholars, in particular, appreciate the need to challenge the academic-industrial complex and its connections to big business, academia, and research funding.[5]

As we discuss below, many of our survey respondents detailed the kinds of pushback they engaged in while managing controversial issues, usually with little institutional support. However, we are not suggesting here that it is only CAS that challenges the neoliberal academy. We are aware that others working in politically contentious areas are also at risk of marginalization. However, it is our contention that working for animal equality is ultimately more confronting because it challenges the very idea of human superiority. From this vantage point, it is not only white, cisgender, heterosexual, non-disabled men who receive unearned privilege. To some extent it is all humans. This may be why we don't always receive the support from other marginalized scholars that we might expect. For instance, ecofeminists have detailed their experiences of being shunned at feminist conferences through largely misguided fears that they were equating women with animals and/or were diverting precious resources away from women's issues.[6]

2. Strategies Used to Navigate Complexities

Our survey respondents spoke of several strategies that they actively deployed to optimize their teaching of human–animal issues considered controversial. These included: respecting difference; making space for dissent; and maintaining curiosity and remembering history, particularly the positive changes that have taken place.

Respect for Difference, Space for Dissent, and Ongoing Curiosity

Respondents indicated that to teach controversial issues "well" in human–animal studies, educators need to be genuinely interested in exploring different ways of seeing the world, including—or perhaps especially—ideas that do not accord with their own. Various expressions were given, such as: "A climate of mutual respect and shared engagement to deal with a controversial topic is vital"; "I have experienced interesting and constructive debates in class, where students have challenged my views and articulated their own very different ones"; "I can take a particular position and I explicitly show how it confronts mainstream thinking about animals. But I do invite controversial discussions and I do honor and value students' views."

Emphasis was placed on educators maintaining their own curiosity with their subject matter and encouraging that curiosity in their students. The facilitators' capacity to engender trusting, respectful relationships in the classroom was an important part of the process, particularly the capacity to empathize with students holding different positions. One respondent described it as, "Trying to be in the skin of people at both ends of the [animal rights] spectrum." Another explained it like this:

> Developing [. . .] curiosity to seek understanding. Determining where I can locate myself and the emotions it raises in me [can be] confronting to people who are thinking [about the topic or issue] in another way to me. [. . .] Here again, [I'm] seeking to elicit empathy for others. [. . .] And after that, [exploring] difference. [. . .] Curiosity is a key.

Educators may find their curiosity piqued by examining some of the learning processes, such as students incorporating new information into existing knowledge bases: "I am often surprised by the insight of students encountering the challenges of these issues for the first time."

Remembering History, Recognizing Changes

Remembering history, including continuities and discontinuities, was a theme for some respondents who spoke of the need to notice changing cultural attitudes to animals and their treatment, including greater acceptance of animal rights, animals as sentient beings, and animals as nonhuman persons:

> In the late 90's, seeing emotions in animals was a crime or a sin. Working with the intersubjective bond between human and nonhuman was perceived as esotericism. [Now there is more] sensibility for animal suffering. [. . .] It changes—a bit at least.

In many circles there is a growing awareness of animal rights and welfare in mainstream Western society.[7] There are several knock-on effects from the more positive cultural attitudes towards animals and humane treatment of them, including greater respect for the service and care work that many animals perform. Greater acceptance of vegetarianism (and to this we might add veganism) is also apparent, particularly in Australia, where the rates of both have risen rapidly in recent years.[8] Respondents recognized these changing trends, including which issues were classified as controversial. For instance, one respondent wrote: "Ten years ago, Animal Assisted Therapy was seen as flippant by almost everyone, and vegetarianism as an extremist position. Both are at the fluffy edges of [the] mainstream now." Another noted: "Veganism is not as strange of a diet as it used to be [. . .] yet people still feel that they don't want to be told (or feel they have to) make an 'extreme' change to stop eating animals."

Getting Support to Sustain the Work

As well as the personal strategies adopted to resist the demoralization incurred by the neoliberal university, respondents also demonstrated an ability to find and/or create differing levels of support from their institutions and peers. We asked, "Are there specific forms of institutional support you can recommend as effective?" One respondent wrote: "Tenure; Supportive Chair, Dean and/or colleagues who share commitment to social change." Worryingly, many of our respondents equated their support and/or ability to get critical animal studies content into the curriculum with their ability to secure tenured positions. Refusing to be silenced about so-called controversial issues in critical approaches to human–animal relations, as well as attendant refusal to play the "academic sausage factory" game,[9] increases the possibility of vegan scholars being sidelined from these employment opportunities. Over time, this may lead to more conservative curricula.

In the face of little/no support or even opposition, some respondents began re-interpreting what organizational support might mean—seeing the lack of institutional interference as a form of support: "They mainly leave me to get on with it, which is helpful. No censorship is [a] form of support these days." Another respondent explained the need for subversive strategies: "Animals have to be snuck into syllabi and teaching sessions." Also highlighted was the need to work with others to develop courses: "Collaboratory efforts with other instructors [help], which means setting up opportunities for discussion and interdisciplinary interaction." Many sought support outside the academy: "[U]nions are key, as are supportive directors/chairs."

Passionate but Patient Alliance-Building

Teaching controversial issues can be highly emotive work, as can the navigation of an increasingly controlling, neoliberal academy. In the face of resistance, alliances within and across our respondents' disciplines were crucial. Part of this alliance-building involved the need to be patient with students and other staff about understanding human–animal relations in non-normative ways: "The animal rights viewpoint [may] stand out as strange but it is appealing to many or they get the ethics of it. I think they have trouble seeing it as a priority or seeing how we can actually create a fair world for animals."

The passion respondents felt for the areas they taught motivated many to pick their way through these challenges, rather than succumb to de-politicized teaching. Many linked their passion to a desire for transformative social change, on behalf of other animals. One wrote: "The ability to speak knowledgeably and respectfully about controversial issues is key to lasting social change. It draws others into the conversation rather than alienating them, creating allies rather than people who dismiss the topic at hand." For many, teaching *is* vegan praxis, strengthened by working in alliance with like-minded others. Finding ways to connect emotionally and intellectually with (potential) allies also meant allowing space for the expression of joy. Said one: [I]t is important to start wherever students are, be generous with them, and to not see resistance as a problem but as part of a journey." Passion was the anchor that kept them challenging a sector not particularly receptive to radical pedagogy on behalf of/about other species. As one respondent put it: "I believe it is the most pressing political issue of them all. It is my life's work and purpose."

3. Ideas for New, Critical Animal Studies Educators

Educators new to animal studies are right to wonder about how they will approach their teaching practices and how they might navigate them within the increasingly neoliberalized academy. From our survey findings, they would be right to assume that the degree of difficulty of the work is higher than if they were to try to sidestep or dilute controversial material. However, we are not suggesting that we/they give up in the face of hostile environments. As we have argued elsewhere, such adversity often leads to friendships and alliances that not only help with the work but also enrich our lives.[10] In this survey, we were keen to ask respondents to think about how they go about solving problems, and how they maintain their passion, patience, and "spark." Suggested ways forward are offered below.

Prioritizing Justice Rather than "Balancing" and Avoiding Dualisms

We asked questions about respondents' perceptions of classroom politics, including whether educators should reveal or conceal their ideological orientations. The common thread for our critically oriented respondents was that the aim should be fairness rather than balance or neutrality. The sheer weight of speciesism in popular culture was the reason cited by some for not being tied to the notion of balance:

> Students are marinated in an anthropocentric status quo, so I see no problem in offering a counterpoint. I am clear about that with them—that they get plenty of the "other side" elsewhere so that my courses are a place to name and address oppression (of various forms) since I take an intersectional approach.

Other respondents emphasized the problem of dualisms: "First, there are never two sides, always at least seven or eight. I think it is essential that educators acknowledge other perspectives, but they do not need to always give them equal weight." Also emphasized was the need to explore ideas rather than proselytizing:

> I think it's more about presenting the story fairly: so not looking for both "sides" if actually the weight of current opinion falls one way. I also dislike [. . .] presenting stories as dualistic (pro or anti, for or against). [It] is unhelpful for the issues I teach about, which are so nuanced. However, I think it's important to present, for example, a theory and the criticisms of that theory. Normally, a topic is controversial because there are views in tension, and it wouldn't be a fair representation of that topic if teachers only discussed one set of views and dismissed the others.

Yet, sometimes the exploration of non-normative ideas was interpreted as proselytizing, especially when presented by women educators. We mention gender here because it still has a habit of patterning how expertise and authority are imagined, and therefore constructed. Whereas male educators with privilege status—such as white, heterosexual middle-class, non-disabled men—are usually accorded authority, women across intersections of privilege and oppression (class, race, sexuality, ability, etc.) are still liable to be positioned as secondary and subsidiary—implicitly, if not explicitly. The gendered nature of this marginalization of voice then taps easily into stereotypes about (overly) emotional women focusing on so-called trivial issues.

We have experienced this ourselves, even from apparent supporters, when they laugh and refer to us as the fluffy researchers, or those who focus on pets, and by implication, avoid "hard" and sensible topics affecting human beings. Often we brush it off, or even laugh along, believing that they mean no harm. To do otherwise also risks us being stereotyped as humorless feminists who can't take a joke. Yet, we know that the same "playful" treatment is not given to other colleagues, especially the men. Having been embroiled in these dynamics of marginalization ourselves means that we appreciate the emotional sensitivities and ideological landmines that vegan educators may face in the course of their work. We think it explains why so many respondents emphasized the great care they took allowing a plurality of views to be expressed in the classroom:

> I do not impose a single political perspective, welcome and encourage debate, etc. yet one or two always say I force "veganism" or "vegetarianism" on them. It's a silly and incorrect accusation. Without question, this dynamic is gendered because there are male professors at my university who are much more emphatic (insistent?) about their political views, who are not critiqued for doing so online (though I have no idea what appears in their evaluations). At the same time, the issue has never been raised in my teaching evaluations (even though they are anonymous) and my scores are always very high. I know that male professors of color who teach

about complex issues experience more push-back (e.g. hateful comments online and right in the evaluations in a critical race studies course), and there is, of course, plenty of research to support what I've experienced.

Intersectionality, Compassion, and the Possibility of Personal Transformation

Our research participants collectively expressed their desire to facilitate classes that were educationally and personally transformative—classes that valued compassion and respected intersectional analyses, inclusive of speciesism. As a consequence, they suggested critically analyzing student reactions to animal rights, in relation to the oppression of humans across the axes of class, gender, race and ethnicity, sexuality, ability, and age. They understood that ideas about, but also lived experiences of, intersectionality can help students make sense of the interconnecting patterns of privilege and oppression, for humans and animals. For one respondent, navigating the intersections of privilege and oppression across human–animal categories opened up discussions designed to offset the potential elitism of human–animal studies in university settings:

> I'm concerned that HAS is seen as elite. Where it is taught in UK universities this tends to be in elite institutions (I know this to be true in the US, too). In non-elite places like mine, there is limited student interest unless you tap into issues around forms of capitalist exploitation or colonial formations.

Another related and useful suggestion was to enable students to explore their own reactions to "controversial" material in relation to their own experiences of privilege and oppression. This can help students make sense of emotions such as anger, compassion, and the distress that can surface when students open themselves to ideas about animal liberation:

> There are always mixed responses. There are those students who transform in compassionate ways. Always. Seeing their anger and sadness along with their newfound awareness and political commitment is very rewarding. There are many who at least take the blinkers off and begin to shift their ideas. And there are those who become hostile or perhaps not angry but embarrassed/resistant/some complex combination. About one third of the class looks down (literally) even with basic photos of gestation crates, for example. That is not unique to my classroom, of course. No-one has said anything to me in person, but every now and then someone writes something hateful on an anonymous site. And this happens despite me introducing them to a range of political perspectives on animals as things to study and understand.

As this respondent goes on to suggest, critical self-reflexivity, or the interrogation of personal beliefs and assumptions from alternative perspectives, does not always occur smoothly:

> One recent experience of note: We do an exercise involving different slogans used by a range of animal advocates—ranging from ADOPT DON'T SHOP, to I'D RATHER GO NAKED THAN WEAR FUR, to FRIENDS NOT FOOD—and we unpack them to identify the advocates' goals, the intended audience, the relative effectiveness, etc. Half deal with food and half are about other animal issues (ivory, fur, rescue/adoption). Yet one student said, "As a meat eater, and someone who isn't ashamed of that, these slogans were all about meat and make me feel like I should feel bad." I noted that they weren't all about meat, and asked whether advocates' goals with some of the slogans are, in fact, to get people to reflect on their own assumptions and behaviors (which, of course, are

precisely the goals). I imagine that despite all the happy stuff, cute animals, etc. the food issue is what will be that student's main recollection from the course, though I'm not sure how exactly she will remember it (with anger or more self-reflexivity).

Conclusion

Aware that the neoliberal environment is no friend to vegan scholars who teach critically oriented animal studies and the vegan praxis that underpins it, respondents provided many insights about their role as educators, and how they navigated the complexities of teaching issues considered controversial. Many of our respondents reported how they depended on the personal and professional alliances with educators from other disciplines but also local community and activist groups, trade unions, and others with shared interests. They show that though there are (still) opportunities to engage in this work and to follow individual passions, it is inherently political in nature, requiring skill, care, and thought. Finding ways to resist the conservatizing forces associated with the neoliberal academy, individually and collectively, is a major part of the challenge.

10

WHAT WE CAN LEARN ABOUT VEGAN EDUCATION FROM ANARCHIST PHILOSOPHY AND ANIMAL LIBERATION ACTIVISTS

Will Boisseau

I have always had empathy for other animals; I became vegetarian as a child and was always concerned about the welfare of animals. Despite being a vegetarian, the political nature of animal rights and the connections with other social justice issues were not something I really considered, until I stumbled upon the English South Coast punk scene. As I became more involved in writing zines and putting on shows, it dawned on me that almost everyone I met was either vegan or vegetarian. It was also at this time that I was introduced to anarchist ideas. Being a punk was hugely significant in my activist education, partly because I read anarchist and animal liberation zines and leaflets on distro stalls, but mainly because of the prefigurative aspects of DIY culture.

Here were groups of people organizing for themselves, without (or with less) hierarchy. Punks put on shows and benefits for hunt saboteurs and other leftist causes. They created safe spaces and attempted to organize production and distribution outside a capitalist framework—exchange and gift-giving were encouraged. It was through punks that I learnt about squatting and Food Not Bombs, and it was through punk that I saw the inspirational things that small groups of people could achieve through horizontal grassroots networks and direct action. The instructive value of this experience has convinced me of the collective educational worth of activism in helping people see how we could work together in a free society, and what we can achieve through solidarity and mutual aid.

Drawing on these experiences, as well as my educational work, this chapter focuses on the confluence of veganism, animal liberation, and anarchism and considers collective vegan action as a site in which practical tools, direct action skills, and radical approaches to pedagogy are developed and exchanged. Throughout the chapter, I argue that vegan solidarity (collective vegan action that includes a critique of capitalism and adopts non-hierarchical organizational approaches) is a form of prefigurative politics, and that animal liberation has acted as a form of "anarchist outreach" by introducing anarchistic ideals, theories, and tactics to a wider audience.

"Prefigurative politics," as understood by anarchists, denotes that the *means* used to create a new society must be consistent with the desired *ends*. For anarchists, this means that a free society cannot be created using authoritarian methods, and cannot be enforced from above; instead, people should act and organize in ways in which they wish the future free society to be organized.[1] The combination of veganism/animal liberation and anarchism has enhanced the educational value of both movements, because in combination anarchism and animal liberation highlight the politics of total liberation. The ideals of both movements—emancipation, liberty, and autonomy—are valuable when applied not only to educational settings but more so in any social context.

In this chapter, we will discuss specific work undertaken within the anarchist and vegan movements, which forms a useful starting point for pedagogues interested in teaching and learning about anarchism, animals, and society. I am offering a cross-section of authors and approaches to the topic that critically engage both non-vegan anarchists and vegans who—inadvertently or not—perpetuate hierarchies through their politics, in the classroom, and beyond. Let us first consider traditional anarchist movement educators, to show you where my understanding of anarchism comes from.

I suggest that whereas there has been a notable history of theorists who aimed to combine anarchism and animal advocacy—most notably feminist thinkers who have worked on anti-speciesism throughout history—a greater impact on the connection between veganism and anarchism has been made by the practical experience of activists taking part in vegan solidarity and collective vegan action.[2] This will lead us to discover significant connections between current anarchist and animal liberation theories and practices that are found within collective vegan action: in particular, the concepts of total liberation, anti-capitalism, opposition to the state, and protection of the planet.

Throughout the chapter, I draw on insights gained from interviewing over fifty animal activists, mostly from the UK, over a three-year period to 2016. These interviews gave me a sense of what motivated animal activists, why they became involved in animal liberation activism, and what they saw as the most important organizational and educational elements of their activism. At the end of the chapter, we will consider the educational and prefigurative nature of collective vegan action as a site of anarchist outreach and education.

In particular, I discuss the common tactics and shared action repertoire of anarchist and collective vegan action groups; these include the use of affinity groups, the stress on consensus decision-making, and most importantly the use of direct action as represented by the Animal Liberation Front (ALF) and the Hunt Saboteurs Association (HSA). The analysis as a whole will show that the combination of anarchism and animal liberation has—in theory and practice—increased the educational value of both movements as vegan anarchists act in solidarity with other oppressed groups.

THE MOVEMENT'S EDUCATORS

What can we learn from the classic anarchist movement educators, especially drawing on their attitudes towards animals? In what ways was animal advocacy included in the development of anarchist thought? The thinkers presented in this chapter are still regarded as influential "sages" of anarchism by British academics and activists.[3] These thinkers provided the "diverse beginnings of anarchist thought," some of which "continues to inspire anarchism to this day, and some of which is no longer relevant."[4]

Interestingly, only a few of my interviewees who identified themselves as anarchists gained their political awakening from reading the classic thinkers. Activists typically become anarchists through social circles, punk music, or mainstream campaigning, before they read works by libertarian writers after a number of years in activism. However, there were those who were convinced by key texts. For instance, one activist for Stop Huntingdon Animal Cruelty (SHAC) describes her political awakening:

> When I was twelve or thirteen I babysat for my mum's friend, and she had this book by [Italian anarchist] Errico Malatesta and I read it in one night and it's the first time I really heard or understood anarchism explicitly and I was like "fuck, this has got to be it. This is, you know, without any authority, self-organizing."

The connection between anarchism and animal liberation is now so prevalent that it is sometimes presumed that the earliest anarchist theorists held "generous opinions" towards animals; and that the "anarchist view that emerges from the nineteenth century anarchists [. . .] fits very well with the eco-anarchic projects of a [Critical Animal Studies] framework."[5] John Sanbonmatsu has argued that, "Mikhail Bakunin and Pierre-Joseph Proudhon held similarly generous opinions of the cognitive and social capacities of other species."[6] However, it would be a stretch to suggest that either of these figures were interested in what would now be called animal liberation. Bakunin believed in the "decisive inferiority of all animal species, compared to man."[7] Bakunin argued that evolution did not mean that humans had a special kinship with animals, but that "man's whole historic mission, his dignity and liberty, consist in getting further and further away from that [animal] state."[8]

Proudhon made a number of different claims about the status of animals. Proudhon argued that some animals "can be seen aiding, protecting, and warning each other" when in danger, and this was evidence that "the social instinct and the moral sense is common" to humans and other animals.[9] However, despite Proudhon being the first, self-declared anarchist, self-respecting anarchists now reject him because of his anti-Semitism and sexism. Proudhon was not interested in raising the status of animals; in fact, he evoked the lowly status of animals when degrading other humans. For instance, he claimed: "[W]omen is a mean term between man and the rest of the animal realm."[10] Proudhon is also reported to have asserted: "[A] woman knows enough if she knows enough to mend our shirts and cook us a steak."[11]

With countless examples like these, it is understandable that anarchists seek their ideological education outside of these thinkers' texts. I argue that the connections between collective vegan action and anarchism, and their ideologies, stem from practice rather than theory. For instance, the ALF (Animal Liberation Front) implemented a non-hierarchical structure based on affinity groups after a process of trial and error, in which most activists "recognized that that way of operating was the most effective in terms of doing the most action and also avoiding [arrest]. [I]t meant that the authorities couldn't destroy what was going on just by arresting one or two people."[12]

It was through taking part in direct action, rather than by studying moral and organizational theory, that the ALF built its anarchistic structure and framework.[13] However, it is still true that many anarchist educators, from the nineteenth century to the present, have included concern for animals within their anarchist vision (even more so if we include thinkers such as Percy Bysshe Shelley, Leo Tolstoy, and Mahatma Gandhi within this canon). This makes them a valuable source for vegan pedagogy. More than any other early anarchist, Louise Michel embedded animal concern within her socialist thought. Michel described how "the origin of [her] revolt against the powerful was [her] horror at the tortures inflicted on animals."[14]

Michel developed what would become a total liberation approach. She recognized that workers and animals are exploited in much the same way: "[H]eavy work bends both men and oxen over the furrows, keeping the slaughterhouse for worn-out beasts and the beggar's sack for worn-out humans."[15] Even when Michel witnessed workers abusing animals, she recognized that they were trapped in an oppressive and hierarchical system in which the most vulnerable are always abused by those with more power:

> Labour crushes the parents; their fate grips them the way their child grips an animal. All around the globe people moan at the machine they are caught in, and everywhere the strong overwhelm the weak.[16]

This observation is particularly important because the current vegan anarchist movement relies on the concept of total liberation to resist the interwoven oppressions underpinned by capitalism and the state. Anarchists' tactics put total liberation into practice, for instance in anti-McDonald's campaigns, which highlight the murder of animals, effects on the environment, and poor conditions of workers in the fast food industry.

One theoretical underpinning for the sympathetic outlook towards other animals by many anarchists is the belief that the natural world, including animal societies, provides a model that proves that, in a state of freedom, humanity would exist through cooperation and solidarity. This belief stems, for example, from the writings of Pyotr Kropotkin, who argued that in the natural world "we already find the feature which will also be distinctive of human societies—that is, work in common."[17] Although Kropotkin himself did not interpret his research as an argument for animal advocacy, a significant lineage of anarchist interest in animal issues springs from his work. Indeed, it is within the literature of Élisée Reclus, Brian Dominick, and Bob Torres that anarchistic animal activism begins to shape itself in ways that can be witnessed in the praxis of current collective vegan action groups.

Élisée Reclus developed what would become a total liberation approach. He believed that humans exploited "all Nature" in the same way in which they exploited animals; moreover, he believed there was a "cause and effect" between the exploitation of animals and the waging of wars.[18] Reclus believed that educational work should be the anarchists' highest priority, and this educational role involved both encouraging fellow humans not to exploit animals, and attempting to raise the intellectual and moral powers of other animals. Brian Dominick, in his influential pamphlet *Animal Liberation and Social Revolution*, detailed an anarchist approach to animal advocacy that supports direct action and a total liberation approach, in which "each form of oppression has become interdependent upon the others. The infusion of these different oppressive dynamics has served to enhance and complement each other in versatility as well as strength."[19]

The anarchist animal liberation tradition was further developed by Bob Torres, who focused on the property status of animals who become super-exploited living beings under capitalism. Torres links animal abuse to all forms of socially constructed hierarchy. According to Torres, it does not make sense for those on the left to embrace a "hierarchy of the species, while simultaneously working to reject other hierarchies."[20] Torres draws on the work of Murray Bookchin to develop "an approach which challenges hierarchy that we exert not only over animals, but also over one another."[21]

An anarchist education based on the canon would be insufficient, however, if our goal is total liberation, that is, the emancipation of all. Increasingly, more vegan activists realize this and so collective vegan action is particularly inspired by feminist scholarship and praxis. A diverse range of ecofeminists and socialist/anarcha-feminists have shaped the movement, from Emma Goldman to Angela Davis.[22] Animal liberation scholarship, such as Critical Animal Studies (CAS), has "ecofeminist roots," which have led to the "foregrounding of intersectional analysis and politics" (which includes species in the case of CAS) and the combination of theory and practice by supporting direct action and radical total-liberation politics.[23]

Anarcha-feminists, who challenge patriarchy both within anarchist circles and in society, have similarly shown concern for other animals. Peggy Kornegger explains that these feminists work together "to expand our empathy and understanding of other living things and to identify with these entities outside of ourselves."[24] Indeed, anarchism has had a strong influence in feminism (particularly in the UK) from the Second Wave onwards. Josephine Donovan believes that this influence partly stems from key thinkers such as Emma Goldman and includes the belief in prefigurative politics and "the integrity of the process of change as part of the change itself."[25]

Emma Goldman saw genuine parallels between the oppression of humans and other animals. In her own experience of patriarchal society,

Goldman felt that there was a connection between the exploitation of women and animals. Goldman believed that due to the structure of society, men treated women in the same way that farmers might treat their herd. Goldman remembered that, as a child, a relative "came over and tried to feel my arms. It gave me the sensation of being naked on the market-place."[26] Even in later life, men would praise her "as if [she] were a horse you wanted to sell," and romantic liaisons were often thwarted because Goldman "would not be bound and kept in a cage"—the metaphorical fate that befell women after marriage.[27]

Despite this connection, Goldman continued to engage in practices that are exploitative to animals, and only briefly became a vegetarian when meat was scarce in Bolshevik Russia. Goldman's example is important because she explained that structural change (through social revolution) was vital to ensuring that humans live in a state of freedom and dignity. However, everyday behaviors that re-create and perpetuate social hierarchies should also be stopped by anarchists before the revolution.

Other socialist feminists have noted the intersections between their own struggle against patriarchal oppression and the systemic exploitation of animals. Rosa Luxemburg felt empathy and solidarity for a water buffalo who had been denied freedom.[28] Angela Davis incorporated veganism as part of her "revolutionary perspective" in order to "develop compassionate relations with the other creatures with whom we share this planet," because that would mean "challenging the whole capitalist industrial form of food production."[29]

Vegan Activism

Now that we have a brief overview of anarchist thought and its usefulness for a vegan pedagogy, let us consider connections between current anarchist and animal liberation theories and practices that are found specifically within collective vegan action. Before examining the key conceptual connections that emerge between anarchism and vegan action, it is interesting to consider the ways in which activists first become politically aware. Of the fifty animal activists I interviewed, the most common feature in the political awakening of vegan anarchists was involvement in the UK punk and hardcore scene, with over 25 percent of activists having some involvement in the scene. Over 15 percent of activists gained their political awakening through involvement in wider, often more mainstream, political organizations, including pacifist groups. Other key reasons were: a love of childhood pets, arguments with vegan friends, and exposure to pro-animal rights documentaries. Less frequent reasons were: the exposure to philosophers, an aversion to meat following the death of a human friend or relative, and an instinct to question social norms.

The social circles and sense of collective identity in the punk scene led to a strong connection between anarchism and veganism. One activist from Southampton explained his political awakening through punk:

> I never cared about animal rights prior to discovering punk rock and it was never my primary focus politically. [. . .] When I got involved in hardcore in my late teens, it was hard to find anyone who wasn't at least vegetarian, and I was surrounded by those ideas all the time. This led to a greater understanding of what I was supporting by eating meat, but that wasn't really an isolated process. I was engaged with finding out about a lot of political issues for the first time as well as developing really strong ideas about DIY culture and politics. A lot of these ideas had a strong anarchist influence. But it was through hanging out with other punks that I became vegetarian. I want to say it's just what you did, which sounds horrible and trendy, but it's true. You became punk, you found out about animal rights, and you quit meat.

Other vegan anarchists describe the imperative to "question everything" that emerged from punk's DIY ethics. The connection is particularly strong for many UK hunt sabs. The number of punks that became active in sabbing led to the anarchistic nature of the movement. As one activist told me:

> There's always been that push within the punk movement to support animal rights, and because the punk movement is by its very nature anarchist, they push towards organizations like the Hunt Saboteurs Association and not the more [mainstream] organizing groups.

This connection is partly practical. For instance, punk bands often host benefit gigs for animal rights causes, and these gigs provide an opportunity for new activists to meet and socialize with more seasoned campaigners.

Many activists explained that they'd had a strong moral concern for animals since childhood. This was sometimes because of parental influence. One activist explained that she'd "been vegan since [she] was four and both of [her] parents are vegan and they always said that animals have rights." Other activists described a "gut feeling" that ultimately led them to participate in the animal rights movement. One said that "rescuing wasps in the classroom" was the "spark" that led to their animal rights work; others recalled saving injured animals when they were young, or growing up with companion animals. One activist told me: "I had a cat at the time; my first real pet. I looked at Buster and I thought 'Whoa, I wouldn't want to eat you, really.'" These are sentiments that educators in all capacities can convey and encourage as part of a vegan pedagogy.

In my interviews, animal activists told me they often became involved in vegan politics after early participation in other social justice causes. CND (Campaign for Nuclear Disarmament) and peace organizations, as well as anti-fascist/anti-racist groups, were the most common gateways to vegan anarchism. One activist joined SHAC after seeing "the interconnection between issues" and participating in ecological, class, and anarchist struggles. Another was initially involved in the peace movement but "shifted over to animal rights because [he] figured there were people to fight against nuclear weapons but there weren't many people to fight against animal exploitation." Others began their political journey with animal rights and moved to wider activism. One activist from Brighton told me that it was through animal rights that she became politically aware:

> It was just straight up single-issue animal rights. But through them, I found other anarchist vegans whom I felt affinity with. I ended up much less involved with animal rights and more with community organizing, ecological direct action, and anarchist politics.

Interestingly for vegan educators, only one activist among my interviewees joined the movement after being handed a leaflet from street campaigners. It was more common for them to experience a "Eureka" moment after watching a documentary, such as *Earthlings*. The final common theme was that people became vegan after discussions with close friends. One activist recalled:

> I was already involved in leftist activism by the time I learned of veganism, and one of the young guys in some of the groups I was organizing with was a vegan and animal activist. I lost an argument with him about humane treatment of animals, and I've always been very keen to live my principles. I was twenty years old when I lost that argument. I went vegetarian for a month, then vegan, thinking that was the best way to live consistent with the new moral understanding I'd arrived at through argument.

The political development of activists was enhanced by the desire to align their actions with their ideological beliefs. Activists often noted the prefigurative aspects of veganism. They wanted to create a society free of hierarchical domination and oppression, and so they wished to have relations with others (including other animals) that did not involve oppression.

The Connection between Anarchism and Collective Vegan Action

Through discussions with animal activists, reading animal liberation literature, and drawing on research from the fields of anarchist studies, critical animal studies, and ecofeminism, we can identify five key conceptual connections between anarchism and collective vegan action:

1. Total liberation
2. Intersectionality
3. Anti-capitalism
4. Anti-statism
5. Pro-environmentalism

These concepts are valuable for anyone who teaches veganism in any form. If we are truly interested in creating a world free of hierarchy and injustice, these ideas should be urgently incorporated into the vegan and anarchist ideology and they should guide our teaching.

The first connection between anarchism and animal advocacy is a belief in the politics of "total liberation," "which grasps the need for, and the inseparability of, human, nonhuman animal, and Earth liberation and freedom for all in one comprehensive, though diverse, struggle."[30] Total liberation is strongly influenced by anarchist theory and practice "in that it is opposed to all forms of oppression and domination and is also not reformist."[31] The call for a politics of total liberation was voiced in the 1960s by a diverse range of "radical political organizations, and was used to describe an uncompromising multifaceted approach to complete freedom and justice for all suffering from oppression and domination."[32] The main principle of total liberation is that different forms of oppression intersect and must be simultaneously opposed.

The concept of intersectionality, the second connection between veganism and anarchism, was coined by Kimberlé Crenshaw. As we have read in earlier chapters, specifically speaking about the experience of black working-class women, the concept outlines the way that different social categories of power such as gender, race, and class function in an overlapping way or rely on the same groundings, such as the dismissal of the "other."³³ Intersectionality could theoretically show how categories such as gender, race, and class overlap, or focus on how intersectionality is experienced by an individual who is oppressed in a variety of ways.

Intersectionality has been developed by theorists such as Amie Breeze Harper and the Sistah Vegan network. Harper's work reveals how racism and sexism operate within veganism and discusses "how being racialized as Black women affected Black women vegans." Harper's work "frame[s] veganism in an intersectional way [. . .] that is inclusive and inviting to a majority of non-white people who are trying to survive through and fight against systemic racism."³⁴

Other activists and educators at the forefront of intersectional approaches to racial justice, social justice, and environmental justice include the contributors to *Veganism in an Oppressive World: A Vegans of Color Community Project*, as well as the Black Vegans Rock and Vegan Hip Hop Movement networks.³⁵ Their organizers, who experience oppression at the intersection of race, gender, and class, have critiqued the way that white social justice activists—including vegans—have used intersectionality in a tokenistic way. Aph and Syl Ko explain: "*Intersectionality* may be a fun word to toss around, but people are scared to make connections in their movements because they will have to create new blueprints for their activism." For instance, sections of the predominantly white vegan movement have attacked the Black Vegans Rock network because it would "distract from helping 'the animals.'"³⁶ Ko and Ko explain that although intersectionality remains a useful tool to navigate current systems of oppression, it does little to help dismantle these oppressive systems:

> Intersectionality maps out the world that has been *imposed* on us; it doesn't begin the process of mapping out the future. More importantly, intersectionality deals with the external conditions of racism and oppression that impact our lives, but doesn't speak to the internal struggles that arise after colonization.³⁷

Anarchists, often embracing ecofeminism, recognize that the concept of intersectionality is pivotal to understanding multifaceted systems of domination and attempting to resist them. Anarcha-feminists would agree "that all oppression, whether based on race, class, sex, or lesbianism, is interrelated and the fights for liberation must be simultaneous and cooperative."[38] Significantly, ecofeminists have included species within their understanding of intersectionality. Carol Adams and Josephine Donovan were also among the first to argue that the power relations of gender and species intersect.[39]

A third commonality we can identify between anarchism and veganism is the opposition to capitalism. Anarchists are opposed to capitalism, and this creates a connection with vegan action because many, though by no means all, animal rights activists are hostile to capitalist structures. Bob Torres argues that the hegemonic order of capitalism means that society has "not only come to devalue our fellow humans and animals as mere laboring machines, but we also are led to believe that this is the only option for human survival and happiness."[40]

As well as resisting capitalism, anarchists also oppose the state. Anarchists view the state as a complex array of social and political institutions that uphold internalized power relations. The state also has interests of its own; the state is a "psychological phenomenon" that creates a certain "way of thinking about the world and understanding social organization."[41] David Nibert argues that the oppression of animals is fundamentally linked to the capitalist state because "the physical, political, economic, ideological, and diversionary powers of the state support and build such entangled oppressions while giving such atrocities legal and social respectability."[42]

Finally, radical environmental politics regularly embrace anarchist elements, including a "criticism of authoritarian politics and capitalism and an emphasis on collectivism, individual freedom and self-fulfilment."[43] The belief in a shared world where everyone can be free extends here towards Earth and nature, as well as its inhabitants, human and animal. There are numerous groups who promote human, animal, and Earth liberation. The two movements unite around their shared tactical use of direct action and belief in total liberation. Through vegan outreach work and collective action, anarchists are able to put these theories into practice while educating the wider public about anarchist concepts of autonomy, solidarity, and collectivity.

Having considered some conceptual overlaps between anarchism and animal advocacy, let us now have a look at the ways that collective vegan action can be used as a site of anarchist outreach. Vegan activists can promote anarchism in two ways: first, by using an anarchist organizational framework, and secondly by discussing anarchist ideas with members of the public who might not usually engage with anarchist issues. This is particularly significant because the microcosmos of a teaching/outreach environment (often consisting of a classroom or family setting or a focused campaign) offers an ideal space for prefigurative politics to emerge. Practical tools deployed by activists can be useful in any teaching context and should become second nature for us when communicating and exchanging knowledge in any capacity.

Both anarchists and animal liberationists may use a consensus decision-making structure, utilize affinity groups, and, most significantly, engage in various forms of direct action. These tactical similarities cannot be regarded as a mere coincidence; in fact, the tactics employed are a central component of the activists' collective identity and political philosophy. David Pellow explains:

> Direct action is a core part of earth and animal liberation movements' tactical and philosophical repertoire, a defining feature of their cultures of resistance—those shared understandings, ideas and knowledge that inform and support individual and collective practices of dissent.[44]

This seems clear for radical animal liberation groups like the Animal Liberation Front (ALF), who are defined by their non-hierarchical structure and use of affinity groups and consensus decision-making. The non-hierarchical structure of the Hunt Saboteurs Association (HSA) in the UK, and of individual groups of hunt saboteurs who typically operate in groups of about ten members and use a consensus decision-making approach, helps explain the overlap between anarchism and hunt sabotage. One HSA activist told me that some activists will become involved in hunt sabotage and subsequently become anarchists because they are attracted to the possibilities of organizing without hierarchical structures.

This connection is important because the structures and actions of the group provide educational value to group members, and help them develop an anarchistic worldview. Anarchism and veganism emerged as key components of the collective identity with hunt sabotage. The desire to achieve social change through collective action without relying on elected representatives was a common trait among the hunt sabs I spoke to. One activist told me that sabs "aren't prepared to sit back and wait for a campaign to be successful to get a change in legislation [or] to get convictions. [. . .] Most people who come to us want to do something, there and then. They know on a day out with us they can stop something dying, there and then."

The desire to achieve change through direct action links other animal groups to anarchism. One SHAC activist explained:

> When SHAC started it was very clearly a direct action grassroots movement. It was like: We're not asking the government to stop testing, we're not asking the government nothing; we're closing this company down ourselves. And so the grassroots movement then was very vibrant and alive and kicking.

Hunt sabbing enables activists to build trust and solidarity in small groups that typically use consensus decision-making and a non-hierarchical framework, while attempting to achieve social change through collective action without relying on elected representatives. People who already subscribe to an anarchist philosophy may be attracted to hunt sabotage as a starting point for activism. Collective education is also facilitated through the activism. Hunt sabbing is easy to get involved with. The issue of hunting has been heavily discussed in the UK media, particularly in relation to a ban, and so people interested in such politics will be aware that such actions are taking place, and potential activists are able to contact the HSA or local groups.

Moreover, unlike other forms of direct action associated with the animal rights movement, hunt sabbing is unlikely to have the same legal repercussions and as such may be a good way for activists to get involved in direct action. Hunt sabbing has been described as the "gateway" to other forms of animal rights activism; it is also a gateway to wider anarchist politics because people see what can be achieved by small non-hierarchical groups working together and ensuring that their structure reflects their ideological commitment to decentralization and autonomy as linked to a rejection of social hierarchies.

Vegan outreach (encouraging people to adopt a vegan diet by providing sample vegan food, often at vegan festivals but also as part of wider political campaigns) can also be used as a site of anarchist outreach. One reason why so many anarchist animal advocates participate in vegan outreach is because it is not reformist; it is not asking for slightly better conditions or "bigger cages." As such, it might appeal to those who believe that revolutionary change is necessary. Like other forms of direct action associated with the ALF and HSA, vegan outreach can be situated in anarchist approaches because there is no appeal to elected representatives; instead, activists themselves are immediately making positive changes. This is certainly the case for groups operating under the Food Not Bombs banner, who do not simply aim to share free food with protesters and those who are hungry, but also practice prefigurative ways of "working together using consensus and implementing their visions independent of government or corporate control."[45]

This way of thinking ties in with the Gandhian notion that activists should be the change they want to see, which has been used to explain prefigurative anarchist projects. If anarchists wish to create a society in which sentient beings are not exploited for profit, and in which citizens do not rely on those with authority to dictate their cultural and consumption habits, then collective vegan outreach may be seen as a positive strategy.

The collective educational role of vegan outreach can also enable activists to engage the public with anarchist ideas and concerns. In particular, anarchist vegan activists have highlighted the fact that animals have become commodities under capitalism. They have linked veganism with a deeper opposition to private property; they have explained connections between government and big agribusiness; and they have suggested positive alternatives such as community gardening. Of course, concern for the suffering of animals is an overriding priority for vegan activists.

Collective vegan action also provides anarchists with the opportunity to suggest sustainable, non-hierarchical alternatives to the existing system. For instance, Food Not Bombs activists believe that:

> [The] skills required to collect and share food can be translated into the growing of food, providing safe fresh water, providing shelter, healthcare, education, entertainment and all the things a healthy, free community would desire.[46]

Therefore, with these collective vegan action groups it is both the structure of the group (non-hierarchical relations and horizontal) and the message delivered that are of educational value to members of the collective and the public.

Direct action enables groups of activists to grow and educate themselves about the possibilities of self-organization and collective action; veganism is particularly significant here because it can help sustain an activist community's sense of collective identity. Such identity politics have often been dismissed as "lifestyle politics," but there is nothing to prevent activists from simultaneously participating in lifestyle activism and radical dissent. Indeed, there are numerous examples of anarchist groups who do both, such as the Anarchist Teapot collective, who aim to build a movement infrastructure by setting up a mobile kitchen that provides vegan meals at various sites of resistance, particularly those connected with anti-globalization protests.

Other activists believe that making veganism a shared part of a movement's collective identity helps strengthen that movement—and enables movement participants to gain a sense of "who we are" and "who we are against"—and this strength will sustain future actions.

Using veganism in this way, like other forms of lifestyle activism, enables activist communities to "encourage collective shifts in ways of living that both align with radical ideas and establish more just relations in the here and now."[47]

Conclusion

We began by considering the most famous anarchist educators and theorists. Although some early anarchists were ambiguous about the status of animals, anti-colonial and anarcha-feminists and ecofeminists have demonstrated the connection between human and nonhuman oppression. Anarchists have been able to educate the public about key concepts through vegan outreach. These concepts include: total liberation, intersectionality, anti-capitalism, anti-statism, and pro-environmentalism. Through vegan outreach, anarchists have reached members of the public who would not otherwise engage with anarchist ideas. For instance, anarchistic animal rights activists have provided vegan meals at environmental camps or to those who are hungry, and in these instances vegan outreach provides an opportunity to put total liberation into practice. However, the greatest educational opportunities emerge in the structure and practice of collective vegan action groups themselves; in particular, the use of affinity groups, consensus decision-making, and direct action. These tactics allow activists to build confidence and experience and witness firsthand the potential of non-hierarchical organization.

Anarchists seek to put their ideals into practice in all aspects of life, and this includes conducting research or in a formal pedagogical context. Research can follow a prefigurative approach in the horizontal nature of the research methodologies, interview techniques, sampling methods, and main questions that arise from activist movements. Through involvement in higher education, anarchists are also able to challenge speciesist approaches in academia and promote veganism through research, teaching, and by organizing conferences and gatherings. When anarchists have the opportunity to act as educators, they can put principles into practice, including using a consensus decision-making approach, creating non-hierarchical spaces, encouraging students to participate in direct action outside the seminar room, and in creating an atmosphere in which participants listen to and learn from the life experiences of other members of the group.

Vegan outreach provides activists with an opportunity to challenge the perception of animal rights as an insular movement by building alliances with other social justice issues. These solidarity alliances are particularly important for activists who combine animal activism with a wider anarchist philosophy. Groups like the Anarchist Teapot and Food Not Bombs provide this solidarity that simultaneously encompasses educative elements, by distributing vegan food at protest sites, at environmental or peace camps, on picket lines, and at benefit gigs. Collective vegan action allows activists to create innovative ways to campaign for animals, from film and music to opening animal sanctuaries.

Animal activists have also combined their promotion of veganism with other initiatives focused on local communities growing their own food, such as the Transition Network, which fosters an experience in which different groups can listen to and learn from each other while building solidarity and trust. From an anarchist perspective, collective vegan action is at its most successful when it combines overlapping social justice issues; for instance, anti–fast food groups have highlighted the unethical targeting of children, exploitation of workers, animal cruelty, damage to the environment, and the global domination of corporations. Networks that allow different activist groups to learn from each other and share ideas, as well as promote anarchist ways of organizing, are vital as the animal liberation movement continues to educate, agitate, liberate, and organize.

11

TEACHING MEN

WHAT MEN (AND ALL OF US) NEED TO CONSIDER WHEN COMMUNICATING FOR VEGANISM

Agnes Trzak

This chapter is addressed to all the men in the vegan community, but especially the white, cis, non-disabled ones among you.[1] You have many valuable abilities that we need in the animal liberation movement. Some of you might be great teachers; others might give spectacular speeches. Some might be good writers; others may be really talented at organizing a coherent campaign strategy. We are happy that you are bringing your skills to our movement. You might be wondering what warrants me to address a whole chapter in this book to you. The reasons behind this are simple.

The first is that only a small percentage of vegans are white cis men, yet you seem to be at the forefront of most lectures or seminars, most syllabi are packed with your work, and you often dominate animal liberation actions.

The second reason for my writing to you is that too often in areas such as the academy, animal advocacy organizations, or small local activist groups, you make use of your privileged stance in our community (and society at large) to contribute to the economic, social, and physical harm towards all those of us who are not born with favored identities. This means that the masculinisms you partake in, the learned attitudes and behaviors that are cherished and encouraged in patriarchal societies, are inhibiting the development of the animal movement.

This is why, next to animal liberation, I, like so many other vegans, have another motive behind teaching anti-speciesism: human liberation. In both areas, which are not clearly separable, I work to dismantle the concept of *animality* from its oppressiveness. Not being constructed as human-enough (as favored, represented, and powerful) as you—a white guy—might be, makes the rest of us *Homo sapiens* suffer from speciesism, too. Our minds and bodies are often sexualized, racialized, disabled, and at times even animalized, so that we can be treated as objects to be consumed. Just like animals, sometimes we are not seen as human-enough by the standards you set for this concept of *humanity*. I can only hope that instead of being furious with me and perceiving what I am writing as a gross exaggeration and an insult to nonhuman animals who suffer from speciesism, you will bear with me throughout this text.

This chapter will show you what you can do to communicate for animals without harming those of us who fight for the same cause but at the same time have to ensure our own safety. Some of the previous chapters in this book make clear to what extent you are the most favored and thus most powerful group in Eurocentric neoliberalism, which is the reason you are being singled out. However, any of us who find ourselves in a privileged position of power in certain contexts (as educators, guardians, and parents often do) will find useful ideas in the suggestions in this text.

Reforming Our Language to Reform Our Thoughts

Language is the basis of our communication with students and colleagues and underpins our thought processes to a great extent. If we are not aware of the symbols we use to educate, we run the risk of alienating or even harming our audiences. If we consciously shift our language away from masculinist, and specifically white masculinist, expression in the form of colonialist thought and action, we create a more horizontal learning experience in which the audience will be more responsive.

We all grow up to be socialized in specific ways, and although our genetics play a role in the way we present ourselves and communicate with the world around us, the behaviors that are encouraged, discouraged, or even rewarded and punished in us also determine the ways we relate to one another. To make sense of all that we encounter, we create meaning and knowledge about one another based on comparisons to something we already know. That which we know best in neoliberal Eurocentrism is the white, non-disabled, cis man. He is dominantly present and represented in most areas of life: politics, education, media, religion, and business. He achieves this status through colonialist methods of occupation and exploitation of "the other"—metaphorically and literally.

We learn from Mel Y. Chen that we already create privilege in our communication by assigning degrees of humanness, aliveness, and ability to the subjects we refer to. The grammatical structures of many languages position the adjectives that I am using to describe you ("cis," "white," "male") at the top of the hierarchy of animacy, which means that you are an "active agent within grammars of ordering."[2] Chen writes that the linguistic prioritization of the masculine genus has real-life consequences dictating how society understands this type of masculinity: grammatically ascribing the *active* agent's position to the "masculine," "familiar" subject in a sentence legitimizes the authority of the masculine, white, non-disabled, cis man (the aforementioned "familiar" in Eurocentric neoliberal society) to make and execute decisions.[3]

Although English grammar allows for a less gendered sentence construction than many other languages, it still designates patriarchal value to many words. Let me invite you to do a very simple exercise that demonstrates how language is gendered and how this informs our perceptions of a binaristically gendered world (this is also a good introduction for adolescent and adult students): In a table with three columns, fill the first column with adjectives that come to your mind when you think of the traditional, even stereotypical, image of a man. In the second column describe with adjectives the traditional image of a woman that society conveys to us, and in the last column fill in the adjectives that would fit to an object. With the words in front of you, which—the masculinized traits or the feminized traits—are closer to the ones in the object column?

Chances are that your column dealing with men is filled with words such as "tough," "commanding," "dominant," "loud," "rational," whereas we find words that signify something similar to "emotional," "sensitive," "small," "quiet," or "moody" in your woman-column. The traits you found for objects might be along the lines of "inactive," "inanimate," "dead." Masculinized traits, such as being rational and commanding, are active; they imply agency and action on behalf of the subject. Being emotional and quiet signify inaction, inability, and a lack of vitality or movement, positioning the feminized traits closer to those of an object.

We must not assume that these stereotypes reflect the truth, but should acknowledge that preconceptions do create meaning, in this case patriarchal, colonialist, and disabling meaning. This meaning is created through language and influences our thoughts and vice versa. When teaching about animal liberation (and really also in any other situation), the gendered and speciesist divide between masculinized "rational" and feminized "irrational" individuals has far-reaching consequences. Writing on how to dismantle patriarchal structures in the animal liberation movement, Brian Luke examines the consequences of the division between what is rational and what is not:

> The terms "rational" and "irrational" distinguish between positions worthy and unworthy of debate, and between people worthy and unworthy of being heard. Making and enforcing these distinctions is a substantial form of social control. At stake in the struggle to define rationality is admission to or exclusion from the realm of public discourse, as well as access to professional credentials.[4]

In other words, favoring reason over emotion, and that which is masculinized over that which is feminized and colonized, excludes all who cannot be masculine-enough (regardless of their gender) from any decision-making process that can have an impact on the political makeup of our society. When we inadvertently (re)produce this gendered division in our course-facilitation work, we prevent those stereotypically lumped together in the "irrational category" of our learned preconceptions from expressing their full potential when participating in the course.

The consequences, however, reach beyond the initial didactic moment, and our students will carry these learned behaviors, reinforced in our classroom, into the world and, in this context, into the animal rights movement. As Luke observes:

> The application of patriarchal metaethics to animal liberation takes the following form: a tacit acceptance of sexist derogations of female animal liberationists as overly sentimental or hysterical, leading to a distrust of emotion and an overemphasis on cold reason as the source of animal liberationism. The goal of animal liberationist ethics is then to delineate rational principles of conduct that control our putatively uncaring dispositions toward animals.[5]

When teaching animal liberation, for example, we can observe this mechanism in the classroom. We introduce our audience to our observations on the cruelty of the human–animal relationship and invite them to interact with the new knowledge we provide them with. As course facilitators we are then faced with two general reactions in the audience. Some of our students will express their emotions of shock, horror, or sadness; others will start forming arguments for or against animal cruelty. Next time you find yourself in a situation like this, pay careful attention to the way you interact with the classroom. Are you brushing off, pitying, or belittling the emotional students and engaging with those who are forming and expressing coherent thoughts through language? As teachers and critical thinkers, this is almost an instinctive reaction for us. Especially when addressing sensitive topics such as animal cruelty, we need to take the time to consider "gut reactions," those emotional outbursts and non-verbal nuances coming from our audience.

Although it might be easier to engage with rational content (because emotions are messy, unpredictable, and uncontainable), it is a pedagogically valuable exercise to respond to emotions (regardless of the students' age) with curiosity: "What about the text/picture/video made you cry?" "Why do you think this was your gut reaction?" "Take a second to consider what made you this angry." "I was also very upset when I first learned about this, for me it felt like. . . . How does it feel for you?" Little interventions like these acknowledge the students and their emotions; they also engage them and jump-start their critical understanding of the given material. This will empower our audiences to act upon their emotional response, which is particularly important as it prevents a feeling of helplessness.

The previous pages call into question only a tiny fraction of the mountain of injustice that is patriarchal and colonialist language, but I hope you understand them as an invitation to consider the meaning our communication produces more carefully in the classroom and beyond. Relearning the way we express is a structural process that needs time; however, there are some concrete changes you can implement straight away.

Perhaps you are already living the following suggestions. If not, it's never too late to try them out.

- Allow students to **trust** you, so that they feel comfortable expressing their opinions, which is especially important when talking about veganism or animal rights, as students will have preconceived notions about this topic. To engage their critical-thinking skills, students need to feel that they can express their own opinions without feeling stifled by the teacher's authority. You can signal safety, for instance, through your body language. As a broad rule of thumb, start by not folding your arms across your chest and not crossing your legs. Smile often and make eye contact. To be inclusive, direct your eyes and your body towards students who speak less in class, who speak more quietly than others, and who simply might be shy.

- **Don't dismiss students with your words or body language.** If, politically or morally, you don't agree with a statement made by a student, do not let your body language reflect that. (Challenge, confront, or penalize them if their opinions put the safety of other students at risk—if they express homophobia, for instance.) If speciesist opinions are voiced, for example, acknowledge them and actively invite other opinions, without initially responding yourself. Guide your students' thinking in a constructive direction: that is, after all, your job. Be friendly, non-judgmental, and non-critiquing.

- Value and foster **consent** and **safety** in your language. Be inviting, encouraging, and motivational instead of demanding, commanding, and directive. For example, when giving out tasks, whenever possible do *ask* whether students want to do the assignments (even just as a rhetorical question). If the mood seems deflated, encourage your audience: Speak in terms of "us" instead of separating yourself from them. You are also part of the classroom! "Let's do this. . . !", "Shall we do that . . . ?" When, for pedagogical reasons, physical contact is needed, *always* ask for permission, and give options for people not to participate if there is a group exercise that involves touch. Lastly, refrain from using slurs of any kind, from commenting on your students' clothes, and from comparing one "group of people" to another (e.g. boys vs. girls).

Applying these suggestions in your teaching without adjusting your outlook on your pedagogy and your students will probably be ineffective. So, let us expand upon these points in the next section.

REFORMING OUR UNDERSTANDING, ATTITUDE, AND BEHAVIORS

When you consider your words and gestures more consciously, your cognitive processes will shift, too. As creatures of habit we can't simply shed ourselves of the ideologies and behaviors we learn and so we reproduce this learned masculinism (or the set of ideas implied in performing masculinity correctly) in the animal movement and in our pedagogies. Seeing that if you are reading this you might already be of an anti-speciesist conviction, it is clear that you have the capacity to empathize, come to logical and moral conclusions, and adjust your practice to your ethics.

You might have already managed to turn your back on carnist culture, which is one of the strongest and most ubiquitous and violent systems we have to navigate. You already know that justifying our actions with the argument "this behavior is natural and has always existed" is invalid, and you are proving it by withholding your participation in animal cruelty. This means that you are capable of dismantling and reconstructing your psychosocial habits in order to adjust your thought processes and your interaction with the world to the moral underpinnings of anti-speciesism.

It is that capability for critical thought and self-reflection that you need to harness when relating to your own masculinism. What I would like to ask you is to remember the cognitive mechanisms you applied when becoming consciously vegan (i.e. completely re-evaluating and adjusting your decisions and actions) and bring them with you into a teaching scenario, where you interact with your students but also with colleagues. The aim is for you, as a pedagogue, to empower others to reach their full potential in the area of life that you are supporting them in.

In this case, let's remain with veganism or anti-speciesism being the topic of your teaching. Our aim as educators, then, is for our audiences to understand speciesism and to disrupt it by withdrawing their support from animal industries and ideally even by actively dismantling the ideology, too. For this, our audiences need to be receptive to our pedagogy first, which is where a dismantling of white masculinism on our part (regardless of our gender) comes into play. Dismantling our learned masculinized behaviors means reconstructing them into gentler, less absolute ways of interacting. In other words, we need to shift our understanding of and attitudes towards the world from masculinist to decolonial feminist.

It won't be enough if you explicitly out yourself as a feminist to your audience. In fact, that is not even necessary. Arguably, you already have many feminist behaviors ingrained in you, without even noticing that you partake in them. Perhaps in the next few days you can pay attention to the ways you navigate your world and become more aware of situations in which you might already be able to renounce traits and behaviors that you have adopted when learning how to perform masculinity correctly. One such learned behavior is the consumption of animals. Learning to be vegan is indeed a feminist act and a direct jab at patriarchy, albeit just a tiny one—perhaps nothing more than an unintentional side effect. Obviously, simply being vegan does not turn our personal politics anti-sexist or anti-colonialist.

Veganism is a feminist act for two reasons. First, animal production is based on undermining the reproductive autonomy of animals, and feminism in its most simple definition advocates for bodily freedom. Once we acknowledge species as a construct similar to race and gender, for example, it is easy to extend our concern for physical self-determination to animals. Secondly, veganism disrupts patriarchy in a more subtle way: consuming the flesh, eggs, and milk of certain animals is more desirable than consuming plants, as it establishes dominance and implies active participation in society. As we learn from Carol Adams,[6] plant-based nutrition evokes passivity, and implies a lack and even dullness, traits that we attribute to feminized and objectified individuals. In fact, a study by Annie Potts and Jovian Parry on animal-eating men and their attitudes towards plant-based men documents to what extent masculinist cis-heteronormativity interrogates, ridicules, and objectifies vegan men by feminizing them.[7] The next chapter also interrogates this phenomenon.

Whereas we all learn to apply masculinized behaviors in certain contexts, it is indeed your responsibility as a white cis man to dismantle masculinism and to make feminism a men's issue. The "how-to" of being a feminist man and educator might seem rather abstract, as masculinism (just like speciesism) is an abstract ideology that we might subscribe to without even noticing. To understand how to dismantle it we need to explore the subject of privilege and power. I understand that these are very loaded words and perhaps might seem overused. However, they imply very useful and important concepts that can help us make more room for feminized, racialized, and otherwise objectified individuals in our classrooms and our movement.

As a white cis man you grow up viewing and interacting with the world differently than other people. You are born with traits (such as your skin color) that grant you social capital that people with other traits don't have access to. Additionally, you are more likely to be encouraged to adopt traits (such as determination and persistence) that lead to the accumulation of more social capital. Very quickly in life you are taught that people who are born with similar identities to yours behave a certain way and are, therefore, granted a dominant and even default and normative status in neoliberal Western cultures. As social beings we have an urge to be accepted and belong to a group. This need and your observation of others like you show you what you should desire in order to perform masculinity correctly. Not only does masculinism teach you *what* to desire but also that you are entitled to satisfy that desire. This is how masculinism constructs freedom. And that is precisely the idea of privilege: a benefit in society that is given to you simply due to the nature of your being and that of the system you are placed in—an automatic reward system.[8]

You need to be aware, however, that your freedom, generated through the proper performance of your identity and the entitlement attached to it, comes at a cost for people of different races, abilities, genders, and with lesser economic means, as well as those who don't belong to the human species. You inevitably develop a bias against them, which is expressed in (micro)hostilities that you might not even be aware of.[9] All of us are impacted by your performance of white masculinity and are even actively discouraged from achieving the same freedoms you are granted. That makes your understanding of the world very limited, initially without any wrongdoing on your behalf. When you reach the point in life, however, where you shift from learning your behaviors from others to being the one whom others learn from, it becomes your responsibility to interrupt the reproduction of colonialist masculinity and the power that is ascribed to it. Especially as a person in the position to influence, such as an educator or a parent, it is our responsibility to discontinue the oppressive constructs we have learned. So how can we reform what we have been taught since Day One?

A necessary starting point is reforming the language we use, as described above, which is placed in a symbiotic relationship with our understanding of and attitude towards the world. Both generate and influence one another and manifest themselves in the behaviors we direct outwards into the world. As an anti-speciesist educator you have the responsibility, first, to notice the way you influence power dynamics internally in any social interaction. (Ask yourself: "To what extent am I in a position of advantage and for which reasons?") Secondly, it is your responsibility to recognize external power dynamics, observing the groups you teach (who in the group is in a position of advantage and why?). Once you have identified distorted attitudes, such as an uneven power relationship in a group, you need to take responsibility to dismantle those.

Together with the aforementioned changes to language use, this action can contribute to the development of a new attitude towards your students and your course-facilitation work as a whole. Below you can find some specific examples of how to evoke a more decolonial feminist understanding of the world and how to express it in your own behaviors.

- **Learn about the experiences of others** in the animal movement and beyond. Become a well-mannered guest, so to speak, in the discourse that you, as a white cis able man, are not part of. This will make your attitude and lessons less masculinist.

- **Recognize uneven group dynamics and balance them out**. From your own experience, you might have noticed that the group dynamic of any classroom almost naturally allows one or two (white) boys/men to steer the conversation on any given topic. Pay close attention to interruptions, the volume of the contributors' voices, and the content that is being communicated. It is your job as the facilitator to moderate the conversation in a way that invites other people and opinions, too. It is important to do this without putting individuals on the spot or forcing them to contribute. It could even be appropriate to pronounce that you have noticed an uneven split in contributions.[10]

- **Expect your students to think autonomously** and to be accountable for the consequences of the decisions they make. This process begins by you allowing your audience to critically examine a subject from many points of view without dictating right and wrong. This demands more patience and leniency on your behalf. By that, I mean that whenever possible, be lenient with your students and their performance. This also asks you to motivate them instead of penalizing them. Yes, it is more work on your behalf but it also has better effects on their well-being and overall capacity to engage with the world in a critical way.

- To do so, **establish your position as part of the class**. Do not assume to be an authority—a pedagogue in the traditional, strict sense of the word. Kindle an understanding of yourself that lets you be more of a facilitator, someone who is in charge of providing the logistics and the framework for learning, rather than someone who holds the knowledge your audience wants to obtain. Be open to learning from your students and let them know that you don't know everything. Admit any potential shortcomings you have. In fact, do admit to not having all the answers. Especially when relating to other men and boys, acknowledge your own mistakes and don't present yourself as infallible, as many of them learn that fallibility and vulnerability are unacceptable. Showing them that it is indeed permissible not to have all answers, and at the same time guiding them on the way to find the answers, is one way of leveling the playing field and making the group structure more horizontal. This allows your students to explore their potential in unfolding their thinking and problem-solving skills. Part of being the host or moderator rather than a top–down teacher means leaving room for mistakes. Allow students to voice opinions that might seem funny or plain wrong to you and be gentle in guiding them towards a more nuanced and considered answer.

- Particularly when communicating for veganism, **be accountable for made mistakes and even the harm you have caused**. Show your audience that you have also been "tricked" into masculinism and carnism and make especially clear that you are now taking responsibility for your actions. When you are teaching about veganism, you might find that it is counterproductive to present yourself as a "flawless vegan" to those who eat animals. Admitting your shortcomings not only makes you relatable, but it also shows your audience that change is indeed possible. Try your best not to judge, prescribe, and dictate what students should think and how they should behave. Instead, let them come to their own conclusions, which will cost you much more patience than simply telling them how and why to be vegan, for instance. If they find out on their own, the end result will be more significant.[11]

- When engaging in **small talk or banter** with students inside or outside the classroom or with colleagues, make sure you find ways to bond that **do not include jokes or commentary on someone else's behalf**. When you single out a student or colleague in such a way, others might see it as a validation of their own unspoken opinions and will now have an excuse to voice these, which constitutes bullying. Don't single out a specific individual or group and do not join in when the class makes one person the target of ridicule; instead, take that person's side. Stay clear of bonding over misogyny, sexism, racism, or masculinity with students and colleagues. And if you involuntarily become part of a conversation that uses these topics to strengthen relationships, make sure to voice your unhappiness about it. There are fewer (if any) consequences if a man draws attention to the fact that a conversation is in bad taste than if a woman does the same thing. She might indeed be penalized by having less access to social capital, which can quickly lead to a loss of economic capital.

Leading by Example and Teaching Others

As educators, it is our responsibility to empower our audiences to make informed ethical decisions. We can only achieve this through obtaining and holding their attention, for which they need to trust us. One way of gaining the trust of our audiences is precisely to dismantle colonialist masculinism as described above. Once again, we cannot continue suffering from the effects of white patriarchy if we want the vegan movement to reach its full potential. In other words, for the animals to be free we must ensure human freedoms first, simply because it is humans who are fighting for animals, and there is no better place than education to start developing this thought.

Your younger students especially will inevitably learn behaviors from you, even if you are teaching the driest math class that has nothing to do with psychosocial behavior. These are the moments when you need to be the brave and innovative teacher your students need you to be. When you interact with your audiences, you not only pass on quantitative knowledge but you also model a way of being in the world that your students will pick up on and even replicate. In this context, that is significant, especially for boys. Australian novelist Tim Winton observes the way boys interact with men in teaching positions:

> What I've come to notice is that all these kids are rehearsing and projecting. Trying it on. Rehearsing their masculinity. Projecting their experimental versions of it. And wordlessly looking for cues the whole time. Not just from each other, but from older people around them, especially the men. Which can be heartbreaking to witness, to tell you the truth. Because the feedback they get is so damn unhelpful. If it's well-meant it's often feeble and half-hearted. Because good men don't always stick their necks out and make an effort.[12]

We have discussed above some possibilities on how to "make an effort" to actively be more inviting and horizontal in our pedagogical encounters. We need to practice this through consciously choosing our language, shifting our attitude, and adjusting our behaviors. All these suggestions give you an idea about how to lead by example through structurally implementing changes in your pedagogy. Let us now, in the final part of this chapter, consider some methodological ideas you could implement.

- Make sure your **teaching materials are representative of the world**. Challenge and change syllabi that only refer to the work of white men, for instance. If you have not come across any people of color, disabled scholars, queer people, and/or women producing knowledge in your field, actively seek them out. Incorporate their videos, literature, and other media into your syllabus. Do not use anyone as a token—that is, include authors not only on topics dealing with their specific identity group. Further, make sure your materials are up to date regarding the language they use. If for some reason you have to use material that can no longer be seen as politically correct, justify to your students why that is the case. Allow room for discussion of any problematic content.

- If you have a habit of starting the semester or a class with introductions, **include pronouns**. The Equality and Human Rights Commission (ECHR) issued an advice report for parliamentarians in the UK in December 2016 in which they state that 91 percent of trans boys and 66 percent of trans girls are victims of bullying and harassment (this statistic does not include other trans identities).[13] If we want our students to have the best learning experience, it is our responsibility as teachers to create a safe environment for them. One small step in that direction is introducing yourself with your name and pronoun and inviting students to do so as well. Many students might not be familiar with the idea; some might want to state their pronoun but won't feel like they have the opportunity. Thus, you should lead by example. It might be helpful putting your name and pronoun on the board for everyone to see, or include pronouns on nametags. You might experience challenges from your audience, perhaps mocking or ridicule. It is your urgent responsibility to condemn such provocations and explain the importance of the task.

- If you are working with one group for a longer period of time (either a whole day, a weekend, a semester) it might be useful to establish a **framework of guidelines** together. In activism, this is called a safer space agreement; in an educational setting, depending on the age of your audience, it can be anything from classroom rules to "facilitation framework." This is not just useful for your audience. However, as the teacher you will have a point of reference that could help you justify actions you take in case students participate in hostile behavior. Ask your audience what they demand from you, what they expect of each other, and also include your expectation of them. Ask your contributors to be as specific as possible with their suggestions when it comes to ambiguous terms such as "bullying," "respect," "harassment," etc. If time allows, you could provide examples of behavior that should be deemed unacceptable and ask the group to work out responses and consequences for unwanted behaviors. Ideally, the agreement should be based on consensus.

Now that we have scratched the surface of dismantling masculinism, I am asking you not to take my words as absolute. Listen to other people who are not white cis men and follow their lead, too. Listen to other men who are already in the process of dismantling their own masculinism. Move on from the so-called "fathers" of the animal rights movement, such as Peter Singer, and open your mind and intellect to teachers who are explicitly and implicitly critically engaging with their own identities and displaying the value in traditionally feminized approaches to veganism and animals.

Don't be afraid to ask people for help and advice. Remember, however, it is your responsibility to take what you have learned into the world, show other men how to dismantle their learned masculinism, and indicate how to make room for more people, inside and outside a classroom setting. Foremost, seek the conversation with other men, openly interrogate your own masculinism together, and hold yourself and other men accountable for any and all harm towards other human and nonhuman animals.

12

MUSCLES, MEAT, AND MASCULINITY
OBSTACLES TO A VEGAN TEACHING PRACTICE IN THE SPORTS SCIENCES

Blane Abercrombie

At the end of my career as an undergraduate student, I began to consider why so many of my friends from childhood were turning to bodybuilding as their new hobby, pursuit, or lifestyle choice. What was it that made men, who had not long ago finished their natural growth through the process of puberty, want to continue that physical growth? I began to think about whether it was actually an attempt to continue the process of their own masculinization in the context of a society where that is rewarded and accorded respect and privilege over the smaller bodies of those who are perceived not to work as hard.[1]

This drive towards the perfect male body is often said to be dependent on the ability of the person in its pursuit to consume large quantities of meat due to the effects it will have on muscle size and development. The culture of hyper-masculinity that is performed by bodybuilders was also a major aspect of why I felt the need to understand and discuss this issue with a view to making alternative, safer, and all-round less socially and personally damaging lifestyles more relevant to the young male populace. At a time when 75 percent of people who take their own lives in the UK are men,[2] we must look to understand the difficult nature of maintaining many social identities and acknowledge that men, too, are pressured to behave in line with the collective expectations that gender places on them.[3] Although they are victims of patriarchal gender norms and expectations, it must be remembered that, collectively, they are also the oppressors of women and gender minorities and are the prime beneficiaries of the structure that is the patriarchal social ordering. Without a drive towards the eradication of these societal pressures we cannot look beyond what masculinity means for those who are required to perform it.

In this chapter I explore my experiences as an educator and researcher as well as a vegan man, and the often hostile responses my subject of interest has received within sections of the department I work in and, more importantly, from the students with whom I work. My work considers the connection between masculine gender identities and meat consumption, with a particular focus on the subculture and discipline of bodybuilding. I intend to speak to my experiences of attempting to bridge a gap between gender studies and vegan theory, while working as a researcher and teacher within the discipline of a sport that can often be hostile to both discourses. Much significant work has been done to explore women's and feminized identities' relationships to ethical vegetarianism and veganism, and it is my aim to complement this work and provide insight into the relationship between diet pathways and masculine identities. Foremost, I want to share my experiences of researching and teaching these connections within the academy. However, I must stress that the mechanisms upholding my experiences are already taught and perpetuated throughout Physical Education curricula across secondary and even primary schools.

Although I am writing from my specific point of view, I am sure that many of the themes addressed in this chapter will be valuable to educators in many other fields, too. I invite you to investigate with me the relationship between the construction of masculine gender identities as performed by men who engage in bodybuilding activities and their consumption of high-protein, animal-based diets. This will provide a basis for an exploration of my experiences working within the world of sports research and education; and doing so while positioned in a school/department that incorporates more traditional, masculinist ways of conducting science within the developing world of sports in academia. I will then seek to add to the discussion why it is particularly important that we, as men and as vegan-educators, find space and opportunities to challenge the oppressive masculinist and carnist nature of both sport and academia.

As Raewyn Connell suggests, attempts at attaching a definition to what masculinity is and what its performances mean to the society in which we live have provided nothing but incomplete, vague, and/or poor definitions.[4] Gender performance alludes to the socially and culturally constructed nature of gender roles and identities; this theory was first coined by Judith Butler in her book *Gender Trouble: Feminism and the Subversion of Identity*. Connell, in her hugely important work with James W. Messerschmidt, states that there is one dominant form of masculinity, within any context—"Hegemonic Masculinity"—which in turn is made up of two distinct types of hegemony, internal and external.[5]

"Internal hegemony" exists within gender, and is said to be the hierarchizing of power that some men have over other men; "external hegemony" is "the institutionalization of men's dominance over women and gender minorities," attempting to reinforce and extend the current societal gender order.[6] The fluid nature of the former and its ever-changing performances and the repeated creation and extension of the hierarchies it produces (which favor masculinized behaviors and disadvantage ones which are socially deemed as feminine) allow the latter to exist and flourish as the most dominant form of masculinity within any given context. Whereas the performative and dynamic nature of gender ensures that actions, behaviors, and mannerisms in which masculinity is executed may change, the rationalization behind the power and dominance men possess remains constant.[7]

Thus, the expectation placed on the behaviors of those who are required to perform hegemonic masculinity will continue to be an "expression of the privilege men collectively have over women" and people of other genders[8]—a structural dominance that men also possess over animals. And although the biological makeup of a person does not necessarily determine or dictate the societal performances they engage in, it does not prevent cisgender, heteronormative, predominantly white men from "artificially attaching all manner of power and privilege to [their] biological differences"[9] to safely retain and where possible expand power over women, gender minorities, and nonhuman animals. An example of this would be the supposed higher levels of emotional intelligence human animals have when compared to that of their nonhuman counterparts, which is granted socially constructed importance and therefore becomes representative of the apparent superiority that humans "naturally" have over nonhumans.

Animal proteins, primarily beef and other red meats, have long been associated with masculinity across the world—a narrative mirrored and often magnified by masculinity's many performances within the environment of bodybuilding, as well as men's fitness. My research is very much motivated by my personal interest, which is why I began to train with a number of men engaged in activities to enlarge muscles and enhance their definition, with the aim of understanding this subculture more. They are all what Alan Klein calls "bodybuilders, body-shapers and/or body designers."[10] The lack of research tying muscularity, meat consumption, and masculinity together sparked my involvement with this culture. The findings of my initial studies have indicated that in an attempt to continue and extend the dominance and oppressing nature of the current societal gender order, men within this highly masculinized section of society very specifically use an inverted version of the "absent referent" of which Carol J. Adams writes.[11]

Adams argues that there are three ways in which living animals are forced into absenteeism when being consumed. The first of these is their "literal absence"—by the very nature of them being dead. Secondly, there is their "definitional absence," which is where language is used as a tool to differentiate between the once-living animal and the now food that is for consumption. (An example would be the use of the term *beef* rather than referring to the "cow" who has been killed.) The third is one of metaphorical absence, which describes how animals—their physical bodies, lives, and experiences, as well their subsequent deaths—are elevated to become purely descriptive terms for human experiences. A commonly used example of this is when a person states that they "felt like a piece of meat." The connections between meat consumption and masculinities are not unintentional. Meat consumption is, and will continue to be, a representation of societal patriarchy with its continual and historical associations with manhood, power, and virility.¹² The creation of a dichotomous hierarchy seeks to position a meat-based diet as being more appropriately consumed by men, and through the feminization of plant-based diets perpetuates a binary of men's versus women's food.¹³

In my teaching and learning practice, I have noticed that men who participate in bodybuilding, and the culture it is so closely tied to, are usually proud of the high meat content in their diet and even attempt to make the dominance that they as men have over people of other genders as well as nonhuman animals evident in their justification for that diet. An example of this would be when a young male bodybuilder proclaimed that he prefers his protein "to have [had] a face" and that even though he is aware that "you [can] get protein from a lot of [food he] still prefer[s] [his] to have had a smile at one point."

In stating this, the bodybuilder is making no attempt to separate the food being consumed from the previously living being it was taken from. This suggests a linguistic and conceptual inversion of the "absent referent" into the "present referent," which Kelly Struthers Montford discusses as a characteristic of the white, heterosexual masculinities dominant within the meat industry's advertisements.¹⁴

Through being involved in the world of sports I have personally observed that not content with oppressing all other humans, men, as a collective influenced by and itself influencing the dominant ideas and ideologies of society, strive to broaden their domination to all other living beings—including nonhuman animals. The domination and oppression that occur within the world of bodybuilding is a magnification of the wider society—where men's bodies are judged and subsequently hierarchized based on their adherence to the *perfect male body*. It is a space in which women's bodies are shunned but simultaneously sexualized, where they have to be *muscly* but not *too muscly*, and where the pink "women's section" of the gym is populated by a woman who is whistled at and treated like—and even referred to as—*a piece of meat*. It is a space where bodybuilders boast of their consumption of the flesh of dead animals, to show their own dominance as humans, and more importantly to them, as men. It is for that exact reason I do not believe we can detach our pursuit for the end of the structural violence of the gender order from our goal of freedom from oppression for nonhuman animals. As sport scientists and teachers, it is our responsibility to point out to our students the injustices and lead them on the way to dismantle them.

In a study conducted by Hank Rothgerber, it was found that men utilized more direct tactics to acknowledge the consumption of a previously living being when seeking to justify their own meat eating. Women, by contrast, were much more likely to use evasive answering techniques or avoidance of the question when responding to queries about their meat consumption. Examples of this would be men attempting to justify their meat eating through their use of hierarchical reasoning: for examples, that humans eating animals is *natural*. Women, however, may seek to distance themselves from meat eating or imply minimal meat consumption.

The results of Rothgerber's study, as well as my own research, indicate that in solely discussing the ethical, environmental, or nutritional benefits of a vegan diet, we are ignoring one of the primary reasons men eat meat: because it "makes them feel like real men," implying that without meat a meal is not *real*.[15] Arran Stibbe analyzed six different copies of *Men's Health* magazine and found that meat was repeatedly positioned alongside images of dominant and oppressive masculinities.[16] This attempt to explicitly couple the practice of meat consumption with the attainment of a perfect male body is said to be due to the apparent significance it plays in the building of muscle size. However, we must foremost acknowledge the important role that meat consumption and the perfect body play in the performance of dominant and oppressive masculinities. There are a myriad of different performances of masculinities and, as previously stated, men perform the type of masculinity they perceive is expected of them, one that is the most beneficial to them according to the environment(s) in which they have assumed their position(s).

What does all this mean for our teaching and learning practice? Unfortunately, disrupting hyper-masculinity and myths about bodybuilding, meat consumption, and virility as a sports educator poses a challenge in itself. Just as the athletes themselves are infatuated with constructing the perfect masculine body, the academy is passionate (and very rigid) when it comes to its own masculinism in sports sciences.

Within academia, I believe a culture of *enlightened sexism*,[17] exists, one that although potentially more gender egalitarian and less subjectively violent in terms of gendered behavior than many others, is still heavily dominated by masculinity and the gender order. This is a setting in which the feminist enlightenment of men who occupy the space affords them the freedom from being challenged and allows them to accumulate masculine privilege while simultaneously doing little to nothing to practically confront the structural inequalities they are often keen to tackle in their writings and teachings.

This enlightened sexism as discussed by Michael Armato ensures that masculinity's performance plays itself out in very different ways. In my experiences, many of the enlightened, pro-feminist men who are willing to understand issues of gender inequality and offer a supportive shoulder and ear to those who struggle against it, also gain huge amounts of capital from adopting this position. In short, it makes academic (and therefore professional/career) sense to be a pro-feminist man in academia, even if your actions fall short of your apparently supportive narrative. Negotiating this nexus can be difficult, as someone who identifies as a pro-feminist man working within academia. To avoid falling into the trap of being another academic gender egalitarian who indeed actively practices patriarchy, it must be us, as men in sports departments and beyond, who through learning and reflection look to understand and support those who struggle against the masculinities (and gendered expectations) constructed by us.

As an educator who uses qualitative research methods often deemed unscientific or unreliable, it can sometimes be difficult to engage with both students and staff who don't see the value in what they would call "subjective analysis." The premise that some research is objective and therefore accurate, whereas other methods are subjective and therefore flawed, is inherently gendered. It comes as no surprise that the gender makeup of the two threads of research, often viewed as oppositional, tends to be unequal with regards to sport and exercise science ("hard science") in comparison with the humanities and social sciences ("soft science").

The gendered nature of the hard/soft science binary leads us to a position where the dominant culture is one where *real men do real science*.

This response is a manifestation of the patriarchal nature of the academy, something particularly prevalent in the highly masculinized area of sport and sports studies. As such, it is within a culture established in partnership between students and educators existing within the sporting environment that perpetuates and ensures all students are similarly wired in terms of their patriarchal behaviors.

The response that I cannot be a *real* academic if I am not using quantitative methodologies is similar to the shunning of those who do not perform the expected gendered behaviors, in line with the dominant hegemony of that space. In that way, it is a similar response to the idea that I cannot be a *real man* if I do not consume the flesh of another being. How can I possibly be a real academic if I do not attach so-called *valid* and *reliable* data (percentages, figures, and statistics, etc.) to my findings to underpin them? And how can I possibly be a *real* man if I do not perform actions that underpin the very nature of manhood—power, domination, and virility—through the consumption of the flesh of other beings? There is an expectation placed on me, as a man, that I will eat *real* food and that, as an academic, I will do *real* science—and my failure to do so leaves me at odds with sections of my gender and the academy. This unconscious bias is ideologically constructed and serves a purpose: masculinities and their performances function to maintain oppressive structures of dominance.

As vegan educators informed by feminist practice and theory, we must seek to interrupt these (and all) performances of hyper-masculinities. Through incorporating vegan-feminist knowledge and methods into the work I teach my students, I hope to disrupt the perpetual cycle of patriarchal norms and offer an alternative. However, the responses of students to my research and teaching are also somewhat indicative of the struggles we as vegan educators face in the drive towards animal liberation. The main difficulty I have encountered in looking to integrate vegan feminist theory into my teaching is that of space on the syllabus. Unfortunately, there is little interest from the students that I work with to learn about veganism through an explicitly feminist lens. However, there is an increasing interest from learners to hear about the health benefits of such a diet. (This could be attributed to the health-focused underpinning of so much of the popularized culture of veganism today, as well as a number of high-profile, elite-level athletes who follow plant-based diets.)

Subsequently, I often find myself up against the prevailing research practice of our sector, focusing primarily on quantifiable metrics of health and athletic performance. Whereas the disciplines of social sciences are becoming increasingly more welcome in the world of sport, they are still, in my experiences, sidelined in pursuit of the "hard science" approach, which often neglects the subjective nature of terms like *health*, thereby failing to take into consideration the nuances and negotiation needed to fully understand health in a sociological framework and setting. For these reasons, educating students about veganism and vegan theory usually takes place on the peripheries of my teaching and occurs predominantly when I am explicitly discussing my own research project(s) rather than the course content.

My position is notably one of privilege: I am a white, cis-gender, male working within a highly competitive environment where those identities matter. These characteristics accord me privilege when it comes to my behavior, my ability to work within particular spaces, and the capital attached to me and to what I have to say when involved in pedagogy. However, my positioning with reference to my research is one influenced by my background and upbringing, which allows me to code-switch my language and behaviors in order to move between the academic and non-academic spaces I occupy and better engage with necessary demographics for my research.

My regional accent, for instance, is a benefit to my research that an academic without such an accent, and the access to the social and cultural references that come with it, would not possess. Although this accent does not necessarily correspond to my class position, it does correspond with my social experiences. Therefore my code-switching occurs *upwards* in an attempt to use what is perceived, under classist Anglocentric standards of language, to be a higher level of spoken English. Be it consciously or unconsciously, my use of my accent authentically speaks to my identities and experiences, and importantly serves to bridge the perceived cultural gaps between many lecturers and students.

On reflection, my speaking as I do could be viewed as participating in the *lad* (or *bro*) culture that permeates much of the world of bodybuilding, as a method of proving authenticity in an effort to gain credit and legitimacy within that space. The access that this grants me also affords me the ability to gain the same credit and legitimacy within the classroom with many of my students, who often perpetuate the same behaviors I encounter within my field of research. This assumption reveals a more deeply held belief that it is inherently masculinist, and therefore violent, to speak with a regional, specifically Glaswegian, accent. It does, however, grant me a foot in the door with my students, who might be more receptive to me due to my accent.

Not only do I present students with niche research, but as a young, early-career academic I am often met with dismissal from my students and some colleagues from across the sector. When I try to impart knowledge and engage students with my research, I also find them immediately skeptical of its importance because of the widely held idea that veganism is not natural and irrelevant in a sporting context. For these reasons, I often find myself utilizing the different aspects of my research to legitimize my work to my students and colleagues by neglecting the discussions surrounding the vegan element of my vegan-feminist lens of analysis. This is particularly apparent when I discuss my work with students at a more introductory level of sociology. One of the primary ways I do this is by discussing, often at great length, steroid usage, because I can therefore cross into dialogue employing narratives more fitting of a *hard scientist*.

Discussions around gender and meat consumption in athletes are made somewhat more complex with the rise of celebrity sports stars adopting vegan diets, primarily for health reasons. Well-publicized examples of Mixed Martial Arts (MMA) fighters are the ones my students usually bring up. It isn't particularly common for MMA fighters to be vegan, and when they are it is almost always for health purposes (often associated with performance improvement) rather than because of any ethical considerations. That said, these examples are very interesting to me. MMA fighters exist within a hyper-masculinized section of society where their violence is what makes them marketable. Their veganism is rendered unimportant because of their performances of masculinities and their perceived attainment of the masculine ideal.

In essence, aspects of their performance of masculinities are so strong and powerful that their failure to comply with one very important aspect of its perfect performance—meat consumption—is superseded and pushed into irrelevance. Their hyper-masculinity transcends the need to adhere to all tenets of masculinity. A conversation on how vegan MMA fighters' performance of masculinities differs from the traditional, violent, meat-eating man, who adheres to the expected standards of hegemonic masculinity, usually takes two different routes. Students (principally male) either disregard the abilities of that given athlete to compete at the highest level as a vegan on the grounds that the regimen fails to provide the levels of nutritional benefits to maximize performance. Or, they disregard their own abilities to go vegan (or to lessen their meat consumption) on the basis that they like meat too much and it is *natural* to eat meat. For these reasons, the most convincing argument for a vegan diet that I as an educator can convey is that of the health benefits for a maximization of athletic performance, rather than any ethical or moral argument to halt (or even simply to minimize) animal consumption.

As part of my role as an educator with bodybuilders, one question I must ask myself when I am engaging in research with them, as well as with staff and students, is where I draw the line on challenging behaviors, beliefs, and attitudes. For example, in a focus group with five young bodybuilders I initiated a discussion on the question of how they would react to a vegan bodybuilder looking to work in the same gym environment and space as them. One bodybuilder replied that he would forcibly have the vegan display their genitalia, which he assumed would be assigned female. At this point in my research, I decided to move on with my set questions rather than challenging or further discussing this comment and the violence that it poses. Clearly, this response is both misogynistic and transphobic and behavior like this should be challenged. However, negotiating research relationships while also trying to live as non-oppressively as possible is difficult, especially for someone embarking on field research for the first time in this instance. The path of less resistance can often be appealing.

It can be difficult in situations such as this to negotiate my role as a researcher, there to understand and document the behaviors that take place within my field, while interacting with the moral and ethical implications of letting these statements go unchallenged. So, it is important to understand where to draw the line with regards to how I, the educator, interact with/challenge participants and the field to elicit responses to use for analysis, and knowing when not to do so, for fear of harming researcher/participant relations. The same could also be said of my practice when teaching. To what extent do I allow students the freedom to develop their ideas and language and at what stage do those ideas become so oppressive or violent that I need to challenge them?

In seeking to breach the topic of veganism, I look to incorporate vegan theory into sections of the curriculum where I would usually situate my research. Examining primarily gender and body image in sport, and how they interlink with veganism, I employ the practice of bodybuilding as my go-to example. I do so because of my knowledge of the discipline and all that comes with it: the steroids, the illicit drug use, the vast levels of meat consumption, the body dysmorphia, and the isolation and loneliness bodybuilders feel, as well as the deeply toxic and harmful masculinism that drives them.

However, as I have suggested, I usually lead to the discussion of the performance-benefits of a vegan diet rather than the ethical considerations of not eating the flesh of another being killed for your consumption. I do so out of striving to engage students on the topic of veganism. Unfortunately, due to the constraints of timings and curriculum, I cannot break down the vast topic of vegan theory and practice. It is for this reason that I find it encouraging when students take an interest in the high-profile examples of vegan athletes we discuss, because they are at least showing a degree of curiosity in a diet shunned by so many in society, particularly within sport.

By approaching my students in this way and allowing them to approach veganism in their own way, I hope to have a more permanent impact on their lives when I do begin to introduce them to veganfeminist theory and literature. Through the coupling of their newly found knowledge on how a vegan diet can be undertaken healthily, as well as the ethical vegan-feminist lens through which to analyze meat and dairy consumption, these students will be more likely to interrogate their own food consumption further down the line. I am, however, attempting to undo the decades of teaching that my students and I have gone through, convincing us that to analyze, critique, or understand behaviors, actions, and responses, you must first have something quantifiable and measurable and with data attached to it. It is a process of simultaneous learning and unlearning.

Yes, masculinity is dominant within the sports world and we must work to undo that. However, the goal has to be to understand how masculinity, and with it the concept of virile flesh consumption, permeate all sections of our society and (no matter the environment) is performed to the detriment of people of other genders and to the further privileging of men, particularly those who conform to its expected standards. From a very young age I have engaged, in a multitude of ways, in the highly masculinized environment of sport—an environment marred by the patriarchal social order and every form of discrimination and bigotry imaginable.

Now it is my aim to document and understand these behaviors and practices. I occupy this space in the hope that through knowledge of these ideas we can begin to offer alternatives to and move beyond the current societal order. Raewyn Connell's work on how we must strive to make masculinities more peaceful and less subjectively violent is where I find myself looking for inspiration.[18] The drive to eradicate masculinized and gendered violence is made all the more difficult when we consider the fact that the most violent systems and institutions in existence are those at the core of how we are organized as humans, that is through states (as exemplified by their militaries and governments) as well as the structural speciesism of society that allows the mass extermination of not only specific marginalized people groups for political ends but nonhuman animal beings for human consumption. Without looking beyond the structural violence of our society today and working in a way that seeks to negate many of its effects and influences to the highest possible degree, we cannot build a less violent, oppressive world for all of its inhabitants. Without talking about how human oppressions connect with the oppressions of nonhuman animals, we cannot truly restructure society into something we can be proud of. As educators it is our responsibility to expose the injustices we perceive and actively work against them, so our students won't perpetuate the same systems of which we are part.

13

Working with the Imagination and a Corporeal Pedagogy to Foster Interspecies Empathy

Terry Hurtado

In recent years, I have had the pleasure to co-facilitate a workshop with my dear friend Joana Formosinho for those who are willing to explore (with) their imagination. With the Imagining Cow Being workshop we are inviting participants to move into the corporeal being of a cow from the inside and to experience the world through her eyes, with the aim of opening another pathway to interspecies empathy. Empathy can be a powerful tool to guide human moral action; however, it can be difficult to empathize with the condition of those whose realities we cannot relate to in a bodily, concrete way. In this workshop format, we guide participants in a 35-minute visualization experience where we use sensorial imagination to envision becoming and being a cow. The visualization was developed by anchoring our imagination in a detailed sense perception of a cow's body, her interactions, and the environment she finds herself in, as well as mimicking some of her actions, so as to free the imagination in order to move our corporeal experience closer to that of the animal.

This is an experimental way of imaginative inquiry inspired by the fact that academic study of animal behavior is mostly theoretical and conceptual. Imagination is usually discouraged in the field, not only because it is labeled as unscientific but also because it encourages anthropomorphism, where those empathizing with animals are likely to attribute their own human characteristics to the animal. This makes the power of imagination an unexplored tool, with the potential to open a window of possibilities for a complementary way of coming closer to understanding an animal's experience, grounded in careful, detailed observation of the animal's body, movement, and behavior. Obviously, as humans, none of us will ever truly understand what it means to be a cow. However, the workshop can be used as an extra tool for animal-behavior research, which through fostering empathy, might make the pedagogical approach to the field less anthropocentric.

The Imagining Cow Being workshop was the result of conversations I had with Joana about what we thought wasn't working well in animal advocacy. We both felt it was necessary to highlight the life of the animal in freedom, rather than under domestication or captivity, in order to get closer to their nature. To illustrate this, this chapter will first consider different approaches to vegan education and campaigning; secondly, it will examine the concept of empathy and how we can teach it; finally, it will explore methods of learning to actively include empathy in our vegan education through portraying empathy not only as an exercise of the mind but also of the body. Before we examine vegan campaigning methods, let us first define what is meant by the concept of empathy.

Empathy can be understood in a broad sense as a vicarious affective response to another—that is, an emotional reaction prompted by the experience somebody else might be having. In our workshop, we also bear in mind Martin Hoffman's more specific definition of empathy: "The involvement of psychological processes that make a person have feelings that are more congruent with another's situation than with [their] own situation."[1] Further, the workshop attempts to evoke another understanding of empathy, one used by William Ickes, which is defined as the capacity of one person to accurately deduce the thoughts and feelings of another.[2] To these, we add that the intentions and perceptions of another are inferred correctly through empathy.

It is important to note here that working to evoke interspecies empathy can be problematic for two reasons. First is the aforementioned impossibility of correctly inferring the reality of a cow from a human perspective. Not only will we never know true "cow being," but not every cow experiences the same reality, as each cow has different desires and thoughts. The other problem we encounter with this workshop is that humans have different ways to empathize and do so to different degrees. It is important to bear both these things in mind and also acknowledge that they do not make the workshop less valuable. As the workshop is simultaneously a very personal and collective event, where we discuss our experiences in a safe space, participants usually find a platform to voice any such concerns.

Approaches in Vegan Education Campaigns

As animal advocates, our goal is to achieve a shift in the way people consume. However, if it were simply a matter of exposing animal cruelty and educating people about the horror of killing animals, then most of the world would now be vegan. So why, then, aren't more people refraining from supporting animal cruelty? I suspect this situation might be due to a lack of animal advocates fostering empathy, or the ways they might be approaching this task.

There is a varied spectrum of approaches to vegan education; nonetheless, a considerable number of people don't have a positive response to the methods and/or tactics used currently by vegan campaigners. Of course, it is unlikely if not impossible that our decisions are influenced by a singular impulse. But let us assume that there are four stand-alone ways that encourage people to take a transformative decision and that each person is influenced by only one of them:

- Engagement and change through *emotions/feelings*
- *Highly rational* engagement and change through *rationality/reason*
- *Highly rational* engagement and change through *emotions/feelings*
- Engagement through *emotions/feelings* and change through *rationality/reason*.

Let us consider the two dominant ways of approaching vegan education and animal liberation outreach in general: the *emotions/feeling* approach and the *highly rational* one. The *emotions/feelings* approach is used by some organizations that choose explicit images of cruelty to animals to raise awareness of the suffering we inflict upon other species. This approach usually employs a *negative message strategy* (e.g. making people feel guilty) and often repels individuals because of the strong and violent images. These images disturb people, who would rather not be faced with this violence and, therefore, do not engage in self-reflection. Naturally, we prefer to forget about anything that brings back such horrible imagery to our minds. As part of an anti-speciesist education, environmental issues are also approached through *emotions/feelings*. Ecological disasters, such as the loss of a forest or a species, are examples of *more-than-human-concerned* discourses. These are also fostered by means of a *negative message strategy*.

Other campaigns approach their target audience with a *highly rational* argument, whether animal rights–based or environmental. Such arguments raise the fact that animals feel pain and the science behind it, for instance, or the philosophical argument that demands the inclusion of other animals in our moral consideration. This approach is *more-than-human-concerned* and more neutral, although it usually focuses on what is lacking. Environmental threats, such as global warming, famine, and pollution, are further examples of this. These are, of course, *human-concerned* and employ a *negative message strategy* (e.g. making people fearful or guilty.)

A different approach to promoting vegan food choices is by emphasizing a healthy diet. This seems to be a *human-concerned* way to advertise not eating animals, as the campaigns often emphasize the risks you face by continuing to consume animals. We can distinguish here between a fitness-oriented diet and one concerned with health. Both the fitness diet and the healthy diet rhetoric utilize an *emotions/feelings* discourse, though the latter more often achieves change of behavior by a rational-based response. It is worth highlighting that the fitness and healthy diet approaches, in contrast to the others, are presented through a *positive message strategy*. They don't blame the target audience or make them feel guilty, but point out the benefits of choosing a plant-based diet. Offering samples of appetizing vegan food is another *human-concerned* tactic campaigners use to convince the general public that changing their food consumption to a vegan diet will actually be pleasant. This is another *positive message strategy* approach to attract attention, but is also not itself anti-speciesist.

So, we can see that most of the popular vegan education and campaign methods are based on a *negative message strategy* and/or do not include an anti-speciesist concern for animals in their approach. In our workshop we are interested in generating empathy through *positive message strategies* while simultaneously conveying a moral concern for animals.

GENERATING EMPATHY

Empathy is as a multidimensional and complex phenomenon, consisting of a variety of components such as empathic concern, personal distress, and perspective taking.[3] Although *personal distress* refers to one's experiencing unpleasant feelings in response to witnessing somebody else in distress, *empathic concern* refers to the individual's feelings of sympathy and concern for someone else in distress.[4] Both of these phenomena are part of my understanding of empathy. In this chapter, by empathic distress, I am referring to both personal distress and empathic concern.

It seems that, currently, *more-than-human-concerned* campaigns mainly rely on empathic distress to achieve an empathic response for animals. However, we learn from the field of psychology that empathic distress does not always lead to actions that would relieve the stress of those whose pain we witness. One reason for why we don't always take action if we do indeed empathically perceive somebody else in distress could be the so-called bystander effect: "The presence of other bystanders may interfere with a person's helping by activating the assumptions of 'pluralistic ignorance'—no one else is reacting; it must not be an emergency after all—and diffusion of responsibility—I'm sure someone else has already called the [ambulance]."[5] Other individuals seemingly witnessing the same precarious situation as us seem to play an important role when creating, or rather not creating, an empathic response.

If a person is among those who consider eating animals normal, we can anticipate that that person will share the perception of the others.

These others might not only be the person's main point of reference, but they could also be seen as bystanders who are not interfering in the observed cruelty towards the animal. Thus, the person might justify eating animals by subconsciously applying the principle of pluralistic ignorance, convincing themselves that "the situation for the animal cannot be precarious, as none of these people are taking any action to prevent the animal's possible suffering." Following the logic of the bystander effect, a meat eater among other meat eaters, who might feel empathic distress for the animals they are eating, might also diffuse their responsibility to refrain from animal cruelty because they think that someone more knowledgeable or qualified for intervention has already taken action.

We can also discern another common result of the bystander effect, which is "when bystanders are alone, their motive to help may be checked by powerful egoistic motives revolving around fear, energy expenditure, financial cost, loss of time, opportunities missed."[6] Some of the commonly displayed "egoistic" motives to avoid the shift from an animal-based diet are, for instance, the inability to find food that imitates the taste of animal products; the difficulty of cooking without animal ingredients; the fear of higher expenditures on a vegan diet; the concern about health risks; and the worry that one might be socially ostracized.

As intuitive as it might seem to base our vegan education on graphic texts and imagery that generate empathic distress, the bystander effect and the many complex reasons that justify meat consumption do indeed prevent most of our audience from engaging with the issue of animal cruelty beyond an initial emotional response that might, in fact, be almost counter-productive. We, therefore, need to acknowledge that some of the vegan campaigns that use *negative message strategies* might not even be able to create the right conditions for audiences and students to critically engage with speciesism.

Descriptions of ecological disasters and scenarios of global environmental catastrophes are indeed shocking and create a state of unease to a degree that many might find unbearable. Similarly, most of those we communicate speciesism to—through confronting them with images and sounds of animals suffering and exposing them to the gory reality of speciesism—may well reject any further engagement with the issue. In addition to the mechanisms played out in our minds through the bystander effect, we are prone to protecting ourselves from stress by simply suppressing an empathic response in the first place. This self-preservation can have multiple facets, as Hoffman explains:

> In view of the cost that helping may entail, we might expect people not only to refrain from helping but also to be leery of feeling empathy in the first place for fear of what it may lead them to do: it may lead them to incur the cost of helping, including the cost of experiencing the unpleasantness of empathic distress. People might, therefore, when possible try to forestall feeling for victims in order to escape the motivational consequences of that feeling.[7]

Rejection and avoidance is, in my experience as a vegan educator, one of the most common attitudes when people are exposed to the reality suffered by the victims of the animal production industry.

Nonetheless, empathic distress shouldn't be discarded completely as a way to generate empathy because it can also function as a tool for interpersonal exchange and supportive relationships. As Nancy Eisenberg and others show, empathic distress does actually correlate positively with people's helping behavior and their will to take action, in situations where the act of intervening, helping, or otherwise diffusing a harmful situation arises from the awareness that one would feel better after helping out.[8] In other words, empathic distress can indeed lead to evoking a helping reaction, despite the bystander effect, simply because we might feel better about ourselves after helping, which would contribute to the minimization of the experienced distress.

If we insist on using *negative message strategies* with distressing stimuli in our vegan pedagogies, we must ask ourselves: "When is the right moment to induce personal distress and at what intensity do we run the lowest risk of overwhelming our audience?"

EMPATHY THROUGH IMAGINATION

Above, I have shown the reasons for a shift away from using negative messages when educating people about veganism and anti-speciesism. Although in the right contexts empathic distress might be a useful tool for a vegan pedagogy, as a movement we must continuously strive to appeal to an ever-wider audience. This is why Joana and I were still looking for alternatives to distressing information as part of our non-anthropocentric pedagogy. We became interested in answering the question of how we could elicit empathy towards nonhuman animals in people who engage and change their attitudes inspired by positive messages.

Joana and I believe that "imagination, grounded in careful detailed observation of the animal's body, movement and behavior, can open a window of possibility to a complementary way of understanding an animal's experience."[9] Thus, "recruiting the aid of the imagination, we are attempting a movement into the corporeal reality of a cow from the inside, through her own eyes—opening another pathway to interspecies empathy."[10] We developed the Imagining Cow Being workshop to enable a bodily experience to which we could relate, in order to actively imagine the corporeal realities of animals. The workshop has three moments: toning the senses, imagining cow being, and reflection.

In Martin Hoffman's writing I find support for this workshop. His work was developed through research with children, but it nevertheless provides important guidelines to approaching empathy within other demographics. He highlights the relevance of mimicry, seeing it as a "hard-wired neurologically based empathy-arousing mechanism" and points out that imitation and feedback, its two steps, are directed by commands from the central nervous system. This is valuable for two reasons: first, "a hard-wired mimicry provides a quick-acting mechanism enabling infants to empathize and feel what another feels without previously experiencing that emotion."[11] Secondly, it "is the only empathy-arousing mechanism that assures a match between the observer's feeling and expression of feeling and the victim's feeling and expression of feeling, at least in face to face encounters."[12]

It is this understanding of mimicry as evoking empathy that we apply in our workshop, in the hope it will evoke or strengthen empathy towards nonhuman animals. We invite participants to experience this through imitating the posture of a four-legged animal, imagining the body shape of a bovine, and performing some of the gestures of a cow through one's imagination, so as to feel a cow moving her tail and her massive body. We also encourage workshop participants to imagine the perspective from a cow's eyes as well as to find a way of enjoying the grass and feeding a calf.

The workshop also offers the opportunity to enable "direct association." Direct association "cues in the victim's situation that reminds observers of similar experiences in their own past and evokes feelings in them that fit the victim's situation."[13] This might also be true for positive experiences: joy, freedom, love, and relaxation, for instance. The hope is that humans who go through the Imagining Cow Being workshop will create this direct association with experiences they might have had in the past: the calm of being in a field; the pleasant contact with the grass, the soil, and the air. The affection for an offspring.

We also incorporate Hoffman's concepts of "self-focused role-taking" and "other-focused role-taking." Self-focused role-taking occurs "when people observe someone in distress. [. . .] [T]hey may imagine how it would feel in the same situation. If they can do this vividly enough, they may experience some of the same affect experienced by the victim."[14] However, in order to reach this point of imagination and engagement, the observer should first have to recognize *being*—that is, another existing as an individual with a life of their own, capable of sensations, feelings, and social interactions. What this means concretely within the context of a vegan education that focuses on generating empathy towards animals is that the observer, before entering an empathy-generating situation, needs to acknowledge the other as a sentient, complex being. If this is not given, the person may be driven away from the cause when they become exposed to the suffering of other species through an image or text, or they might simply find it irrelevant. Even worse, the human may interpret that action or condition in which the animal is pushed into distress or intense suffering as normal.

A more difficult empathic response to generate is one that comes about through "other-focused role-taking," which occurs when "learning of another's misfortune. [. . .] [P]eople may focus directly on the victim and imagine how he [*sic*] feels; and doing this may result in feeling something of the victim's feeling."[15] In this case, it is even more fundamental to build up the capacity to acknowledge the other being as capable of very similar psychological and physiological responses, if not the same ones. As Antonio Damasio states: "This empathic response may be enhanced by bringing in any personal information they have about the victim"—that is, in the case of a vegan and anti-speciesist education, not about the individual but about the species, a dominated species, and additionally, if possible, specific beings of that subjugated species.[16]

Imagination and Body

Considering that the biochemistry of the brain and the body as a whole are intimately interlocked, and the brain triggers and modulates bodily states while the body feeds back to the brain, we specifically developed the workshop to involve not just the mind but the body in our visualization practice in order to evoke empathy. As Damasio writes: "The representations your brain constructs to describe a situation, and the movements formulated as response to a situation, depend on mutual brain–body interactions. The brain constructs evolving representations of the body as it changes under chemical and neural influences."[17] This suggests that fostering empathy from a purely conceptual and abstract perspective, which would not relate to the body, might be more difficult to accomplish than an attempt at generating empathic responses that enable the involvement of the body.

We think based on representations: some perceived by our senses in the moment and others recalled. The former come from our interaction with the environment, the latter from our memory. These representations and the thoughts we formulate based on them have an effect upon our actions and behaviors. Thus, a bodily experience appears to be necessary in order to influence the images that are at the base of our thinking.

The challenge in our case is specifically thinking about how to construct interspecies empathy, especially when it comes to a body that is so different from ours. That said, we must bear in mind that, even among humans, we are all different and our minds and bodies function in as many ways as there are people. Nevertheless, many of us find ways of empathizing with one another. You could say that perhaps we empathize comparatively easily with humans because we learn to understand human behavior and language and are highly capable of interpreting somebody else's state with relative certainty, based on us witnessing their testimony, so to speak. One human can tell another how they feel, while a cow cannot, one might think. At the same time, one might argue that it is easier to evoke empathy towards other humans than other animals, as we share a specifically human condition. We might say that an experience is perhaps exclusively human and that the experience of animals is just so different from our own that it is impossible for us to interpret their thoughts, behaviors, and desires.

However, we know today two facts from institutional science that we, the human species, have arguably long known from personal observation: First, animals are complex individuals with relationships, desires, and emotions; secondly, animals communicate within their own species and across species, including with humans. Yes, any interpretation of animal behavior, any relating to an individual of another species on our part, will tend to be anthropocentric, because we are human. But our imagination becomes an aid to fill the gap between our bodily realities and that of others, including animals. Thus, our workshop invites participants to shed themselves of speciesist divides that might prevent us from bearing witness to the experiences of a cow, and to allow ourselves, as social beings, to include animals in our circle of concern.

Based on the thoughts above, we find it reasonable to approach imagining being a cow based on our images referring to diverse elements that constitute a cow, from an embodied perspective. These include the characteristics of her organs and the psychosocial range of interactions she could have. In the workshop, we create images of how we picture a cow. These come from our memory and are not actually perceived through our senses there and then. To imagine a cow we need to recall the image we have of a cow and it doesn't matter that the image is modified. When we recall objects we create a reinterpretation of them rather than an exact reproduction of the original. I believe this reconstructive characteristic of memory might play out in favor of the way the workshop participants see cows, since imagining cow being enables an experience that reinterprets the nonhuman animal.

As argued in Damasio's book *Descartes' Error: Emotion, Reason, and the Human Brain*, emotions and feelings are the bridge between cortical and subcortical structures, rational and non-rational processes. Emotion is the response to stimuli in the world or in our bodies. However, our bodily state and cognitive processing also enact specific features in response to particular emotions. In congruence with the above, research suggests that it is indeed our emotions that play a cognitive guidance role and allow us to communicate meaning to others. Thus, emotions should not be underestimated as a change driver. Let us consider what Damasio thinks of emotions: "I see the *essence* of emotion as the collection of changes in body state that are induced in myriad organs by nerve cell terminals, under the control of a dedicated brain system, which is responding to the content of thoughts relative to a particular entity or event."[18]

The process continues into the *feeling* of the emotion. Feeling is what establishes the connection between the object and the emotion that excited it; feeling is the realization of the link between an emotional body state and an object. As Damasio says: "If an emotion is a collection of changes in body state connected to particular mental images that have activated a specific brain system, *the essence of feeling an emotion is the experience of such changes in juxtaposition to the mental images that initiated the cycle.*"[19]

In other words, feelings give us an indication of what is going on in our body, as an instantaneous image of our own body is juxtaposed with the images of the objects we perceive and situations we find ourselves in. Feelings then modify our cognitive notion of those other objects and situations. By means of such a juxtaposition, body images determine the quality of what we perceive and let us interpret if what we experience is desirable or not, and if the object gives us pleasure or discomfort.

Bodily changes and bodily experience are both facilitated by imagination; it is our imagination that continuously evokes a new set of emotions. Thus the workshop, by connecting the imagination with bodily sensation, attempts to generate a deeper emotion/feeling understanding of a cow, which will hopefully sow the seeds to enable a stronger empathic response to cows in the future.

It is also worth stressing again that the information the body provides the brain is not just about what is within its own perimeter. What we perceive of the environment shapes the representation the brain makes of the body. The mind is the product of our whole organism. Thus, in developing the workshop we agree that it might be worth attempting to mimic, through imagination and movement, some inner aspects and the environmental context of a cow. The cow we imagine during the workshop is not exploited by the milk industry, nor is she domesticated and living in a barn.

We want to reassert an image of animals, particularly that of cows, free from human intervention, because that is an image of animals that domestication has completely removed from both our realities and imaginations. Simply try to think of a time you saw a cow in freedom—without a nose ring, without a tag, without the restraints of a barn or a fence. Chances are your answer will be "never." Even in vegan education we almost exclusively make use of imagery depicting animals under human domination. Further, we feel it's important to describe a free cow in our workshop because it simply makes sense to experience (for instance) the swinging and swishing of a tail in an environment where the cow can freely express herself, and where her interactions would not be covered under the shadow of grief and her body would not be full of sorrow.

PRACTICAL EXPERIENCES WITH THE WORKSHOP

Most workshop participants in the imagination experience have reported feeling serenity, joy, and curiosity. These reactions might be relevant as the workshop seems to be triggering positive body states, which perhaps are enabling the cognitive processes we are hoping for in participants. A woman who had lost her brother a week before she attended the workshop mentioned to us being in a state of unease. However, after the workshop she expressed her gratitude to us, saying that the workshop helped her "find some peace." This "feeling of peace" is actually a recurring theme in the feedback for all sessions regardless of the place where the workshop has been run.

Many participants express curiosity and interest in imagining the size of a cow's body, her posture, and even her tail. The participants' experience indicates that partaking in the workshop brings them positive bodily states, which correlates with my theoretical assumptions about the differences between positive and negative strategies for generating empathy, as illustrated above. As we learn from Damasio, generating distressing empathy and the bodily sensations that come with it is simply not sustainable:

> Along with negative body states, the generation of images is slow, their diversity small, and reasoning inefficient; along with positive body states the generation of images is rapid, their diversity wide, and reasoning may be fast though not necessarily efficient. When negative body states recur frequently, or when there is a sustained negative body state, as happens in a depression, the proportion of thoughts which are likely to be associated with negative situations does increase, and the style and efficiency of reasoning suffer.[20]

This means that a vegan education based solely on the enlightenment of our audiences about the plight of animals cannot be sustainable. In other words, being exposed to animal cruelty might generate empathy in us; however, it also incapacitates us in the long run, as we plummet into recurring or continuous negative bodily states that drain our mental and physical health.

The last part of the workshop is dedicated to reflection and sharing, enabled initially by drawing, painting, or individual writing. Once that reflective, and sometimes cathartic, phase is carried out, participants are invited to a group phase of reflection, in which they might wish to talk about their individual work or their thoughts and feelings during the imagination phase.

These conversations during the reflection are key to explicitly addressing the relationship human societies have established with cows and other animals. This part is always marked by a very somber tone, since people find themselves in a very intimate space after the experience. A Colombian high school student who was thinking about going vegetarian mentioned to us that "after this experience it will be difficult to see things the same way," referring to his food consumption. It is common that participants, regardless of their dietary habits, will mention that during the imagination exercise they experienced moments of concern or even the feeling of fear of mistreatment, based on the knowledge they already had about human–animal relations.

Such observations show that people are aware of the levels of abuse that come with farming, which is all the more reason for us to stress the positive imagery during the exercise and letting our participants enjoy a peaceful experience. Our sessions often allow people to feel raw and vulnerable to the extent that many often break out in tears. An already-vegan activist from Canada opened his eyes after the imagination exercise and gently started to cry. He shared his empathic reaction with us, stating that he had never thought about how free a cow could actually be and that the abuse must therefore be even worse than what he'd ever been able to imagine.

The workshop is, of course, only one way of generating empathy through positive imagery and we continue to adapt and develop elements of it with every new session. As with all educational methods, it will not work with all audiences. Nonetheless, the theoretical background laid out in this chapter and our experience in the workshops continuously shows us that it is a very valuable and urgent approach to teaching empathy across species.

NOTES

Introduction

1. In response to the harassment endured by vegans, the body of literature and other media on ways to cope with carnist violence towards animals and vegans themselves is growing. See for example: Carol J. Adams. *Living Among Meat Eaters: A Vegetarian's Survival Handbook* (New York: Lantern, 2008); pattrice jones. *Aftershock: Confronting Trauma in a Violent World: A Guide for Activists and Their Allies* (New York: Lantern, 2007); Melanie Joy. *Beyond Beliefs: A Guide to Improving Relationships and Communication for Vegans, Vegetarians, and Meat Eaters* (New York: Lantern, 2018).

1. Dismantling the Human/Animal Divide in Education: The Case for Critical Humane Education

1. This chapter draws from educational theory, (eco)feminist, posthumanist, critical animal, postcolonial, and postmodern studies. Given the goals of this chapter, and because of the accountability and responsibilities that I must commit myself to as a scholar of my positionality, it must be explicitly stated that many, if not all, of the ideas that I engage with in this text are not new. Many of the ideas, concepts, and theories put forth here arise from Indigenous knowledges that have been in existence for centuries. Acknowledging that many of these ideas are not new is not meant to discredit the Western academic sources I draw upon. It is rather meant to give credit where credit is due and resist further neo-colonization of Indigenous knowledge by staking claim to these ideas. This is not meant to encourage the cherry-picking of Indigenous knowledge to be used in commodified, romanticized, homogenizing ways to the benefit of Western imperialist academia. It is the goal of this chapter not to partake in such epistemological violence, though given the time and scope of this text, paired with my settler-colonial positionality, this has the potential to occur. This chapter is not meant to serve as a be-all-end-all account of educational critique, but rather an academic project that is entirely open to critique itself.

2. Karen Warren. "The Power and Promise of Ecological Feminism" in *Environmental Ethics* 12 (1990): 127.
3. *Ibid.*: 128.
4. Greta Gaard. "Toward a Queer Ecofeminism," in *Hypatia* 12:1 (1997): 114 <www.pantheresroses.koumbit.org/textes/ecology_toward_a_queer_ecofeminism.pdf>.
5. *Ibid.*: 115.
6. *Ibid.*: 116.
7. Val Plumwood. *Feminism and the Mastery of Nature* (New York: Routledge, 1993): 42.
8. *Ibid.*: 43.
9. Gaard. "Queer Ecofeminism," 116.
10. *Ibid.*: 118 (emphasis added).
11. *Ibid.*: 119.
12. *Ibid.*
13. Maneesha Deckha. "The Subhuman as a Cultural Agent of Violence," in *Journal for Critical Animal Studies*, 8:3 (2010): 28 <www.criticalanimalstudies.org/wp-content/uploads/2012/09/JCAS-Special-Issue-Women-of-Color-November-FINAL-2010.pdf>.
14. Aph Ko and Syl Ko. *Aphro-ism: Essays on Pop Culture, Feminism, and Black Veganism from Two Sisters* (New York: Lantern, 2017): 66.
15. Michael Baker. "Modernity/Coloniality and Eurocentric Education: Towards a post-Occidental Self-understanding of the Present," in *Policy Futures in Education* 10:1 (2012): 13.
16. *Ibid.*: 4.
17. Linda Tuhiwai Smith. *Decolonizing Methodologies: Research and Indigenous Peoples* (Dunedin: University of Otago Press, 1999), 25.
18. This is neither meant to be a universal statement nor to discredit the incredible work of student activists working to liberate marginalized communities in and out of the classroom. Many students are aware of their oppression in school and society. It is more meant to acknowledge that Western educational systems and Eurocentric curricula actively work to whitewash histories and do not *encourage* students to challenge white supremacy and other oppressive colonial systems.
19. Ko and Ko. *Aphro-ism*, 66.
20. Deckha. "The Subhuman," 17.
21. Ko and Ko. *Aphro-ism*, 45.
22. *Ibid.*: 92.
23. *Ibid.*: 94.
25. Vanessa Watts. "Indigenous Place-thought & Agency among Humans and Nonhumans (First Woman and Sky Woman Go on a European World

Tour!)," in *Decolonization: Indigeneity, Education & Society* 2:1 (2013): 22 <www.decolonization.org/index.php/des/article/view/19145>.
25. Kathleen J. Tate. "Integrating Humane Education into Teacher Education: Meeting Our Social and Civic Responsibilities," in *Teacher Education and Practice* 24:3 (2011): 303.
26. Helena Pederson. "Schools, Speciesism, and Hidden Curricula: The Role of Critical Pedagogy for Humane Education Future," in *Journal of Future Studies* 8:4 (2004): 5 <www.jfs.tku.edu.tw/8-4/A01.pdf>.
27. Zoe Weil. "Begin with Children," in *Satya*, November 2002 <www.satyamag.com/nov02/weil.html>.
28. Gert J.J. Biesta. "Say You Want a Revolution . . . Suggestions for the Impossible Future of Critical Pedagogy," in *Educational Theory* 48:4 (1998): 499.
29. The term *citizen* in this chapter is in no way meant to evoke the isolating definition of citizenship as being a "legal" member of a nation or state. Citizenship, as it is used here, has no legal affiliation. It is meant to describe those who inhabit any give space or place, and at times even the world as a whole.
30. Biesta. "Revolution," 523.
31. Jan Masschelein. "How to Imagine Something Exterior to the System: Critical Education as Problematization," in *Educational Theory* 48:4 (1998): 521.
32. Lydia S. Antoncic. "A New Era in Humane Education: Troubling Youth Trends and a Call for Character Education are Breathing New Life into Efforts to Educate Our Youth About the Value of Life," in *Animal Law* 9:183 (2003): 188 <www.animallaw.info/sites/default/files/lralvol9_p183.pdf>.
33. Ko and Ko. *Aphro-ism*, 88.
34. *Ibid.*: 67.
35. Masschelein. "How to Imagine," 542.
36. Deckha. "The Subhuman," 44.
37. Christopher Sebastian McJetters. "Animal Rights and the Language of Slavery," in *Striving with Systems*, December 27, 2015 <www.strivingwithsystems.com/2015/12/27/animal-rights-and-the-language-of-slavery/>.
38. McJetters. "Animal Rights."
39. Ko and Ko. *Aphro-ism*, 89.
40. *Ibid.*: 90.

2. Our Bodies, Complex and Connected: Analyzing Interconnected Oppressions as a Methodological Basis for a Liberating Pedagogy

1. A. Breeze Harper (ed). *Sistah Vegan: Black Female Vegans Speak on Food, Identity, Health, and Society* (New York: Lantern, 2010); Kara Davis and Wendy Lee (eds). *Defiant Daughters: 21 Women on Art, Activism, Animals, and the Sexual Politics of Meat* (New York: Lantern, 2013); Carol J. Adams. *The Sexual Politics*

of Meat: A Feminist-Vegetarian Critical Theory (20th anniversary edition) (New York: Continuum, 2010).
2. One of the most highly visible examples of inaccessibility to academia is the lack of women and girls taking Science, Technology, Engineering, and Mathematics (STEM) subjects beyond a compulsory level. This has implications for women who continue in those fields as a minority. We see it across other areas of study, too: people from lower socioeconomic backgrounds are often unable to continue their studies because of high tuition fees and hidden course costs, as well as the cost of living and the threat of lifelong student debt.
3. Mira Schor. "A Plague of Polemics," in *Art Journal* 50:4 (2014): 36–41.
4. Cherríe Lawrence Moraga and Gloria Evangelina Anzaldúa edited an anthology on the topic of bearing the weight of identity oppression on our backs, specifically from the perspective of women of color: *This Bridge Called My Back: Writings by Radical Women of Color* (4th edition) (Albany: State University of New York Press, 2015).
5. Davis and Lee. *Defiant Daughters*.
6. Harper. *Sistah Vegan*.
7. Marjorie Spiegel. *The Dreaded Comparison: Human and Animal Slavery* (New York: Mirror Books, 1996).
8. Adams. *The Sexual Politics of Meat*.
9. Claudia Jones. "An End to the Neglect of the Problems of Negro Women!" *Political Affairs* (1949): 28–29; Frances M. Beale. *Double Jeopardy: To Be Black and Female* (Pamphlet, 1969); Deborah K. King. "Multiple Jeopardy, Multiple Consciousness: The Context of a Black Feminist Ideology," in *Signs* 14:1 (1988): 42–72.
10. Susan Greenhalgh. *Under the Medical Gaze* (Berkeley: University of California Press, 2001); *When Language Runs Dry: A Zine for People with Chronic Pain and Their Allies* <www.chronicpainzine.blogspot.co.uk/>.
11. Recent cases of sterilization of people of color give us insight into the anxiety that white European-descended settler colonial society has regarding "demographic threat."
12. Rebecca Vallas. "The Mass Incarceration of People with Disabilities in America's Jails and Prisons," Center for American Progress, July 18, 2016 <www.americanprogress.org/issues/criminal-justice/reports/2016/07/18/141447/disabled-behind-bars/>; Abla Abdelhadi. "Addressing the Criminalisation of Disability from a Disabled Justice Framework: Centering the Experiences of Disabled Queer Trans Indigenous and People of Colour," *The Feminist Wire*, November 21, 2013 <www.thefeministwire.com/2013/11/addressing-the-criminalization-of-disability-from-a-disability-justice-framework-

centring-the-experiences-of-disabled-queer-trans-indigenous-and-people-of-colour/>.
13. Nadra Kareem Nittle. "The US Government's Role in Sterilizing Women of Colour," *ThoughtCo*, April 8, 2018 <www.thoughtco.com/u-s-governments-role-sterilizing-women-of-color-2834600>.
14. The website remember.org provides information and further reading on medical experiments of the Holocaust and Nazi medicine" <www.remember.org/educate/medexp>; Victoria Brignell wrote an urgent article, entitled, "The Eugenics Movement Britain Wants to Forget," *New Statesman*, December 9, 2010 <www.newstatesman.com/society/2010/12/british-eugenics-disabled>.
15. The history of eugenics is often erased and forgotten. This is why L. L. Wall provides us with this important article: "The Medical Ethics of J. Marion Sims: A Fresh Look at the Historical Record," in *Journal of Medical Ethics* 32:6 (2006): 346–50. Activists are also seeking to undo this erasure, and the erasure of the many other examples of abuse of people of color and other marginalized groups in the name of research, in works like *The Immortal Life of Henrietta Lacks* by Rebecca Skloot (New York: Crown, 2010) and the NPR podcast "Remembering Anarcha, Lucy and Betsey: The Mothers of Modern Gynecology" February 7, 2017 <https://www.npr.org/2017/02/07/513764158/remembering-anarcha-lucy-and-betsey-the-mothers-of-modern-gynecology> #sayhername.
16. The Big Questions, Mentorn TV. "Is Animal Testing Justified?" <https://www.youtube.com/watch?v=-Q2eYth-mBs>.
17. *Crip theory* is an offshoot from the wider area of disability studies. Disability studies was developed in the late 80s and into the 1990s. At its core is the belief that disability itself is socially constructed (similar to race, gender, etc.), and that there is a key difference between an individual's impairment and their social, political, and economic disablement under systems of ableism and capitalism. Crip theory is a development of these core beliefs, closely related to queer theory (and the practice of *queering*). *Cripping* is a process of analysis through a primarily disabled lens. *Crip* as an identity is a reclamation of the slur "cripple," which asserts that disabled identity is viable and valid and should be acknowledged and celebrated; and that our status as disabled people (crips) is not a lack or a loss, but a difference, which is actually a powerful and transgressive force in undoing systems of oppression. For an insight into *Crip Theory* see Cheryl Green and Caitlin Wood in conversation: "Cripping Capitalism: Disability, Feminism and the Controversy of Work" (https://www.youtube.com/watch?v=8Af8lvfFZQQ) as

well as Sunaura Taylor's *Beasts of Burden: Animal and Disability Liberation* (New York: The New Press, 2017).
18. Kathryn Eddy, Janelle O'Rourke, LA Watson (Eds). *The Art of the Animal: Fourteen Women Artists Explore the Sexual Politics of Meat* (New York: Lantern, 2015). The most affecting and powerful works in the book for me include O'Rourke's "A Life Erased." On a pink background, hand-cut rice paper spells out a disjointed list of terms that permeate our culture, from *butcher* to *menu*, and serve to make us forget the life that once was; to turn parts of beings into "pork rumps ham hocks ribs meat whole cuts short sliced whole pig," etc. This work almost perfectly illustrates Adams' "absent referent," the linguistic magic trick that is performed every time a cow is absent when being represented by "beef."

3: Modeling Dissent: Teachers as Protectors, Activists, and Public Intellectuals

1. Paulo Freire. *Pedagogy of the Oppressed* (New York: Herder and Herder, 1972): 37.
2. bell hooks. *Teaching to Transgress: Education as the Practice of Freedom* (New York: Routledge, 1994): 75.
3. *Ibid.*: 12, 19.
4. *Ibid.*: 110.
5. The work referenced here is Kimberlé Crenshaw's "Mapping the Margins: Intersectionality, Identity Politics, and Violence against Women of Color," in *Stanford Law Review*, 43:6 (1991): 1241–99. This work was the author's attempt to: 1) critique the "identity politics" of contemporary antiracist and feminist movements; and 2) forward an intersectional understanding of the ways in which women of color, specifically black women, are impacted by both sexism and racism. Crenshaw explains further: "My objective there was to illustrate that many of the experiences Black women face are not subsumed within the traditional boundaries of race or gender discrimination as these boundaries are currently understood, and that the intersection of racism and sexism factors into Black women's lives in ways that cannot be captured wholly by looking at the race or gender dimensions of those experiences separately. I build on those observations here by exploring the various ways in which race and gender intersect in shaping structural and political aspects of violence against women of color. [. . .] My focus on the intersections of race and gender only highlights the need to account for multiple grounds of identity when considering how the social world is constructed" (1991): 1244–5.

6. There is an important caveat to this statement: poor and working-class individuals in the United States, including indigenous peoples and people of color impacted by environmental racism and segregation, have longstanding, structural obstacles to accessing healthy and whole foods, including organic vegetables and plant-based alternatives to meat and dairy products. If this remains unaddressed, especially by white teachers/activists, then we inadvertently prop up those same structures of oppression and alienation that are a function of racism and classism in North America. It would also be colonialist to suggest to any indigenous person that their cultural practices are "unethical."
7. Freire. *Pedagogy of the Oppressed*, 19.
8. hooks. *Teaching to Transgress*, 33.
9. For further reading, I recommend Kenneth J. Saltman's "Putting the Public Back in Public Schooling: Public Schools Beyond the Corporate Model," in *DePaul Journal for Social Science* 3:1, Fall 2009.
10. Freire. *Pedagogy of the Oppressed*, 72.
11. Carl Sagan. *The Demon-Haunted World: Science as a Candle in the Dark* (New York: Ballantine, 1996): 59.
12. *Ibid.*: 254.

4. Including an Anti-speciesist Practice in My Work with Neurodiverse Youth

1. I have chosen to use identity first language (autistic person) in relation to autism. Research undertaken highlights that autistic adults choose this over person-first language (person with autism), but obviously each individual might have a different preference. See L. Kenny, C. Hattersley, B. Molins, C. Buckley, C. Povey, E. Pellicano: "Which Terms Should Be Used to Describe Autism? Perspectives from the UK Autism Community," in *Autism* 20:4 (2016): 442–62.
2. Jon Stone. "Government to Cut School Funding for First Time Since 1990s, IFS Says," *Independent*, February 27, 2017 <www.independent.co.uk/news/uk/politics/school-funding-cuts-tories-theresa-may-education-1990s-budget-2017-a7601366.html>.
3. Rachel Pells. "Record Gap between Rich and Poor Students Winning University Places," *Independent*, December 14, 2016 <www.independent.co.uk/news/education/education-news/record-gap-social-mobility-rich-and-poor-students-going-university-vince-cable-theresa-may-gender-a7475256.html>.
4. Kimberlé Crenshaw. "Mapping the Margins: Intersectionality, Identity Politics, and Violence against Women of Color," in *Stanford Law Review* 43:6 (1991): 1241–99.

5. Teaching Various Age Groups about Animals: Observations on How We Learn to Ignore Animal Oppression

1. Plato. *The Laws*. Translated by Trevor J. Saunders (London: Penguin, 1975).
2. Animal Aid is a UK pressure group, campaigning to end all forms of animal abuse.
3. In a recent survey of unhappy children, the UK was ranked fourteenth out of fifteen countries. See Denis Campbell and Sarah Marsh: "Quarter of a Million Children Receiving Mental Health Care in England," *Guardian*, October 3, 2016 <www.theguardian.com/society/2016/oct/03/quarter-of-a-million-children-receiving-mental-health-care-in-england>.
4. Herbert Marcuse. *One Dimensional Man* (London: Routledge, 1991): 13.
5. Martin Heidegger. *On the Way to Language*. Translated by Peter D. Hertz (San Francisco: Harper, 1982).
6. James Rachels. *Can Ethics Provide Answers?* (Lanham, MD: Rowman & Littlefield, 1996): 99.
7. Cahal Milmo and Andre Wasely. "Plummeting Milk Price Prompts 'Stealth' Rise of 2000-cow 'Mega-Dairies' in the UK," *Independent*, November 23, 2015 <www.independent.co.uk/news/uk/home-news/plummeting-milk-price-prompts-rise-of-2000-cow-mega-dairies-in-britain-a6744501.html>.
8. Immanuel Kant. *Foundations of the Metaphysics of Morals*. Translated by Lewis White Beck (Indianapolis, IN: Bobbs-Merrill, 1959): 47.
9. Immanuel Kant. *Lectures on Ethics*. Translated by Louis Infield (New York: Harper, 1963): 239.
10. *Ibid.*: 240.

6. What Zoos Teach Us: Speciesism, Colonialism, Racism, and Capitalism in the Captive Animal Industry

1. Nicola O'Brien is currently Campaigns Manager for Freedom for Animals and Liz Tyson is the former the Director of Organization <www.freedomforanimals.org.uk>.
2. Born Free Foundation <www.bornfree.org.uk>.
3. Dave Hone. "Why the World Needs Zoos," *Guardian*, March 8, 2016 <www.theguardian.com/science/2017/mar/08/why-the-world-needs-zoos>.
4. Robin Ganzert. "Zoos Are Not Prisons. They Improve the Lives of Animals," *Time*, June 13, 2016 <www.time.com/4364671/zoos-improve-lives-of-animals>.
5. Jenni Watts. "Are Animals in Cages a Necessary Evil?" CNN, November 6, 2013 <www.edition.cnn.com/2013/11/06/world/asia/jenni-watts-animals-in-captivity/index.html>.

6. Christie Blatchford. "Opinion: It's a Gorilla, Get Over It," *National Post*, May 31, 2016 <https://nationalpost.com/opinion/christie-blatchford-its-a-gorilla-get-over-it>.
7. Cristina Russo. "The Role of the Zoo in Education and Conservation," *Sci-Ed*, March 11, 2013 <www.blogs.plos.org/scied/2013/03/11/zoo-education>.
8. ADAS. *Review of Zoos' Conservation and Education Contribution* (London: ADAS, p.i., 2010).
9. What constituted "negative learning" was not clearly explained in the work nor was the method by which negative learning was assessed shared in the article.
10. Eric Jensen. "Evaluating Children's Conservation Biology Learning at the Zoo," *Conservation Biology* 28:4 (2014): 1004–11.
11. Zoological Society of London (ZSL). "Education Sessions," ZSL <www.zsl.org/zsl-london-zoo/schools/education-sessions>.
12. Bristol Zoo. "Event Q&As," Bristol Zoo, accessed 2018 <www.bristolzoo.org.uk/event-qa>.
13. Freedom for Animals. Footage from Bristol Zoo. "Bristol Zoo 'Big Night Out'—Zoo Staff States Animals Stressed by Late Night Party Event" <https://www.youtube.com/watch?v=FyYkKQO0NdE>.
14. K. Struck, E. Videan, J. Fritz, and J. Murphy. "Attempting to Reduce Regurgitation and Reingestion in a Captive Chimpanzee through Increased Feeding Opportunities: A Case Study," in *Lab Animal* 36:1 (2007): 35–8.
15. Meghan S. Martin-Wintle, David Shepherdson, Guiquan Zhang, Hemin Zhang, Desheng Li, Xiaoping Zhou, Regui Li, and Ronald S. Swaisgood. "Free Mate Choice Enhances Conservation Breeding in the Endangered Giant Panda," in *Nature Communications* 6 (2015).
16. Conservation threats are, for example: deforestation, climate change, human–wildlife conflict, mineral exploitation, human displacement/migration, or other socio-economic issues.
17. Biaza Zoo. "Love Your Zoo" Biaza <www.biaza.org.uk/campaigns/detail/love-your-zoo>.
18. IUCN Red List <www.iucnredlist.org>.
19. For more information and the full statistics visit Freedom for Animals <www.freedomforanimals.org.uk/con-in-conservation>.
20. Responsible Travel. "The Public Have Zoos on a Take Pedestal, New Survey Reveals," *Responsible Travel* <www.responsibletravel.com/copy/blog-post-twenty-six>.
21. "Zoo Publishes False Information," Freedom for Animals <www.freedomforanimals.org.uk/news/zoo-publishes-false-information>.

22. "Happy Hippos Education Pack," ZSL London Zoo <www.zsl.org/sites/default/files/media/2014-06/Happy%20Hippos.pdf>.
23. See for example the Village WaTuTu at The Living Desert Zoo and Gardens. <www.livingdesert.org/plan-your-visit/things-to-do-and-see/village-watutu>. Another example would be La Terre des Origines at Pairi Daiza, which, oblivious to its own imperialist appropriation, invites us to join, "The Country of Origin [that], glowing, warm and primitive, submerges us in the cradle of mankind. [. . .] A fishing village on stilts, surrounded by pirogues, invites us to palaver in the hut of the chief, the school, the traditional grocery store, the home of the voodoo priests, the music, the meeting hut or the barbershop" <www.pairidaiza.eu/en/worlds/the-country-of-origin>.
24. Jeremy Hance. "Zoos Could Become 'Conservation Powerhouses,'" *Guardian*, December 8, 2015 <www.theguardian.com/environment/radical-conservation/2015/dec/08/zoos-aquariums-conservation-animals-wildlife-funding>.
25. M. Gusset and G. Dick. "'Building a Future for Wildlife?' Evaluating the Contribution of the World Zoo and Aquarium Community to in situ Conservation," in *International Zoo Yearbook* 44:1 (2010): 183–91.
26. Heather D'angelo. "Local People Are Not the Enemy: Real Conservation from the Frontlines," *Mongabay*, November 12, 2014 <news.mongabay.com/2014/11/local-people-are-not-the-enemy-real-conservation-from-the-frontlines>.
27. *Ibid.*

7. Ecocriticism in the Classroom and at Home: Generating a New Ethical and Ecological Consciousness through Fairy Tales

1. Cheryll Glotfelty and Harold Fromm (eds). *The Ecocriticism Reader: Landmarks in Literary Ecology* (Athens: University of Georgia Press, 1996): xviii.
2. *Ibid.*: xix.
3. The belief that considers human beings to be the most significant entity of the universe and interprets or regards the world in terms of human values and experiences.
4. Jožica Čeh Steger. "Ekologizacija literarne vede in ekokritika," in *Slavistična revija* 60:2 (2012): 199–212.
5. Timothy Clark. *The Cambridge Introduction to Literature and the Environment* (Cambridge: Cambridge University Press, 2014): 179.
6. *Ibid.*: 179.
7. Glotfelty and Fromm. *The Ecocriticism Reader*: xix.
8. *Ibid.*
9. *Ibid.*: xx.

10. Donald Worster. *The Wealth of Nature*, cited in Glotfelty and Fromm. *The Ecocriticism Reader*: xxi.
11. Serpil Oppermann. "Ecocentric Postmodern Theory: Interrelations between Ecological, Quantum, and Postmodern Theories," in *Ecocritical Theory: New European Approaches* edited by A. Goodbody and K. Rigby (Charlottesville: University of Virginia Press, 2011): 230. Further, biocentrism, unlike anthropocentrism, affirms "the intrinsic value of all natural life and displace[s] the current preference of even the most trivial human demands over the needs of other species or integrity of place." See Clark: *The Cambridge Introduction to Literature and the Environment*: 2.
12. Serpil Oppermann. "Ecocentric Postmodern Theory": 230.
13. *Ibid.*
14. *Ibid.*: 231.
15. *Ibid.*: 232.
16. Svetlana Makarovič. *Svetlanine pravljice* (Dob, Miš, 2008): 825.
17. For instance, in 1998, 2000, and 2002, Makarovič was nominated for the Andersen Award for her entire work in the field of children's literature.
18. Makarovič. *Svetlanine pravljice*: 827.
19. *Ibid.*: 828.
20. Marjetka Golež Kaučič, "Folklorni in živalski slovar v ustvarjalnem opusu Svetlane Makarovič," in *Jezik in slovstvo* 56:1–2 (2011): 32.
21. Marjetka Golež Kaučič. "Thematization of Nonhuman Subjectivity in Folklore, Philosophical, and Literary Texts," in *Cosmos* 27 (2011): 145.
22. *Ibid.*
23. Makarovič. *Svetlanine pravljice*: 829.
24. *Ibid.*: 830.
25. *Ibid.*: 831.
26. *Ibid.*: 600.
27. It must be noted that the ecocritical approach should not be limited exclusively to literature; it can also be expanded to other disciplines. For instance, the topic of exploitation of farm animals is shown in the animated comedy film *Chicken Run* (2000), in which the miserable life of farm chickens is depicted by means of comedy. Even though the film is defined as a comedy and appropriated for children, it incorporates a strong criticism of the human relationship towards animals, and therefore it can be used as a powerful didactic tool for stimulating an ethical and ecological consciousness in a child.
28. Makarovič. *Svetlanine pravljice*: 599.
29. *Ibid.*: 602.
30. *Ibid.*: 600.

31. The concept of deflection was coined by Ian Hacking and refers to practicing ignorance with regards to what people do to, or with, animals. See Stanley Cavell, Cora Diamond, John McDowell, Ian Hacking, and Cary Wolfe: *Philosophy & Animal Life* (New York: Columbia University Press, 2008): 146.
32. Makarovič. *Svetlanine pravljice*: 599.
33. *Ibid.*: 605.
34. Kuzma the gremlin appears in several of Makarovič's tales.
35. Makarovič, 510.
36. *Ibid.*: 512.
37. *Ibid.*: 516.
38. *Ibid.*: 530.
39. *Ibid.*: 531.
40. *Ibid.*: 533.
41. *Ibid.*: 647.
42. *Ibid.*: 649.
43. *Ibid.*: 552.
44. Larisa Ćavar. *Ekokritika: odnos* človek—žival *v izbranih živalskih pravljicah Svetlane Makarovič* (undergraduate thesis). (Ljubljana, L. Ćavar, 2014): 18.
45. *Ibid.*: 19.
46. Makarovič. *Svetlanine pravljice*: 552.
47. Literary texts, fairy tales, and books for children in particular, in which animal characters and nature play a key role, very likely include (subversive) topics relevant for an ecocritical analysis. Films that include different themes that are part of a vegan pedagogy are for instance: *Bambi* (1942)—hunting; *The Plague Dogs* (1982)—animal testing; *Madagascar* (2005)—wild animals in captivity; *The Book of Life* (2014)—bullfighting, welfare of pigs (pigs as pets); *The Secret Life of Pets* (2016)—domestication and stray animals; *Zootopia* (2016)—modern society represented by anthropomorphized animals with a strong criticism of speciesism; *Ferdinand* (2017), based on Munro Leaf's book for children *The Story of Ferdinand* (1936)—bullfighting.

8. Including Non-Vegans in Developing and Delivering an Anti-Speciesist Pedagogy to Children

1. Luís Paulo de Carvalho Piassi, Rui Manoel de Bastos Vieira, and Emerson Izidoro Dos Santos. "Science Stand: Crossing Borders between Sciences, Arts, and Humanities in a Decentralized Science Dissemination Program" in *Crossing the Border of the Traditional Science Curriculum* edited by Maurício Pietrocola and Ivã Gurgel (Rotterdam: Sense Publishers, 2017): 73–94.
2. Paulo Freire and Antonio Faúndez. *Por uma pedagogia da pergunta* (Rio de Janeiro: Paz e Terra, 1985): 109.

3. Paulo Freire. *Conscientização* (São Paulo: Centauro, 2008).
4. Tânia R. Vizachri. "Animais Humanos ou humanos animais?: Um estudo sobre a representação dos animais antropomorfizados em cultura," Masters dissertation, University of São Paulo, 2014.
5. Steve Baker. *Picturing the Beast: Animals, Identity and Representation* (Champaign: University of Illinois Press, 2001): 138.
6. Jean Piaget. *The Essential Piaget* edited by Howard E. Gruber and J. Jacques Vonèche (New York: Basic, 1977).
7. Maria W. McKenna and Elizabeth P. Ossoff. "Age Differences in Children's Comprehension of a Popular Television Program," in *Child Study Journal* 28:1 (1998): 53–68.
8. Thomas Kesselring. "Os quatro níveis de conhecimento em Jean Piaget," in *Educação e Realidade* 15:1 (1990): 3–22.
9. This is a mosquito of the species *Aedes aegypti*, known to spread the dengue fever, Chikungunya, and yellow fever.
10. Yves de La Taille. *Moral e ética: dimensões intelectuais e afetivas* (Porto Alegre: Artmed, 2006).
11. Diana Barros *Teoria semiótica do texto* (São Paulo: Ática, 2005).
12. Paulo Freire. *Pedagogia do oprimido* (Rio de Janeiro: Paz e Terra, 2002): 57.
13. *Ibid.*: 75.
14. Paulo Freire. *Extensão ou Comunicação?* (Rio de Janeiro: Paz e terra, 2011): 116.
15. Freire and Faúndez. *Por uma pedagogia da pergunta*, 39.
16. *Ibid.*: 106.
17. *Ibid.*: 27.

9. "The Things We Choose to Teach Are Political Decisions. So, Embrace That": Neoliberalism, the Academy, and Critical Animal Studies Educators

1. Nik Taylor and Richard Twine. *The Rise of Critical Animal Studies: From the Margins to the Centre* (London: Routledge, 2014).
2. Heather Fraser and Kate Seymour (2017). *Understanding Violence and Abuse: An Anti-Oppressive Practice Perspective* (Winnipeg: Fernwood Press, 2017); David Harvey. *A Brief History of Neoliberalism* (Oxford: Oxford University Press, 2005).
3. Heather Fraser and Nik Taylor. *Neoliberalization, Universities and the Public Intellectual: Species, Gender and Class in the Production of Knowledge* (London: Palgrave, 2016).
4. Henry Giroux. "Neoliberalism, Corporate Culture, and the Promise of Higher Education: The University as a Democratic Public Sphere," in *Harvard Educational Review* 72:4 (2002): 425–62.

5. Barbara Noske. *Beyond Boundaries: Humans and Animals* (Montreal: Black Rose Books, 1997).
6. Donna Haraway. *When Species Meet* (Minneapolis: University of Minnesota Press, 2007).
7. Robert Garner (ed). *Animal Rights: The Changing Debate* (London: Springer, 2016).
8. Lucy Cormack. "Australia Is the Third-Fastest Growing Vegan Market in the World," *Sydney Morning Herald*, June 4, 2016 <www.smh.com.au/business/consumer-affairs/australia-is-the-thirdfastest-growing-vegan-market-in-the-world-20160601-gp972u.html>.
9. Neil Smith. "Who Rules This Sausage Factory?" *Antipode* 32:3 (2000): 330–9.
10. Fraser and Taylor. *Neoliberalization, Universities and the Public Intellectual.*

10. What We Can Learn about Vegan Education from Anarchist Philosophy and Animal Liberation Activists

1. Matthew Wilson and Ruth Kinna. "Key Terms," in *The Continuum Companion to Anarchism* edited by Ruth Kinna (London: Continuum, 2012): 346.
2. The term *collective vegan action*, used throughout this chapter, refers to different types of organized direct action by vegan activists—from ALF and hunt sabbing to Food Not Bombs chapters. Collective vegan action is distinctive in combining veganism with a wider critique of capitalism and commitment to non-hierarchical politics.
3. Ruth Kinna and Süreyyya Evren. "Unscientific Survey: 7 Sages of Anarchism," in *Anarchist Developments in Cultural Studies: Blasting the Canon*, Issue I (2013): 211–41.
4. Wilson and Kinna. "Key Terms," 334.
5. John Lupinacci. "Recognising Human-Supremacy: Interrupt, Inspire and Expose," in *Anarchism and Animal Liberation: Essays on Complementary Elements of Total Liberation* edited by Anthony Nocella, Richard White, and Erika Cudworth (Jefferson, NC: McFarland, 2015): 183.
6. John Sanbonmatsu (ed). *Critical Theory and Animal Liberation* (Plymouth, MA: Rowman & Littlefield, 2011): 15.
7. Mikhail Bakunin in *The Political Philosophy of Bakunin: Scientific Anarchism* edited by G. P. Maximoff (London: The Free Press, 1953): 86–7.
8. *Ibid.*
9. Pierre-Joseph Proudhon in *What is Property?* edited by Donald R. Kelly and Bonnie G. Smith (Cambridge: Cambridge University Press, 2002): 173.

10. Peter Marshall. *Demanding the Impossible: A History of Anarchism* (Oakland, CA: PM Press, 2010): 269.
11. *Ibid.*
12. Interview with ALF activist.
13. Ronnie Lee and the ALF founders also possessed a good knowledge of the tactics of other revolutionary groups. Lee was particularly inspired by the Angry Brigade.
14. Louise Michel in *The Red Virgin: Memoirs of Louise Michel* edited by Bullitt Lowry and Elizabeth Gunter (Tuscaloosa: University of Alabama Press, 1981): 24.
15. *Ibid.*: 27.
16. *Ibid.*: 25.
17. Peter Kropotkin. *Mutual Aid: A Factor of Evolution* (New York: Black Rose Books, 1989): 45.
18. Élisée Reclus: *On Vegetarianism: The Great Kinship of Humans and Fauna* (Jura Media, 1992): 3.
19. Brian Dominick. *Animal Liberation and Social Revolution: A Vegan Perspective on Anarchism or an Anarchist Perspective on Veganism* (Active Distribution, 1995/2008): 5; see also Brian Dominick. "Anarcho-Veganism Revisited" in *Anarchism and Animal Liberation: Essays on Complementary Elements of Total Liberation* edited by Anthony Nocella, Richard White, and Erika Cudworth (Jefferson, NC: McFarland, 2015).
20. Bob Torres. *Making a Killing: The Political Economy of Animal Rights* (Edinburgh: AK Press, 2009): 116–7.
21. *Ibid.*: 11. See also Murray Bookchin: *The Ecology of Freedom: The Emergence and Dissolution of Hierarchy* (New York: Black Rose Books, 1991).
22. Emma Goldman. *Living My Life: In Two Volumes*, Volume One (New York: Dover, 1931/1970); Angela Davis. *Freedom Is a Constant Struggle: Ferguson, Palestine and the Foundations of a Movement* (Chicago, IL: Haymarket, 2016).
23. Nik Taylor and Richard Twine. "Introduction: Locating the 'Critical' in Critical Animal Studies," in *The Rise of Critical Animal Studies: From the Margins to the Centre* edited by Nik Taylor and Richard Twine (London: Routledge, 2014): 4–6.
24. Peggy Kornegger. "Anarchism: The Feminist Connection," *Quiet Rumours: An Anarcha-Feminist Reader* (3rd edition), edited by Dark Star (Edinburgh: AK Press, 2012): 30.
25. Josephine Donovan. *Feminist Theory: The Intellectual Traditions* (New York: Continuum, 2012): 84. See also Lynne Farrow. "Feminism as Anarchism,"

The Anarchist Library, 1974 <www.theanarchistlibrary.org/library/lynne-farrow-feminism-as-anarchism.pdf>.
26. Goldman. *Living My Life*, Volume One: 12.
27. *Ibid.*: 205.
28. Kate Evans. *Red Rosa: A Graphic Biography of Rosa Luxemburg*. (London: Verso, 2015): 140.
39. Angela Davis. "On Revolution: A Conversation between Grace Lee Boggs and Angela Davis," Pauley Ballroom, University of California, Berkeley, February 2012 <www.radioproject.org/2012/02/grace-lee-boggs-berkeley>.
30. Steven Best, Anthony Nocella, Richard Kahn, Carol Gigliotti, and Lisa Kemmerer. "Introducing Critical Animal Studies," in *Animal Liberation Philosophy and Policy Journal* 5:1 (2007): 45.
31. Anthony Nocella, Richard White, and Erika Cudworth. "Introduction: The Intersections of Critical Animal Studies and Anarchist Studies for Total Liberation," in *Anarchism and Animal Liberation*: 13.
32. *Ibid.*: 12.
33. Kimberlé Crenshaw. "Demarginalizing the Intersection of Race and Sex: A Black Feminist Critique of Antidiscrimination Doctrine, Feminist Theory and Antiracist Politics," *The University of Chicago Legal Forum* 140 (1989): 139–67.
34. Amie Breeze Harper. "Veganism Should Always 'Trump' Intersectionality: Make Veganism Great [and White] Again!" Sistah Vegan, May 21, 2016 <www.sistahvegan.com/2016/05/21/veganism-should-always-trump-intersectionality-make-veganism-great-and-white-again>.
35. Julia Feliz Brueck (ed). *Veganism in an Oppressive World: A Vegans of Color Community Project* (Switerzerland: Sanctuary Publishers, 2017); Black Vegans Rock <www.blackvegansrock.com>; Vegan Hip Hop Movement <www.veganhiphopmovement.blogspot.co.uk>.
36. Syl Ko and Aph Ko. *Aphro-ism: Essays on Pop Culture, Feminism and Black Veganism from Two Sisters* (New York: Lantern, 2017): 30.
37. *Ibid.*: 131–2.
38. Carol Ehrlich. "Socialism, Anarchism and Feminism," in *Quiet Rumours: An Anarcha-Feminist Reader* (3rd edition), edited by Dark Star (Edinburgh: AK Press, 2012): 57.
39. Carol J. Adams and Josephine Donovan (eds). *Animals & Women: Feminist Theoretical Explorations* (Durham, NC: Duke University Press, 1995).
40. Torres. *Making a Killing*, 6.
41. Erika Cudworth. "Anarchism: The Politics of Anti-Statism," in *The Modern State: Theories and Ideologies* edited by Erika Cudworth, Timothy Hall, and John McGovern (Edinburgh: Edinburgh University Press, 2007): 142–6.

42. David Nibert. *Animal Rights/Human Rights: Entanglements of Oppression and Liberation* (Lanham, MD: Rowman & Littlefield, 2002): 185.
43. Elisa Aaltola. "Green Anarchy: Deep Ecology and Primitivism," in *Anarchism and Moral Philosophy*, edited by Ben Franks and Matthew Wilson (Basingstoke: Palgrave, 2010): 161.
44. David N. Pellow. *Total Liberation: The Power and Promise of Animal Rights and the Radical Earth Movement* (Minneapolis: University of Minnesota Press, 2014): 127.
45. Keith McHenry. *Hungry for Peace: How You Can Help End Poverty and War with Food Not Bombs* (Tucson, AZ: See Sharp Press, 2012): 12.
46. *Ibid.*
47. Laura Portwood-Stacer. *Lifestyle Politics and Radical Activism* (London: Bloomsbury, 2013): 142–3.

11. Teaching Men: What Men (and All of Us) Need to Consider When Communicating for Veganism

1. Chances are you might find it peculiar, perhaps even annoying, that I am using all these adjectives to address you. But, like all words, they are placed in the sentence to help the reader narrow down the meaning of the text. In other words, the more descriptive words I use, the more precisely I can express myself. More importantly, however, I hope that if you do experience unease or anger when you hear these identifying words, you see it as an invitation to check what kind of adjectives you use in your day-to-day life and whom you refer to with them, in which contexts and for what reasons. People who are not white, cis, non-disabled men are confronted with this language every day. Most of the time, it serves no other purpose than to stress their difference from the dominantly constructed individual. This is not what I am doing here: Yes, I am singling you out, but only because I am speaking directly to you and the format of our conversation in this chapter makes this the most precise way of indicating who I am writing to. So, no hard feelings: being white, cis, and able-bodied simply means that your presence produces a very distinct meaning, as this chapter explains.
2. Mel Y. Chen. *Animacies: Biopolitics, Racial Mattering, and Queer Affect* (Durham: Duke University Press, 2012): 27.
3. *Ibid.*
4. Brian Luke. "Taming Ourselves or Going Feral? Toward a Nonpatriarchal Metaethic of Animal Liberation," in *Animals and Women: Feminist Theoretical Explorations*, edited by Carol J. Adams and Josephine Donovan (Durham, NC: Duke University Press): 299.
5. *Ibid.*: 291.

6. Carol J. Adams. *The Sexual Politics of Meat: A Feminist-Vegetarian Critical Theory* (20th anniversary edition) (London: Continuum, 2010): 60.
7. Annie Potts and Jovian Parry. "Vegan Sexuality: Challenging Heteronormative Masculinity through Meat-free Sex," in *Feminism and Psychology* 20:1 (2010): 53–72.
8. For a fundamental understanding of the idea of privilege and specific examples of its manifestation I urge you to read W. E. B. Du Bois' *The Souls of Black Folk* (Amherst, MA: University of Massachusetts, 2018/1903), as well as Peggy McIntosh's work on white privilege and male privilege, *White Privilege: Unpacking the Invisible Knapsack*. This is available through McIntosh's SEED Project <www.nationalseedproject.org>.
9. Based on the work of Derald Wing Sue, Tori DeAngelis provides us with an extensive vocabulary on racial microaggression and an outline of its repercussions in "Unmasking 'Racial Micro Aggressions': Some Racism Is So Subtle that Neither Victim Nor Perpetrator May Entirely Understand What is Going on—Which May be Especially Toxic for People of Color," in *Monitor on Psychology Volume* 40:2 (2009): 42.
10. In his book on consensus-building, Peter Gelderloos shows us how to formally assess whether or not a group dynamic is uneven, so as to train our own sensitivity to the issue as well as to draw our audience's attention to it. In *Consensus: A New Handbook for Grassroots Social, Political, and Environmental Groups* (Tucson, AZ: See Sharp Press, 2006): 64.
11. Melanie Joy provides us with a handy list of tips for effective communication for anti-speciesism in *Strategic Action for Animals: A Handbook on Strategic Movement Building, Organizing, and Activism for Animal Liberation* (New York: Lantern, 2008): 121.
12. Tim Winton. "About the Boys: Tim Winton on How Toxic Masculinity Is Shackling Men to Misogyny," *Guardian*, April 9, 2018 <www.theguardian.com/books/2018/apr/09/about-the-boys-tim-winton-on-how-toxic-masculinity-is-shackling-men-to-misogyny>.
13. House of Commons. "Tackling Everyday Transphobia," UK Houses of Parliament, 2016 <www.publications.parliament.uk/pa/cm201516/cmselect/cmwomeq/390/39009.htm>.

12. Muscles, Meat, and Masculinity: Obstacles to a Vegan Teaching Practice in the Sports Sciences

1. Nancy Galambos, David Almeida, and Anne Petersen. *Masculinity, Femininity, and Sex Role Attitudes in Early Adolescence: Exploring Gender Intensification* (Hoboken, NJ: John Wiley and Sons, 1990): 1905–14.
2. Samaritans. *Suicide Statistics Report 2017*: 12.

3. See Lee F. Monaghan. *Bodybuilding, Drugs & Risk* (London: Routledge, 2001).
4. Raewyn Connell. *Masculinities* (Cambridge: Polity Press, 1995).
5. Raewyn Connell and James W. Messerschmidt. *Hegemonic Masculinities: Rethinking the Concept* (Thousand Islands, CA: Sage, 2005): 844.
6. *Ibid.*
7. For further reading on gender construction, performance and the lived experience tied to it see: Michel Foucault. *Discipline and Punish: The Birth of the Prison* (New York: Vintage, 1979); Judith Butler. *Gender Trouble: Feminism and the Subversion of Identity* (London: Routledge, 1990); Demetrakis Z. Demetriou. "Connell's Concept of Hegemonic Masculinity: A Critique," in *Theory and Society* 30:3 (2001): 337–61; Arthur Brittan. *Masculinity and Power* (Oxford: Basil Blackwell, 1989).
8. Raewyn Connell. "Teaching the Boys: New Research on Masculinity, and Gender Strategies for Schools," in *Teachers College Record* 98 (1996): 209.
9. Alan Klein. *Little Big Men: Bodybuilding Subculture and Gender Construction* (Albany: State University of New York Press, 1993): 5.
10. Alan Klein. "Pumping Irony: Crisis and Contradiction in Bodybuilding," in *Sociology of Sport Journal* 3:2 (1986): 115.
11. Carol J. Adams. *The Sexual Politics of Meat: A Feminist-Vegetarian Critical Theory* (New York: Continuum, 1990).
12. Matthew B. Ruby and Steven Heine. "Meats, Morals and Masculinity." *Appetite* 56:2 (2011): 447–50.
13. Richard A. Rogers. "Beasts, Burgers, and Hummers: Meat and the Crisis of Masculinity in Contemporary Television Advertisements," in *Environmental Communication: A Journal of Nature and Culture* 2:3 (2008): 281–301.
14. Kelly Struthers Montford. "Nonhuman Animal Sacrifice & the Constitution of Dominant Albertan Identity" (2013) <https://www.youtube.com/watch?v=AE0nrjaI_BM>.
15. Hank Rothgerber. "Real Men Don't Eat (Vegetable) Quiche: Masculinity and the Justification of Meat Consumption," in *Psychology of Men & Masculinity* 14:4 (2013): 363. See also, Jeffery Sobal. "Men, Meat, and Marriage: Models of Masculinity," in *Food and Foodways* 13:1–2 (2005): 135–58.
16. Arran Stibbe. "Health and the Social Construction of Masculinity in *Men's Health* Magazine," in *Men and Masculinities* 7:1 (2004): 31–51.
17. Michael Armato. "Wolves in Sheep's Clothing: Men's Enlightened Sexism & Hegemonic Masculinity in Academia," in *Journal of Women's Studies* 42:5 (2013): 578–98.
18. This very short interview with Raewyn Connell on YouTube gives us a good first insight into the topic: <www.youtube.com/watch?v=OYboMmQS0tU>.

13. Working with the Imagination and a Corporeal Pedagogy to Foster Interspecies Empathy

1. Martin Hoffman. *Empathy and Moral Development: Implications for Caring and Justice* (Cambridge: Cambridge University Press, 2000): 30.
2. William Ickes. "Measuring Empathic Accuracy," in *Interpersonal Sensitivity: Theory and Measurement* edited by Frank J. Bernieri and Judith A. Hall (Mahwah, NJ: Erlbaum, 2001).
3. Mark Davis. "A Multidimensional Approach to Individual Differences in Empathy," in *JSAS Catalog Selected Documents in Psychology* 10 (1980): 85.
4. Amanda Williams, Kelly O'Driscoll, and Chris Moore. "The Influence of Empathic Concern on Prosocial Behaviour in Children," *Frontiers in Psychology* 5 (2014).
5. Hoffman. *Empathy and Moral Development*, 33.
6. *Ibid.*
7. *Ibid.*: 34.
8. See, for example, Nancy Eisenberg, Natalie D. Eggum, and Laura Di Giunta. "Empathy-Related Responding: Associations with Prosocial Behavior, Aggression, and Intergroup Relations," in *Social Issues and Policy Review* 1:4 (2010): 143–80; Nancy Eisenberg and Paul A. Miller. "The Relation of Empathy to Prosocial and Related Behaviors," in *Psychological Bulletin* 1:101 (1987): 91–119.
9. Joana Formosinho and Terry Hurtado. Imagining Cow Being, 2017 <www.imaginingcowbeing.com>.
10. *Ibid.*
11. Hoffman. *Empathy and Moral Development*, 44.
12. *Ibid.*
13. *Ibid.*: 47.
14. *Ibid.*: 54.
15. *Ibid.*
16. Antonio Damasio. *Descartes' Error. Emotion, Reason, and the Human Brain* (New York: Avon, 1994): 228.
17. *Ibid.*: 241.
18. *Ibid.*: 139.
19. *Ibid.*: 145.
20. *Ibid.*: 147.

Glossary

This brief glossary explains some of the words that we might not come across in everyday conversations or texts. The book as a whole and this glossary contribute to equipping us with a liberation vocabulary that will make it easier for us to coherently create and communicate emancipatory knowledge.

ALF
Animal Liberation Front: an umbrella term for all those who use *direct action* (see below) to physically liberate animals from conditions of imprisonment by removing and rehoming them. Anyone can operate in the name of the ALF, as most actions are taken out anonymously. The condition, however, is that the action must be nonviolent: that is, no lives must be harmed.

Animalization
In the context of this book, animalization is used to imply a process of *othering* (see below). Animalization works similarly to objectification, where a living individual is turned into a thing, metaphorically and literally deprived of desires and life. The process of animalization begins with the conceptual invention of "the human" and the attribution of traits, such as skin color, ability, gender, and sexual orientation to "humanness." The social construction of these categories orders them hierarchically, leaving those not "human-enough" animalized. Any individual who cannot or will not fit into "humanizing" categories falls victim to objectification. If this objectification includes ascribing traits that imply animality, we can speak of "animalization." Many individuals who are categorized as *Homo sapiens* are animalized to different degrees. Further,

among nonhuman animals themselves we also find differing degrees of animalization. This is how degrees of "humanness" and animalization dictate the moral consideration different individuals are given.

Anthropocene
The Anthropocene is the current geological period. The specific denotation of this epoch acknowledges the damage humans have caused to the geology and ecology of this planet.

Carnism
Carnism, a term coined by Melanie Joy, denotes the ideology of eating meat. In her book *Why We Love Dogs, Eat Pigs, and Wear Cows* Joy illustrates that meat-eating culture is indeed just as ideological as veganism. Being as ubiquitous and normalized as it is, however, the sociopolitical impact of eating flesh is very well hidden. It is important to say that carnism/carnist is not to be understood as a slur—although, at times, it is (mis)used or (mis)interpreted as such. The word simply helps us name what has previously gone unnamed and so makes it easier for us to critically engage with its meaning and social impact.

Consensus
In a decision-making process with more than one party, consensus is reached when all parties agree upon the decision made. This approach to making decisions ideally empowers all parties to actively participate in coming to a decision. There are many methods to reach consensus for different contexts. Practicing consensus-based decision-making is valuable not only in activist groups but also in a classroom or family setting.

Critical Pedagogy
Critical Pedagogy can be understood as a movement and a teaching method. The concept explicitly acknowledges that knowledge is subjective, political, and social. Educators applying a critical pedagogy in their teaching and learning practice are particularly interested in equipping their students with critical-thinking skills that will allow them to liberate themselves and others from oppressive power structures.

Direct Action

Direct action is a form of activism that involves interference with a subject—be it a person, a company, an interaction, or relationship. In the widest sense, activists participating in direct action interrupt, sabotage, or prevent behaviors and events that cause harm. There is no absolute consensus within activist communities as to what exactly constitutes direct action: Is a low-key peaceful protest against the government's immigration policies to be equated with high-risk actions such as chaining yourself to a charter flight to stop deportations? Both are of value and significance; however, questions often arise about what constitutes "direct" action in the form of an unmediated and immediate interference with a subject. Direct action can take forms such as a strike, occupations, the destruction of hunting towers, phone blockades, or the removal of an animal from a laboratory, for example.

Ecocriticism

At once a literary movement and a method for critical thought and pedagogy, ecocriticism is defined by analyzing the relationship between literature and that which is embodied, particularly the natural environment. Ecocriticism acknowledges the symbiosis between both. It is a useful tool for educators, including parents, who work with texts, as a critical engagement with texts in respect to their portrayal of and impact upon the environment and animals will train our ecological awareness.

Ecofeminism

Ecofeminism as a philosophy and political movement started as a feminist concern for the environment and now also includes concern for animals. Ecofeminists believe that the effects of the *Anthropocene* (see above) are caused by masculinist and capitalist ideology.

Humane Education

As a pedagogical movement, Humane Education employs learning and teaching methods that are specifically designed to foster compassion and care for others, including animals and the environment.

Intersectionality

Generally, the concept of intersectionality refers to the idea that identity is made up of many traits that are all intertwined. Therefore, intersectional activism acknowledges the fact that no individual is oppressed in only one way (that is exclusively for being black or just disabled) but that different identity markers marginalize people as a whole without being separable. Multiple chapters in this book go into more depth regarding intersectional theory, which gained popularity with Kimberlé Crenshaw, a legal scholar writing on the multilayered oppression of working-class women of color. White activists often appropriate the concept when producing knowledge on identity and the interconnectedness of oppressions, eroding the important contribution the conceptualization of the word made to the liberation of racially and economically marginalized women.

Kyriarchy

Coined by Elisabeth Schüssler Fiorenza, *kyriarchy* denotes the master's (*kyrios*) rule/reign (*archos*). The term contributes to a social justice vocabulary, in that it expands the idea of a single source of oppression (such as masculinist violence under patriarchy). Instead, *kyriarchy* lets us acknowledge that oppression is multifaceted and interconnected.

Meat Paradox

This concept denotes the process of cognitive dissonance that occurs when we have an affinity for animals but still knowingly partake in harming them by consuming their flesh.

Othering

When perceiving and constructing another individual as intrinsically different, we *other* them. Othering specifically occurs when an individual with dominant, widely represented identity traits construes another as deviating from these traits, inevitably making them marginalized and minoritarian. Forms of othering include, for example, racialization, feminization, animalization, and objectification. It is through a process of othering that the dominant power-holder remains unidentified, which makes it harder to critically engage with them and deconstruct their power.

Prefigurative Politics

Prefigurative politics are practiced every time a community reflects the ideal state it aspires to achieve within its activism. In other words, prefigurative moments happen when communities are created in which the oppressive structures from dominant society can be left behind, albeit temporarily.

Privilege

Privilege is the advantage we are given without technically earning it. We obtain it simply based on the nature of our identity and that of the system we find ourselves in. It could be seen as the structural currency of power that allows us to access social, political, and economic capital.

Social Justice Warrior

The term originated on social media and is often abbreviated as SJW. Generally, SJWs are people who are fighting for social justice by being unapologetically outspoken about often very personal struggles concerning liberation and identity politics. They are activists for political correctness and inclusivity. The term can have a derogatory connotation, implying that SJWs are simply proliferating themselves through censoring hate speech and offensive commentaries on the Internet out of spite or supposedly for personal gain, such as fame and power. Many of those who have been called SJWs, however, decide to reclaim the term and use it to refer to themselves, implying their dedication to evoking a shift towards a more just world.

Speciesism

Speciesism is an ideological system based on the assumption that all living beings can be divided into species, some of which are regarded as more valuable and hierarchically ordered than others. Speciesism is a form of discrimination, similar to ableism, sexism, or racism.

Total Liberation

The anarchist roots of total liberation connect the concept to ideas of horizontality, anti-authoritarianism, and freedom. Based on the principles of non-harm towards other people, animals, nature, and the planet as a whole, total liberation learns from *intersectionality* (see above) that identity is complex, as is oppression and—as a logical conclusion—so is liberation. The concept acknowledges, in line with that of *intersectionality* and *kyriarchy* (see above), that single-issue liberation and campaigning for isolated identity groups are not the most effective ways to evoke emancipatory moments.

Trauma

After finding ourselves in distress, we experience psychological as well as biological changes. If these changes are so severe that they interfere with our mental or physical well-being, we speak of a traumatic experience. As social justice activists, many of us experience trauma. If we don't go through it ourselves we might still have to cope with secondary trauma, which is induced through bearing witness to someone else's traumatic experience and perhaps even supporting them through it. This is something to be aware of as educators for social justice, as it is our responsibility to provide the appropriate care to those we teach: The goal of our education should be for our audiences to be empowered rather than left behind, traumatized by the long-lasting effects of "aftershock." Aftershock consists of the repercussions activists and their allies are left with after a traumatic response, as pattrice jones writes in *Aftershock: Confronting Trauma in a Violent World: A Guide for Activists and Their Allies.*

About the Authors

Blane Abercrombie is currently a postgraduate research student at the University of the West of Scotland, where he works primarily in the field of sports sociology and gender studies. His research looks at the link between the construction of masculine gender identities in bodybuilders and meat consumption and the domination of other living beings. Blane has taught at both his own institution as well as the University of Edinburgh and seeks to embed both human and nonhuman animal liberation into his teaching practices wherever possible.

Jacqueline Adamescu is a high school English teacher, writer, and activist who spends her free time reading books, watching films, and practicing yoga. Her favorite genres are sci-fi and horror. She earned a B.A. in English literature and education from Marietta College (2010) and an M.A. from the New York University Gallatin School for Individualized Study (2013). She has published personal essays in two books: *Letters to a New Vegan* (Lantern, 2015) and *The Vegan Studies Project: Food, Animals, and Gender in the Age of Terror* (University of Georgia Press, 2015). She founded the vegan anarcha-feminist crit-lit zine *Project Intersect*, published quasi-annually, and sometimes speaks at book fairs and conferences on topics such as anarchism, feminism, ethical veganism, embodiment, and punk politics. Jacqueline lives with her partner and three rescue animals in Los Angeles.

Tanja Badalič works as an assistant with doctorate at the School of Humanities at the University of Nova Gorica, Slovenia. Her teaching domain is world literature, while her main research interests are women writers, women's literature, ecocriticism, ethical and ecological functions of literature, and animal studies, as well as representations of the nonhuman world in literature. She also writes poems that deal with the ideas of animal liberation, veganism, and ecocriticism.

Will Boisseau completed his Ph.D. at Loughborough University. His research focuses on the place of animal rights within the British left, particularly on the relationship between the anarchist/direct action and legislative wings of the movement.

Adriana Regina Braga is a biologist and holds a Ph.D. in the psychology of human development and education from UNICAMP (Campinas University) Education College. She is a member of LPG (Laboratory of Genetic Psychology), GEPEM (Research Group on Morality of Unesp e Unicamp) and INTERFACES (Thematic Nucleus of Fantasy Studies and Resources in Arts, Sciences, Education and Society—USP). She is a professor at Education College of UNIFESP (Federal University of São Paulo). As an author she specializes in environmental education, emphasizing sustainability, ethics, and consumption.

Beti Scott Brown is a queer and disabled artist, making socially engaged art that empowers people to fight against ableism, sexism, and speciesism. She understands art as a way to communicate politics, which she reflects in her pedagogical practice. She also holds an M.A. in fine art and art history. In engaging critically with the course content and methods during her studies, Beti has developed a radical understanding of education, which informs her own learning and teaching facilitation with disabled people.

Heather Fraser is an associate professor in the School of Public Health and Social Work at Queensland University of Technology (QUT). Heather started her career three decades ago working with women and young people who are surviving violence and abuse. She is a critical social worker who supports intersectional feminism and for the last six years she has been working in the area of Human–Animal Studies. Heather can be contacted via heather.fraser@qut.edu.au.

Terry Hurtado is an activist and independent researcher based in Cali, Colombia. He holds an M.Sc. in holistic science. His research has been on ethnomathematics, water footprint, and currently on animals in warfare and peace building in the Colombian war. Terry is a board member of the Institute for Critical Animal Studies (ICAS) and the Federación de Liberación Animal (Colombia), from which he runs the Animal Liberation School. He is the director of the magazine *Vida Libre* (*Free Life*) as well as a member of the International Anti-bullfighting Network, and Human Rights Committee of Cali. He is also a long-term activist for indigenous autonomy and is interested in anarchism, social ecology, and deep ecology.

Nicola O'Brien is a UK–based animal advocate and fundraiser, dedicated to helping non-profits and grassroots groups work effectively for nonhuman animals. Her interests in animal–human interactions and intersectional politics also guide her work. Over her fifteen years in the field, Nicola has worked extensively with non-profits focused on ocean conservation, animal rescue and rehabilitation, sanctuary, advocacy, and campaigning. Covering a variety of roles, she has experience in small non-profit management, campaigning, volunteer management, administration, and fundraising. Nicola completed her B.Sc. in animal welfare at Lincoln University in 2012. Since 2015, she has been in post as campaigns director at Freedom for Animals, an animal rights charity working to end the captivity of animals and animals used as entertainment.

Sarah Rose Olson holds a B.A. in comparative history of ideas with a tri-focus in critical animal, environmental, and gender studies from the University of Washington. She is currently pursuing an M.A. in environmental education at Western Washington University. Sarah's interests include incorporating critical animal studies into everyday curricula and exploring speciesism in tandem with other social justice movements. She can be contacted at solson208@gmail.com.

Luís Paulo de Carvalho Piassi is associate professor (full professor) at the School of Arts, Sciences and Humanities of the University of São Paulo USP. He holds bachelor's and master's degrees in physics (1990) and is a doctor of education (2004), and full professor in arts, culture, and recreation for the School of Arts, Sciences and Humanities (2012). He is a supervisor of graduate studies in the education program and in the cultural studies program at USP. He conducts research on the cultural studies of science communication and education, with an emphasis on youth and children's cultures, pop culture, science fiction, and fantasy. He also works in non-formal education in school environments, as well as with science communication and inquiry-based science education.

Susan M. Roberts practiced law for a few years and then returned to university to further her interest in philosophy. She lectures in moral philosophy and has spoken at the International Conference on Animal Rights on the subject of animals and technology. She is also a volunteer school speaker on the subject of animal rights. In addition, she has written articles on political and philosophical topics for online publications such as *Counterpunch*, *The Socialist Viewpoint*, and *The Journal of Natural and Social Philosophy*.

Nik Taylor is a critical and public sociologist whose research focuses on mechanisms of power and marginalization expressed in/through human relations with other species and is informed by critical/intersectional feminism. Nik is currently associate professor in the Department of Human Services and Social Work at the University of Canterbury, New Zealand. She is the author of *Humans, Animals, and Society: An Introduction to Human–Animal Studies* (Lantern, 2013).

Riley J. Taylor is a queer-feminist and anti-speciesist activist who works as a key worker at a school. She also holds a degree in English literature. Riley currently lives with her partner and their rescue cat in the South of England.

Agnes Trzak is an educator, activist, and scholar, specializing in anti-speciesist theory and the deconstruction of the *(Hu)man*, a term originating from her doctoral thesis. She is also the founder of the Anti-Speciesist Collective, a grassroots group run for and by non-binary people and women to facilitate accessibility to knowledge and, through this, empower those on the margin to take action for humans and animals. She works as an integration pedagogue with primary school children and is currently located in Berlin.

Liz Tyson is an animal advocate with over fifteen years of experience working for animal protection and conservation. She acted as Director of Freedom for Animals (formerly CAPS) 2010–2015, after working in primate conservation in the UK and South America for various years previous. From 2015 to the present day, she has worked as a freelance consultant for various animal organizations and groups. Her clients have included: the ISPCA, Comunidad Inti Wara Yassi (Bolivia), Santuario Wings of Heart (Spain), World Animal Protection, and Eurogroup for Animals. She currently works with the Born Free Foundation (UK) and Born Free USA. In 2007, Liz co-founded UK registered charity Entropika UK, and acted as legal representative of the organization's Colombian partner, Fundacion Entropika, based in the southern Colombian Amazon, until 2009. She is also an Associate Fellow of the Oxford Centre of Animal Ethics.

Tânia Regina Vizachri is the coordinator of DIAN (Debates and Investigations about Animals and Nature) and member of INTERFACES (Thematic Nucleus of Fantasy Studies and Resources in Arts, Sciences, Education and Society—USP). She is a Ph.D. student at the Faculty of Education of University of São Paulo (USP), where she researches the process of conscientization on animal rights in early childhood. She holds a master's degree in cultural studies and a bachelor's degree in social science. She works also as a high school teacher.

About the Publisher

LANTERN PUBLISHING & MEDIA was founded in 2020 to follow and expand on the legacy of Lantern Books—a publishing company started in 1999 on the principles of living with a greater depth and commitment to the preservation of the natural world. Like its predecessor, Lantern Publishing & Media produces books on animal advocacy, veganism, religion, social justice, and psychology and family therapy. Lantern is dedicated to printing in the United States on recycled paper and saving resources in our day-to-day operations. Our titles are also available as ebooks and audiobooks.

To catch up on Lantern's publishing program, visit us at www.lanternpm.org.

facebook.com/lanternpm
instagram.com/lanternpm
twitter.com/lanternpm